T0244945

KILLING
NAPOLEON

About the Author

Jonathan North's degree focused on Italian history and he has spent much of his life studying the era from 1789 to 1815. This has led to a dozen books on the period, including *Napoleon's Invasion of Egypt* (Amberley) and *Nelson at Naples: Revolution and Retribution*. As well as many years' experience writing and translating, he has spent some of his career as a commissioning editor of modern history. The author's website is www.jpnorth.co.uk

KILLING NAPOLEON

THE PLOT TO BLOW UP BONAPARTE

JONATHAN NORTH

AMBERLEY

First published 2019
This edition published 2024

Amberley Publishing
The Hill, Stroud
Gloucestershire, GL5 4EP

www.amberley-books.com

Copyright © Jonathan North, 2019, 2024

The right of Jonathan North to be identified
as the Author of this work has been asserted
in accordance with the Copyrights, Designs
and Patents Act 1988.

ISBN 978 1 3981 2254 3 (paperback)
ISBN 978 1 4456 8377 5 (ebook)

British Library Cataloguing in Publication Data.
A catalogue record for this book is available
from the British Library.

Origination by Amberley Publishing
Printed in India

CONTENTS

LIST OF ILLUSTRATIONS AND MAPS

Illustrations

1. A heroic image of Napoleon, First Consul of France.
2. An image of Napoleon, mounted, dating from the time of the Infernal Machine.
3. Napoleon in uniform.
4. The British view of Napoleon and his fellow consuls.
5. The Minister of Justice, Joseph Fouché.
6. The Prefecture of Police.
7. The courtyard of the Prefecture of Police.
8. The Tuileries Palace.
9. A review before the Tuileries.
10. A row of houses in Rue Nicaise.
11. The street itself.
12. A map of the Rue Nicaise.
13. A crowd before the theatre.
14. An artist's impression of the explosion.
15. A and B. Two contemporary versions of the explosion, produced by the French media.

Maps

ACKNOWLEDGEMENTS

I would like to thank Steven H. Smith for providing me with countless texts. I also owe a debt of thanks to the staff of the National Library of Scotland; the British Library; the London Library; Dr Clare Lappin of the Warburg Institute; Peter Harrington of the Anne S. K. Brown Military Collection; Isabelle Rossez of the Service de la Mémoire et des Affaires Culturelles at the Préfecture de police in Paris; the Archives de Paris; the Bibliothèque Historique de la Ville de Paris; and the Archives Nationales. Incidentally, the Museum of the Prefecture of Police in Paris is also worth a visit. It has on display a collection of prints and documents relating to the Infernal Machine, and the rebel Georges Cadoudal's wallet, but there is little in the way of police evidence relating to the actual bomb, as most has been lost or destroyed over the years.

I would also like to thank participants at the Napoleon Series forum, in particular Daniel Lamblat, Susan Howard and Tom Holmberg, for all their assistance over the years, and the anonymous people who make the Bibliothèque Nationale de France's Gallica repository of rare texts such a splendid resource.

Acknowledgements

I am grateful to the professional team at Amberley, particularly Jonathan Jackson and Shaun Barrington, and would like to thank all those who commented on the manuscript and who provided advice. I am, however, responsible for any errors or lapses in continuity. The process of research, translation and writing has been one that has lasted many years, something which has caused a physical and mental absence from family life. For that I owe a great debt to Evgenia and Alexander for their forbearance. It may be a poor consolation, but I hope to pay some of that debt out of the royalties.

AUTHOR'S NOTE

Translations within the text are my own and, in most cases, I have converted dates to the more familiar Gregorian style (there is a helpful converter at www.1789–1815.com/cal_conc.htm). Most contemporary writers, aside from the royalists, followed the republican calendar, but there was much confusion about days off, holidays and the starting and ending of years.

Confusion reigned, too, when it came to currencies. It may be worth bearing in mind that, roughly speaking, an écu was worth 5 Francs or 100 sous and a Louis was worth 20 Francs (and a Pound Sterling was worth around 25 Francs). As for purchasing power, André Guilmot, a frugal medical officer, baulked at paying three sous to have his shirt washed and two more to have it ironed, albeit badly. The more prodigal Chevalier de Mautort calculated that he could live modestly in the Paris of 1800 on 20 écus per month, including rent and food (with a decent meal costing 24 sous), although many a labourer was having to live off 20 sous a day.

If currencies continued to be referred to with a mixture of the old and new styles, then it should come as no surprise that a similar situation pertained with weights and measures and street names.

Rue Nicaise was relatively easy for Parisians, as it was a simple shortening from Rue Saint-Nicaise. Other streets in that quarter had, however, been transformed into more revolutionary-sounding thoroughfares. Rue Rohan may have become Rue Marceau, and Rue de Chartres-Saint-Honoré the Rue de Malte, but many of the locals continued to use the old names.

As many examples in this book will show, contemporaries also had problems when it came to spelling surnames. This led to puzzlement, and some cases of wrongful arrest. Forms of address also proved problematic. Although *citoyen* and *citoyenne* dominated in official documents, Monsieur and Madame were becoming increasingly common in everyday speech under the Consulate and, indeed, some of the older forms of address, based on pre-revolutionary hierarchies, were creeping back into use. In 1800, when asked how he should prefer to be addressed, the Bishop of Coutances remarked, 'As Monsieur in public, but, in private, one may call me Monseigneur.'

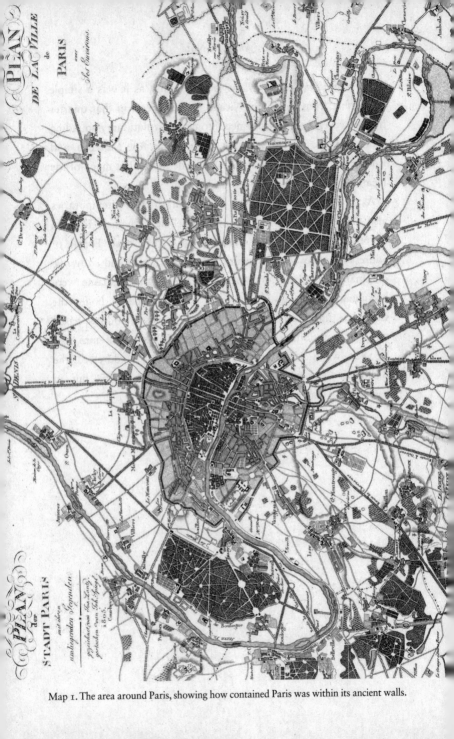

Map 1. The area around Paris, showing how contained Paris was within its ancient walls.

Map 2. Central Paris.

A   Rue d'Aguesseau
B   Rue Paradis Poissonnière
C   310 Rue Martin (Carbon's house)
D   Rue Neuve Egalité
E   Place des Victoires
F   The Opera, or Théâtre des Arts et de la République, on Rue de la Loi
G   Rue Croix des Petits Champs
H   Hotel de Mayenne in Rue du Four-Saint-Honoré
I   Rue des Prouvaires
J   The Louvre Museum
K   Rue Nicaise
L   The Tuileries Palace

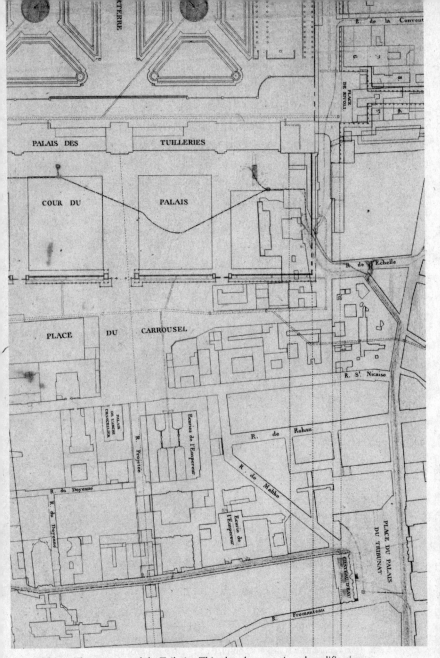

R. de la Convent...

PLACE DE RIVOLI

PALAIS DES TUILLERIES

COUR DU PALAIS

R. de l'Echelle

PLACE DU CARROUSEL

R. S^t. Nicaise

PALAIS DE L'ANCⁿ CHANCELLERIE

R. Projetée

Ecuries de l'Empereur

R. de Rohan

R. de Malthe

R. du Doyenné

R. du Doyenné

Ecuries de l'Empereur

PLACE DU PALAIS DU TRIBUNAT

CHÂTEAU D'EAU

R. Fromanteau

Map 3. The area around the Tuileries. This plan shows projected modifications to the city's streets but gives a good view of the layout as it was in 1800. Napoleon's coach exited the Tuileries gates, then crossed the square into the Rue Nicaise.

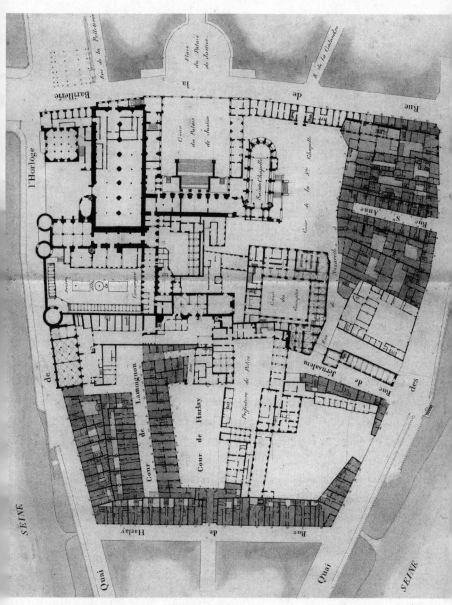

Map 4. A plan of the Prefecture of Police.

INTRODUCTION

War may be politics continued by other means, but sometimes assassination will do just as nicely. Indeed, such a targeted act of political violence is often less risky, and arguably more effective, in destroying rival leaders and leading enemy states to ruin. It is therefore unsurprising that history has produced a rich stream of such acts, all differing from one another in motive and means. Opportunists have seized their moment to kill tyrants whilst plotters in foreign pay have brought to a bloody culmination months of tense and deliberate work. Fanatics have taken careful aim to kill and by doing so placate a god, and men of reason have lashed out to hurry on their idea of liberty. Human ingenuity, too, has been applied to tip the balance of life and death in favour of the attacker, with assassins employing the weapon they thought most suitable to their self-appointed task. Balthasar Gérard chose pistols to silence William the Taciturn; Czar Paul I was strangled; Admiral de Coligny was merely tipped from an upper-floor window;[1] and a gunpowder plot put an end to the life of Henry Stuart, Lord Darnley. But in all these varied cases the purpose was clear, the target defined and the human cost largely limited to the participants. However, political violence evolves alongside other aspects of power and more recent developments have turned the precision of targeted killing on its head. Terrorism does not care who it kills and, although it continues to view assassination as a useful tactic, this basest form of killing prefers the shock of indiscriminate death to convey its sanguine message. The disaffected and deranged now measure success through numbers killed and terrorise through their indifference to the sanctity of human life. Today we live with that scourge, but demanding political change with bombs and murders on city streets is still a relatively new concept. Indeed, before the French Revolution the word terrorism was simply unheard of.

It was the aftermath of that singular example of political violence, the storming of the Bastille on the morning of Tuesday 14 July 1789, that planted the word terrorism in the public lexicon. As the trees of liberty went up, both sides sought new ways to describe the shock waves following in the wake of the destruction of the old order and the building of the new. Robespierre's rule of liberty and oppression was the first to be tarred with the term; his Terror, and that of the Jacobins, defined state ruthlessness for centuries to come. The Jacobins, the most radical revolutionary sect, were, for a time, proud to be terrorists, seeing in Terror the means to hasten their objectives. Their enemies, on the other hand, saw such extremism as a reflection of the anarchy and lawlessness that could be expected from handing power to the people. For those who rejected the revolution, and there were many, branding the government as being one of terrorists served as a warning that those seeking revolution, and the overturning of social order, would rather shed blood than tolerate defeat. Whatever the viewpoint, it is clear that this developing form of political conflict, now branded as terrorism, had imposed itself on the popular imagination.

All that was to change. As that early definition of terrorism as a purge of the body politic was gaining currency in the late 1790s, something happened. A new kind of atrocity took place, one which would eventually transform the meaning of that nascent word. In 1800 a singular act of violence, designed not only to do away with the intended target but to kill and maim any innocent civilian in the vicinity, was perpetrated on the people of Paris. This attack, aiming to intimidate a population and to warn and destroy a government, was carried out by royalist gentlemen who had made cold-blooded killing for a cause a way of life. This was their final, desperate attempt to bring down a government, to topple an ideology, that they loathed. As a tactic, a would-be catalyst for political change born out of failure, it was something new, something indiscriminate. And something terrifying.

This act of terrorism occurred in the French capital on Christmas Eve in 1800. Royalist conspirators packed a barrel with gunpowder, musket balls and bits of old iron, dragging it into the busy streets on a covered vehicle. They intended to detonate this improvised explosive device just as Napoleon's carriage passed by on the way to the opera. Whilst Napoleon escaped with his life, the explosion wreaked death and destruction on one of the busiest streets in the capital, as the perpetrators knew that it must.

It not only marked the birth of a new and brutal age, but, as with all acts of violence, there were unintended consequences. Napoleon survived. Far from the conspiracy subverting or breaking his government, he tightened his grip, channelling the surge in public anger not only against the perpetrators but against his more immediate political rivals, the men of the revolution, purging and harassing them until these tired dissidents were an entirely broken force. Then he had his police move against the real instigators of the crime, royalist extremists, hunting down the plotters and maculating them and their cause as the tools of perfidious Albion. His police, for once, proved adept, and their vigilance, surveillance and energetic harassment of enemies of the State were rewarded with ever-widening powers. Having vanquished such opposition, and won popular approval for having done so, Napoleon's regime grew stronger, more ruthless and more resolute. But he and it did not rest there. Soon after this attempt at killing Napoleon, the First Consul of France had himself elevated to first consul for life. Then, lending an ear to ambition and to those who feared that another similar attack might deprive the French of their saviour, and siding with those agitating that only a new dynasty could bring security in these restive times, he crowned himself emperor. It is not as though the infernal machine that detonated in Rue Nicaise on 24 December 1800 obliged Napoleon to don the imperial purple. But it did away with much of the potential resistance to that act of authoritarian ambition.

In an age of terrorism, it is not enough to be wary of the terrorists. There are unintended, as well as intentional, consequences stemming from political violence, and opportunities await those bold or ruthless enough to make use of them. The First Consul was not a man to let such an opportunity pass. So it was that Napoleon Bonaparte stepped out from the smoke and dust and made use of the confusion to fashion an empire from the ruins of a republic.

I

REVOLUTIONARY FEVER

It was cold that Wednesday morning. The steel-grey sky, however, was the least of the capital's concerns. For Paris was on holiday and the crowds were out in force, shouting, cheering, waving their reds, their whites and their blues. Towards the edge of that noisy excitement, and soon rolling into it, came a lumbering cart, heading for where the mass was densest and deepest.

Accompanied by the solemn and erratic music of anticipation, the cart had crossed the Seine and turned into Rue Saint Honoré, a street fringed by luxurious houses and named after the chapel dedicated to Saint Honoratus, the seventh bishop of Amiens and patron saint of bakers. There the crowd, mouths agape, watched this anonymous vehicle as it trundled past the house of François Chabot, the Capuchin monk who had authored the catechism of the sans-culottes, and passed the birthplace of Jean-Baptiste Poquelin, the irreverent Molière. Then came the pharmacy where the Swede Fersen had brought his invisible ink to write to the empty-headed young Marie Antoinette and the cart was soon making its way past the café where Diderot and his enlightened friends had waited whilst their encyclopaedia was published next door. The cart trundled on, leaving behind it the former Oratory of the Louvre and that more celebrated ecclesiastical relic, the cloisters of the Jacobins, where one of Paris's dominant political sects would meet in the church. A little further on, it crossed in front of the gates of Maurice Duplay's house where Maximilien Robespierre found it convenient to reside, close as it was to his club.

And so the cart continued along a street lined by Parisian history and on towards a square to be haunted by it.

The vehicle moved laboriously, the metal rims on its wheels knocking against the loose cobbles and shaking its fragile load, or sliding as it cut through the squelching ordure of the kind which then graced all the capitals of Europe. It seemed as though it was being deliberately slow, unhurried by the sense of expectancy that had won out over the cold at its bloody destination, the Place de la Révolution. Indeed, those awaiting it in the square were growing increasingly impatient. For the innocuous little vehicle carried an important cargo.

A wooden plank slotted between the sides of the ominous tumbrel bore a confessor and Queen Marie Antoinette. This grim vehicle was bringing the queen of France to her place of execution. That overcast morning, 16 October 1793, would see the execution of the Bourbon queen, who would thus join her husband, poor Louis XVI, beheaded ten months before, in the Madeleine cemetery, as well as in the hardly modest pantheon of royal martyrs. As the queen's blood trickled from the scaffold, and her head was held aloft by Henri Sanson, the world was sent a clear message that the kingdom of France had ceased to exist, and a popular revolution had replaced it with a republic, one and indivisible.

The radicals rejoiced, their message a provocation to defiance. Defiance would soon follow for there were many who could not accept a republic, and there were more who stood aghast at such revolutionary violence. This apparently final act of bloodshed therefore polarised France and launched a decade-long struggle to see who might stoop and collect the crown of the Capets from the mud into which it had fallen.

For a short time, as the smoke from the storming of the Bastille cleared and the revolution gained popular impetus, it seemed as though the people might be permitted to be their own sovereign. That was, after all, what they had been promised, seduced as they were by the allure of all being equal. Indeed, in those early years of revolution, it seemed as though the people were in charge as the meagre, stale, forbidding ways of custom, law, statute and Bourbon corruption were being swept away. The revolutionaries were acting on behalf of progress, humanism and reason[1] and few could maintain that this was not being done for and by the people. But despite the stirring slogans, and the sense amongst many that it was bliss to be alive, such uncomplicated progress was not fated to last.

The revolution had to go forwards or wither and, aware of such danger, it was inclined to rush headlong into the unknown. The further it pushed, the more its careless democratic steps tripped over an increasing array of obstacles. Those raised to power by the revolution, too involved in factionalism and Parisian intrigue, did not heed such warnings and their recklessness spawned a violent reaction. All sides mobilised but only the most ruthless, and most organised, could win in such a struggle and so, by the summer of 1793, popular sovereignty had slipped into the hands of a sect of radicals convinced that they were the only ones who could safeguard the revolution. This Society of Jacobins, Friends of Liberty and Equality[2] made judicious use of the mob, and exploited divisions amongst the new republican elite, to wrest power and form a government. These Jacobins had a radical agenda, and employed terror to ward off threats, but they were bold and violent enough to assume sovereignty over Paris and every other part of France that they thought mattered.

Elsewhere, however, and particularly in the countryside, the revolutionary impetus had already lost its way even before the Jacobins had unleashed their version of equality on the masses and atheism on the congregations. Here, the radicalism of the Jacobins provided fertile ground for counter-revolution. Resistance was to be centred on the surviving core of the old order, which would not give way lightly, but increasing frustration with the new republican institutions, a breakdown in the economy and now fear of the extreme dictates emanating from Paris all added to the distrust the provinces had always felt towards the centre and gained new converts to the resistance. Indeed, the clumsy carelessness of the government allowed all enemies of the republic to position themselves as moderates and as saviours who could secure the provinces from the wicked republican trinity of atheism, conscription and taxes.

As the banners proclaiming loyalty to God, King and Country, or meeker banners demanding self-rule or federalism, went aloft, the nation was very much in danger of splitting apart at the seams. Paris and the cities urged revolution on vast swathes of a country prepared to risk the France of 1793 in order to restore that of 1788. Civil war seemed the only possible outcome, especially when the great powers of Europe also turned on the republic.

That war to restore the Bourbons and purge Europe of revolutionaries had, in fact, been launched in a desultory way in April 1792 but it was given impetus when the crowned heads of Europe, shocked by the sight of their executed kin, summoned their fugitive courage and prepared to strike in unison. Soon Austrian, Prussian, Spanish, Dutch, British and various Italian armies sent columns of men marching across the French frontiers whilst within them, the forces of reaction, coaxed into life by the promise of foreign support, now felt sufficiently emboldened to launch their revolt.

The campaign to topple the republic would be supported both within France and without by those Frenchmen who had fled into exile. Clusters of resistance had formed along the French frontier with exiled royalists lavishing gold and ink on fighting the republic. Amongst the first to leave France had been the Count D'Artois, who had quit Paris on 16 July 1789, even before the smoke from the Bastille had dissipated. His departure was soon followed by thousands more. Indeed, the numbers of those leaving swelled from 1791, battalions of young officers, including the 23-year-old Joseph Picot de Limoëlan, voting with their horses' feet by riding over the frontier. Over time, the number of such individuals would increase to 145,000 and they would prove useful, and tenacious, auxiliaries in the fight against the revolution.

Some would remain part of the fraternity of royalist exiles established in Germany or Italy, or, for those who could afford to place the Channel between themselves and the scaffold, London. At Turin, D'Artois established a counter-revolutionary committee, sending other emigrants back to France to stir up dissent in the conservative western provinces. These agents and officers began to form, cajole and command the forces of reaction.[3] To counter such foes, the republic decreed death for any emigrant caught with a weapon in his hand as part of a suite of sweeping measures – there would be 53 laws enacted against fugitives from the revolution in the first 10 years of the republic – designed to secure the French Republic from subversion and to frustrate the return of a king.

The possibility of such a return was brought closer when the internal enemies of the republic chose to take to the field in open revolt, launching a series of popular uprisings across the provinces. Thousands who preferred the fetters of custom to the confusions of liberty and the republic's insatiable appetite for conscripts and cash, took up arms, with the territories on either side of the Loire being amongst the first to rise in the spring of 1793. Taking to the field in an armed struggle, punctuated by appalling massacres, the peasantry of Brittany and La Vendée, goaded on by priests and returning emigrants, were initially successful. The Chouans, as these royalist rebels in the west soon became known, received succour from foreign powers, particularly London, and hope from the outbreak of royalist or federalist rebellions in other parts of France. Robespierre's Terror kept Paris loyal to the republic, and federalist Bordeaux was quietened under Tallien's fist, but other urban centres were soon overrun by chaos. Lyon was only returned to republican rule by brutality, with the former priest and revolutionary zealot, Joseph Fouché, making sure that this Ville Affranchie (Liberated City) was free of rebels by executing them en masse. In the south Marseille fell to the reaction too but was razed in revenge in October 1793, the victorious government renaming the remains Sans Nom, whilst just along the coast Toulon shared a similar fate. There the royalists seized the port and called for the intervention of foreign powers. These, eyeing the French fleet, were for once quick to respond and an Anglo-Spanish fleet sailed in to safeguard the revolt. The republicans, alert to the danger but short of resources, began a desultory siege which only came to life when a youthful artillery captain, Napoleon Bonaparte, galvanised the blockade and helped drive off the Allies and their royalist friends. To the hard-pressed republicans in the south, it looked as though the Corsican had saved the republic.

Royalists, and royalist hopes, withered before so brutal an offensive and, even though Robespierre and the Jacobins were swept from power in 1794, the pragmatists realised that the restoration of a monarchy receded with each republican victory. The symbol of that monarchy, for he was king in name only, was Louis Stanislas, the Count of Provence, raised to the title of Louis XVIII in June 1795 following the death of the child king Louis XVII in prison. Plump Louis Stanislas, nursing his self-pity at Verona, was as inactive as his brother, D'Artois, was sharp, and it was this count who counted for most in the royal camp. D'Artois, shivering in Scotland, had surrounded himself with a like-minded coterie of militant royalists, known to friends and enemies alike as ultras, and they stood for a France returned to 1788. That would be for a France with the old frontiers restored and, within them, vengeance. He was fanatical enough to be prepared to countenance any method to achieve such an outcome and to thus regain his seat by the throne.

The natural method for the chivalrous was war but military defeat had dented the power of the royalists, with even the Chouans of the west now wavering and signing treaties, such as those at the manor house of Jaunaye and at La Mabilais, which sent the rebels home with promises of peace. Only the ultras and Britain did what they could to cheat France of her tranquillity. Whitehall constantly channelled agents, counterfeit money, guns and powder into Brittany and, in the summer of 1795, went further. The British called up the few thousand émigré troops encamped along the coast of the southern counties and summoning the royalist officers from the coffee houses of London, sent a seemingly impressive force across the Channel to the Quiberon peninsula. The expedition was a disaster, and only a few of the rebels emerged with any glory, among them Colonel Georges Cadoudal, a gigantic Breton, and Pierre Robinault de Saint-Réjant, who, sporting a red English coat, cut his way into the hinterland rather than surrender.

It was a significant setback to regime change through conventional means. Having failed, the royalists turned to politics – of a kind developed in Paris. Their early attempt at influencing the elections to the new legislative bodies replacing the Jacobins was frustrated, so they emulated the sans-culottes and hired a mob to storm the centre of power. The royalists, including the impressionable young Hyde de Neuville, marched across the River Seine on 4 October, heading for the Tuileries and ready to massacre or depose the National Convention. It was again Napoleon Bonaparte, kicking his heels in Paris after refusing to go and fight fellow Frenchmen in Brittany,[4] who thwarted their plans. He collected some guns and gave the order to open fire, sweeping Rue Saint Honoré and Rue Florentin with his whiff of grapeshot and massacring a knot of stubborn royalists outside the Opera. As the smoke cleared from the crimson streets, 300 dead royalists were testament that Napoleon had again saved the republic.

That republic had changed beyond recognition. Sovereignty had been completely wrested from the people and their representatives by the Jacobins but their demise in 1794 saw the proclamation of the Constitution of Year III and the establishment of the Directory. Power had therefore slipped to a clique of oligarchs sheltering behind a government of five, men who promised freedom to all whilst guaranteeing appropriation for the few. With the Jacobins broken and the royalists defeated in battle and in the streets, the Directory was glad to get on with life, liberty and the pursuit of money. General Bonaparte was wise enough to side with this avaricious sect and, rewarded with the challenging command of the republic's armies in Italy, he paid them back handsomely by killing Austrians and robbing Italians.[5]

The blatant accumulation of gold – and the concentration of it in the hands of the five most unworthy men in France – exasperated many and created unusual allies. One such alliance of royalists and republican moderates saw General Pichegru as a potential saviour and he toyed with opposition hopes before being discovered and, with 53 deputies, expelled to the penal colony of Guiana.[6] Government anger at this apparent betrayal gained in intensity and a harsh purge followed, the regime of the corrupt conducting a limited terror and introducing more laws targeting émigrés. This reaction, and more demands for conscripts and money, provoked the sensitive west into another rebellion and the royalists of Brittany, Normandy, Maine and La Vendée once more entered the fray. This time they were being led into action by General Georges Cadoudal, that enormous Breton miller who had been in and out of republican prison and trounced at Quiberon. He had scores to settle with the Blues and, as he went about settling them, he was ably supported by experienced subordinates such as Pierre Robinault de Saint-Réjant, Guillemot, Sol de Grisolles - and the golden guineas of Britain. Pierre-Joseph Pièche, who served under Saint-Réjant, describes what a difference this gold made to the cause: 'From then on he [Cadoudal] continued to pay us 36 Francs a month and the others different amounts. This money had come from England.'[7]

Still, it was not the glory days when armies and fleets had conspired with rebellion, and the Chouan bands proved reluctant to stray far from their homes, or heed the promises of luckless princes who could neither see nor know the risks of rebellion.[8] But the uprising prospered, nevertheless, encouraged by the feebleness of the government response and an increasing sense that the republic, and her people, was on the verge of exhaustion.

Frustration did not mean that France would welcome the return of a king as desirable – indeed many feared royalist revenge and a White Terror as much as they feared the return of a Robespierre

– but the debased kleptocracy that ruled them was evidently incapable of acting in the nation's interests. Continuous war, rebellion and a series of unpopular measures, including enforcing conscription in September 1798 (the Jourdan Law) and heavy taxation and duties on alcohol, further discredited the notion that the French lived in liberty and enjoyed equality. It was apparent to most that France was as disappointed with the Directory as it was jaded by a decade of political turmoil, and, for now, only victory abroad kept the wolves from the door. Napoleon played his part in staving off disaster by sending the riches of Italy home; but even the legacy of his successes was thrown into question when the conquering hero suddenly quit Europe.

The ambitious general had sailed eastwards in order to barter lives for glory in Egypt. But his plans and his navy went up in smoke when Admiral Nelson destroyed the French fleet at Aboukir in August 1798, trapping the expedition and, before long, encouraging a new coalition against France. A shaken and unpopular Directory, deprived of their finest general and facing campaigns on multiple fronts and hostility at home, recoiled. The royalists rejoiced and a year after Aboukir an enthusiastic D'Artois declared that, with Allied armies now converging on France in the north, south and east, the time had come for a general rising in the west. His loyal lieutenants heeded the call, Louis de Frotté crossing over from England to Bayeux for the conquest of Normandy whilst in Brittany Cadoudal again galvanised his legions, taking command of the 2nd Legion himself and entrusting Saint-Réjant with the 5th Legion and Édouard de La Haye-Saint-Hilaire with the grenadiers. The royalist commanders put aside any divisions for a show of unity at the château de Jonchère on 14 September 1799 and to support these warlike preparations the British mustered aid of all kinds. The Royal Navy landed a huge shipment of arms on the bleak and barren coast by Saint-Brieuc on 25 October. So with weapons in their hands and gold in their pockets, Georges Cadoudal and his Chouans went on the offensive.

By then another valuable cargo had landed on the welcoming shores of the south of France. Napoleon had returned from Egypt. He arrived in Paris on 16 October, embracing his mother and rescuing his fractious marriage before doing the same for France. As the republic's enemies had closed in during that terrible summer of 1799, Sieyès, the greyest of the republic's éminences grises, had put himself forward as kingmaker, turning to the generals to salvage the revolution. Young General Joubert was suggested as the kind of man who might rescue the republic, or replace it with a Cromwellian regime, but his body had been unhelpfully mangled at Novi in August. The next candidate, General Moreau, disappointed the politicians by refusing to become involved, preferring the comradeship of the bivouac to the duplicities of the salons. Bonaparte therefore arrived just in time, and proved more than willing to sacrifice himself in order to save France. But by doing so, he would destroy both the republic and any hopes for the restoration of the monarchy.

One Frenchman's saviour was at once another's tyrant.

2

A COUP OF GRACE

Sunday 10 November was misty and cold. Some 500 men of the ponderously named Grenadier Guards of the Legislative Corps were marching at speed from their Parisian barracks at the Boulevard des Capucines towards the palace of Saint-Cloud. Tasked to escort and protect the lawmakers of France, they would that autumn morning form the cortège for the interment of the republic.

They left behind them a capital under martial law. The Minister of Police, Joseph Fouché, the former Jacobin zealot who had punished Lyon, had been told to secure Paris against what rumour said was a Jacobin coup, but he hedged his bets by doing nothing. Instead of his police, it was the army, or those elements of it loyal to Bonaparte, which was out patrolling the streets. The gentlemen of the republic's Council of Ancients and the Council of Five Hundred were hastily transferred to the safety offered by Saint-Cloud on the fringe of the capital. Their deliberations on the various emergencies afflicting France began after lunch, with the Council of the Ancients convening on the first floor. News that the Directors were to be dismissed was announced and caused consternation, into which strode General Bonaparte, followed by his secretary Bourrienne and a limping General Berthier.

Beneath a fresco of the muse of music and poetry Bonaparte attempted to deliver a prepared harangue on liberty and equality but, for once, his nerve seems to have failed him and his few disjointed sentences were shouted down by the rising clamour of the legislators. Red-faced, Bonaparte took the opportunity to retire, determined to try again, this time with the Council of Five Hundred then sitting in the orangery.

Napoleon's brother Lucien, president of the Council, recounted what happened next:

> General Bonaparte entered. He had with him four grenadiers from our guard; some other soldiers and officers occupied the entrance to the orangery. The entire assembly, indignant at the sight, jumped up. A crowd of them shouted 'armed men, in here?' and they surged towards the general, grabbing at him, pushing him back. A few raised daggers[1] against him but the grenadiers acted as a rampart against them.

Whilst the enormous representative of Toulouse, Hugues Destrem, was shouting and throwing punches towards the general, the deputy Barthélemy Aréna made a grab for Bonaparte's collar and only the presence of grenadiers Thomas Thomé and Edme-Jean-Baptiste Pourée, who had their uniforms torn, allowed the general to beat a retreat through this disorderly sea of lawyers towards the exit. To shouts of 'Down with the tyrant!' and 'Outlaw!' the humiliated general was finally bundled out, and perhaps just in time, for the Jacobin deputy Grandmaison, opting for a pistol to the preferred weapon of Brutus, took out his firearm and brandished it towards Lucien. The young Corsican chose discretion over valour and promptly retreated to join his infuriated brother.

To be humiliated twice was enough but Bonaparte was almost humbled a third time when the horse he mounted to harangue the assembled troops reared up and nearly threw him. This was too much and it transformed Napoleonic rage into action. As darkness fell, the general gave the order to clear the improvised chamber. Captain Ponsard's grenadiers fixed bayonets and, to Joachim Murat's crude order of 'Throw those buggers out,' advanced on the orangery. With drums rolling the soldiers marched in and hundreds of deputies scattered, many exiting directly through the 12 windows, and the legitimacy of the government went with them.

Ten years of revolution had been swept away in an instant. Sovereignty had not slipped into Napoleon's hands. He had reached out and seized it for himself.

After the dust settled, the man nobody liked but everyone preferred had himself declared First Consul. A revolution cannot survive such a coup, and Napoleon was glad to mouth the required eulogy, declaring: 'Citizens, the revolution is established upon the principles with which it began: it is ended.'[2] He saw his coming to power as an opportunity to rally France behind him, and for him to see whether the French might not support his own preference for glory over liberty. The moderate middle, used to sighing that something must be done, was glad to find someone else to do it, and this hero seemed ready to lift them from the anarchy into which the revolution had degraded.[3] Napoleon could charm such subjects, but even to his enemies and rivals he first preached concord in soothing tones of patriotism, declaring that 'the simple title of French citizen is worth more than that of royalist, Clichyen, Jacobin, Feuillant, and the other thousand and one denominations which breathe life into the factionalism which has, for the last ten years, pushed the nation into the abyss from where it is high time it was rescued.'[4]

Most French citizens were, however, yet to voice an opinion. The majority, more curious about the government than confident in its abilities, seemed inclined to wait and see, after all it was clear that affairs could not get any worse. However, a sizable minority were perturbed by this blatant grab for power. The royalists would of course resist, but many of the true sons of the republic were equally incensed by Napoleon's dismissal of ten years of democratic rule. Although the Directory had discredited the idea of republicanism, with their fraternity of expropriation reserving liberty and equality for themselves alone, there were still many who owed all to the republic and who were sceptical of this Corsican arriviste and his clan. Some on the left were indeed suggesting that the English had escorted Bonaparte back from Egypt just to weaken her old enemy. Others took a more principled stance against a man who had, after all, seized power from the people. Bertrand Barère de Vieuzac, an unrepentant Jacobin and occasional police informer, suggested that Napoleon was not helping by assuming princely airs, which, accompanying republic slogans, exposed the new government to ridicule. He was perhaps right, for the early examples of consular pomp aimed for the sublime but achieved only the ridiculous. On 19 February 1800, in a display of quasi-royal mummery, Napoleon swept towards the Tuileries in an imperial Austrian coach drawn by six white horses. Reaching the palace, the chief magistrate of France, who just five years before had been shivering in rented rooms in the seedy Rue de la Huchette, marched past the two trees of liberty in the courtyard and established himself in royal apartments still pockmarked with the bullets of 1792. By taking up quarters in Louis XVI's rooms the First Consul immediately disappointed both royalists and revolutionaries but evidently amused himself, supposedly telling Josephine 'well, my little creole, come and lie down in the bed of your masters.'[5] Sleeping in the bed of tyrants and walking in the shoes of kings was all very well but as the new ruler remarked, the difficulty was not in getting into the Tuileries. The difficulty was remaining there.

To do so, he turned to men who came from the broad spectrum of French politics but shared the common trait of ruthlessness. Fouché, the regicide and proponent of terror, was retained as Minister of Police. An avowed republican later at ease in an empire, thin-lipped Fouché was a man who would make a fine minister of all talents, even some of the darker ones.[6] Talleyrand, the lame old priest who had found the catechism of control and rituals of power more to his liking, settled into his aristocratic office at the Ministry of Foreign Relations. The other two consuls, Jean-Jacques-Régis de Cambacérès and Charles-François Lebrun, shared Ancien Regime tastes.[7] Apart from these collaborators, Napoleon placed his trust in his popularity, for he had only the crudest means to stifle dissent, and his empty coffers offered few inducements to reward loyalty. His police force was still a work in progress and the army was more republican than Bonapartist. 'If he is popular with the soldiers,' wrote on observer, 'it is only with those he has commanded' – and most of those had been abandoned in Egypt.

Fortunately, Napoleon's seizure of power had taken many by surprise and opposition to it was riven by factions developed over a decade of struggle. This was particularly true of the republicans and Napoleon soon tested the loyalty of his supporters by using them to harry the republican opposition into political oblivion. On 12 November, at two in the morning, orders went out to seize and deport 61 former deputies of Jacobin tendencies and on 17 November a further 37 Jacobins whose presence undermined the new order were declared outlaws. No hand was raised to resist this latest purge and those who had once been sans-culottes remained rooted to the likes of Bully's café in Rue des Mauvais Garçons, more successful at downing wine than governments.

Having thus warned the men of the left, Napoleon had a free hand to placate those traditional props of order, the Church and the aristocracy. Napoleon's concessions to the Catholics and his expressed support for freedom to worship were rewarded with a degree of clerical support, particularly from Abbé Étienne Alexandre Bernier, who proved himself useful by winning over the Norman and Breton clergy. Some nobles also submitted to servitude through honours, finding lucrative positions as prefects, and others, such as Lafayette, felt optimistic enough to return to France, with Napoleon encouraging loyalty by removing many of the returnees from the list of those banished by revolution.[8] However, as with the republicans, those obstinate enough to reject Napoleonic largesse and insist on a restoration of the Bourbons could expect just one outcome. They would be chastised.

Those most committed to the Bourbon cause hated Napoleon, not only because his whiff of grapeshot had shredded their hopes and supporters, but also because he, a man made by the revolution, had placed himself on the throne of kings. The militant set of royalists around D'Artois were against any kind of compromise with the Corsican. One of D'Artois' men, Nicolas-François Dutheil de Telmont, hoped that those making their peace with the new regime 'would get what cowards deserve'. As with the republican grumblers, such antipathy to the usurper would perhaps not have mattered except for the fact that, in this case, these royalists had foreign backers intent on keeping the conflict alive for reasons of state. London was still at war with France, and her belligerent ministers Pitt, Grenville and Windham were intent on making use of discord to weaken France. For now their best option still lay in the restless west of France. The rebels there were kept on a short lead, and unleashed with funds and guns whenever London and D'Artois wished to convert discord into opportunity. In late 1799, as the Chouan rebellion rumbled on in Brittany, the royalists' most obedient hound seemed to be Georges Cadoudal. He had championed war at Jonchère in September, and enjoyed the support of several competent lieutenants. These included François-Gaspard de La Nougarède (known as Achille Le Brun); Picot de Limoëlan (known as Pourleroy), a 30-year-old officer intent on revenging his executed father;[9] Louis de Frotté, who had come over from Portsmouth on 12 September; Pierre Mathurin Mercier, known as La Vendée; and Colonel Pierre Robinault de Saint-Réjant. These rebels made considerable progress whilst France's best armies battled the Allies on the French frontiers in the autumn of 1799.

However, as winter began, it was the turn of the foreign armies to quit the field,[10] a sign to the Chouan captains and their sponsors that they had little cause to be optimistic in a struggle against the more formidable Napoleon. The First Consul exploited their nascent doubts with a two-pronged approach, offering peace whilst noisily preparing for war. The gentlemanly General Théodore Hédouville, veteran of Valmy, had replaced the incapable commanders of government troops in the west. He had arrived in Angers to see that 'the situation of our forces is abysmal.' To win time, he opted to launch a charm offensive, agreeing an armistice with some key Chouans which would run from 25 November to 21 January 1800.[11] The royalists D'Autichamp from the Vendée and Châtillon from Maine, both as tired of war as most of France,[12] hoped this was the start of a more comprehensive peace. Cadoudal, however, was incensed, his subordinate, Mercier, telling Bourmont 'this truce is a mortal blow to the Bourbon family ... Georges [Cadoudal] speaks for both of us when he says we do not want any kind of peace.'[13] Cadoudal eventually bowed to the inevitable compromise and outwardly adhered to the armistice on 10 December, but he evidently saw it as an opportunity to sharpen his claws.

A truce was not the same as peace. Still Napoleon's policy of divide and rule paid dividends and rescinding the law of hostages, and tempting the pessimists among the Chouans with offers of preferment, won some new supporters. The more embittered royalists dismissed such advances as double-dealing, Bernard de la Fréjolière speaking for them when he expressed his fear that 'If that tyrant wants peace it is only because he wishes to divide us and have us climb the steps to the scaffold silently and one by one.' Such legitimate concerns would dominate the royalist conference at Pouancé in Anjou in mid-December. There Cadoudal naturally advocated resuming hostilities and made use of D'Artois's name to offer British muskets and money[14] to sway the undecided. He was out-voted, D'Autichamp and Châtillon had already sought terms, whilst Bourmont, Frotté and 30 other royalist captains, including Joseph de Limoëlan, agreed to negotiate with Paris and set their names to 39 articles that would perhaps form the basis of a future settlement. Frotté's man, the Chevalier Louis Gaérin de Bruslart, was sent to London for its views whilst D'Andigné was nominated to head to Paris to see Napoleon. He first met Hyde de Neuville, an agent of the crown who had been sent to Paris with the blessing of London to see whether Napoleon might be persuaded, for suitable compensation, to relinquish power to the royal family. This was not as far-fetched as it seemed, after all General Monck had done exactly that in 1660 and General Pichegru provided a more recent example of a republican general promising to restore the Bourbons. However, the royal agents relied on hope rather than any actual evidence that Napoleon was biddable. Even so, Hyde and other poor judges of character were determined to try and rumours eventually reached Napoleon that he would be offered the rank of Constable, or Grand Duke of Milan, as the reward for stepping aside.[15] In the meantime, as Napoleon stifled his laughter, Hyde put aside his own ideas in order to act as broker for D'Andigné, making use of a connection to that venal Minister of Foreign Relations, Talleyrand,[16] to arrange a meeting between the rebel envoy and the First Consul. On the evening of 27 December 1799, D'Andigné entered the Luxembourg Palace:

> We entered a room on the ground floor. A short man, rather mean-looking, came in a few moments after us. He had an olive complexion, straight hair and an air of considerable negligence. Nothing in his appearance led me to think that he was anyone of note. So I was quite shocked when Hyde announced that this man was the First Consul.[17]

The interview began with Napoleon paying heed to the royalist terms for peace, and D'Andigné, spurning Hyde's optimism that Napoleon would voluntarily relinquish power, stuck to the more pragmatic task of finding mutually acceptable ground for some kind of agreement:

> We discussed several articles of the proposed treaty and agreed on some principles, including: exemption from conscription for the rebel provinces; payment of arrears in tax; deletion from the list of emigrants for those royalist captains which featured on it, and the return of their unsold property (Bonaparte told me, however, that he wanted to limit it to 100 names); forbidding the courts to prosecute any royalist for any act carried out during the war; recognition by our representatives of the rights of those who had acquired national property to enjoy it. The point I insisted on most was for the free exercise of the Catholic faith without our ministers being required to swear loyalty or send in any kind of submission.[18]

Napoleon willingly participated in this debate, and happily added terms and conditions of his own. Indeed, D'Andigné found it difficult to keep up as Napoleon 'had a vivid imagination which meant that he jumbled his sentences so that it was difficult to follow the conversation and to concentrate. His manner of speaking was as swift as his ability to create projects, and he jumped quickly from one subject to another. He opened a theme, dropped it, returned to it, seemed not to be listening to you whilst not missing a thing you said, and he did not forget anything either.'[19]

What D'Andigné would not forget was that Napoleon was negotiating from a position of power, and it was clear enough that London, Hyde and their ilk had been overly optimistic[20] about Napoleon stepping down. Indeed, as the discussion continued, the First Consul was clearly telling the Chouans that it was they who should be surrendering to him, almost as a personal act of obedience. When D'Andigné asked why the First Consul would not put his signature to any agreement, Napoleon told him that his word was enough. The royalist insisted that the treaty should become law, and Napoleon, fuming, told him 'the government has been sufficiently humiliated by treating with you and will not codify its shame into law.'

Here the interview cooled, only to warm again when Napoleon, who was evidently expecting complete submission, questioned why royalists like D'Andigné were still true to their oaths of obedience to the princes of France. He became animated and, in an impassioned monologue, wondered why they were remaining loyal to the undeserving whilst they spurned his advances, he who had done so much for the glory of France:

They have done nothing for glory. They are forgotten. Where were they during the Vendée? Their place was there! Their heart was always with you but the politics of foreign powers always kept them away! They should have thrown themselves into a fishing boat ... If I had been in the Vendée I would have fought for them. But you cannot understand how little Europe cares. There was a time, I confess, when I wanted to do something for them. After the treaty of Campo-Formio, I spoke about creating a court for them. But they would not make any sacrifices.

Napoleon had a point, but an honourable man such as D'Andigné could not be expected to turn coat so quickly. Still, his stubborn commitment to his oath of obedience irked Napoleon, who evidently had a more flexible approach when it came to self-interest, and the First Consul demanded to know whether the Chouans were 'ashamed of wearing the same uniform as a Bonaparte'. D'Andigné replied that of course he was not, but that he would find it difficult to bear arms against countries who were so recently allies. Napoleon struck again, accusing the royalists of being in league with foreign powers and D'Andigné closed the debate with 'you know that we were obliged to accept the support of England and we cannot forget that so quickly.'

With both sides having made some progress, but with any agreement breaking on the rocks of loyalty, the meeting reached an impasse. For the royalists, Napoleon revealed himself to be implacably in charge, ready to trade concessions, but unwilling to relinquish any of his newly acquired power. To break those who would stand in the way, he would shout, rage and offer lucrative inducements. Indeed, soon after that interview Napoleon wrote to D'Andigné:

Tell your fellow citizens that the revolutionary laws will no longer devastate the beautiful land of France, that the revolution is over, and that liberty of conscience will reign absolute, that all shall be protected and held free from prejudice and that, as for me, I shall recognise and be grateful to those who have given France peace and tranquillity.[21]

For all the promise and for all the charm, there was an iron hand in the velvet glove proffered to D'Andigné and his comrades. Napoleon could make life worth living for those Chouans willing to sheath their swords, or pursue them to the grave should they resist. The choice was theirs but before decisions could be made time ran out and with the truce expiring, hopes for a lasting agreement died away too. For the hotheads in the royalist camp, eager to drag their comrades back into the fray, this was the desired result and Cadoudal, supported by D'Artois,[22] was again leading the call to arms. The government had also been preparing for war whilst talking peace and Napoleon had assigned General Brune, fresh from victory over the Duke of York in the hills of Holland, to replace the conciliatory Hédouville and lead the infernal columns against Brittany. General Lefebvre was also to advance and was given free rein to treat Normandy like occupied territory. Napoleon, thinking that 'weakness is inhumane', suspended the constitution in 18 rebellious departements and, hoping for a quick victory,[23] instructed Brune to do his worst:

The Army of the West has 60,000 men under arms. March on the Morbihan, where you will find the 22nd and 72nd. Disperse Georges' men. Seize his cannon, and his grain stores (he keeps a great deal on the coast and sells it to the English). In short, make sure the rebels of the Morbihan feel the full weight of the horrors of war. The departments of the Ille-et-Vilaine, Loire Inférieure, Cotes du Nord and Morbihan are placed outside the constitution. Anyone who surrenders, make them welcome ... tolerance for the priests ... no mercy to those communities which behave badly. Burn a few farms and a few of the larger villages in the Morbihan, and make a few examples. Your troops shall not want for bread, meat or pay. There is enough for your troops in those guilty departments. It is only by making war terrible that the inhabitants will, of their own accord, unite against the brigands and make it clear through their disposition that the game is up.[24]

The First Consul then told his subordinate to 'make sure that by the last week of February, the bands of Georges, Frotté and Bourmont have been annihilated or, if not, then Georges and Bourmont have, like Frotté, no more than 60 or 80 men, wandering about and too afraid to show themselves. Here [Paris] some five or six Chouans are shot each day.'[25]

Aghast at this approaching storm, some of the exhausted royalists, along with the realists, promptly surrendered, concluding peace treaties, receiving amnesties, and swapping the rigours of camp life for the comfort of forgiveness. The tired Charles D'Autichamp, who had been beaten in La Vendée and signed a peace treaty at Montfaucon on 18 January 1800, was, with Châtillon and his Bretons, brought back to the fold by the intercession of the Abbé Bernier.[26] Frotté and Georges Cadoudal, emboldened by English subsidies and arms, proved more intransigent, Bernier thinking: 'as for Georges and Frotté, we know who manages them. England does not hide it, saying openly that their armed opposition will prevent at least 30,000 men from being sent to the banks of the Rhine when the campaign opens.'[27] For now, Napoleon, like a veteran lion, sensed that Bourmont was the one most easily plucked from the Chouan herd and told Hédouville 'don't remove your boots until you have destroyed him [Bourmont].' Bourmont was surprised and beaten by General Chabot at Meslay on

23 January and gratefully surrendered, asking for the same terms as D'Autichamp on 4 February.[28] Frotté and his 2,000 men were next. He fought an indecisive battle at Cossé and, seeing with alarm how the government forces progressed, offered a truce. General Guidal was authorised to treat, but Napoleon sent special orders via an officer of his Guards. These instructions are missing from the archives, but the First Consul's sentiments were already known. He had told Brune to offer a reward of 100 Louis for Baron de Commarque, Chevalier de Monceaux, Lavi Dubois, d'Hauteville, Memecourt, Picot, Rues, Hugon and Des Essarts and 1,000 for Frotté.[29] As to what would follow, Napoleon was of the opinion that 'These men should no longer exist within a fortnight.'

Frotté, issued with a safe-conduct to pass through republican lines, rode into Alençon, staying at Guidal's headquarters at 10 Rue du Cygne. There he was seized by his host on 16 February and he was sent to Verneuil, tried by a military commission of five officers and, with six of his comrades, ceased to exist on 18 February. Napoleon denied that he had ordered the Chouan shot, forgetting perhaps his remark to Brune on that same day that 'Frotté has been taken with his staff, at this very moment he should be being shot.' Whether Guidal was guilty, or his superior Lefebvre, mattered little to the royalists, who instantly blamed Napoleon for what they saw as a betrayal.[30]

Whether betrayed and slain, or persuaded and pacified, most Chouan captains were ending their fight, with even those who believed in the *lex talionis* rethinking their vendetta. Indeed, many of the senior officers were busy gaining favourable terms for themselves and their subordinates, and brought with them petitions to the Napoleonic regime listing those of their officers who should be removed from the list of émigrés, thus restoring their rights and, in many cases, their family's income. Châtillon requested this favour for 20 officers, the Chevalier de la Prévalaye sought amnesty for three, one of whom was Joseph de Limoëlan, an officer who had signed his peace with Brune on 18 February. La Prévalaye noted that 'he is the serving officer under my command who has contributed most to the pacification and who was the first to consult General Hédouville on this matter.' Limoëlan, with many of the other Chouans, set off for Paris, riding out on 12 March to settle his status and to await the decision of the committee established a fortnight before to weigh the merits of each request for reintegration.[31]

By then even Georges Cadoudal, dubbed 'the leader of the English faction ... the most dangerous of all the enemy, just as the Morbihan is the military and political key' by an angry First Consul, seemed prepared to relent. Cadoudal, with his four pieces of artillery and 7,000 English muskets, had barely escaped being beaten by Harty at Pont-du-Loc and following this stalemate, Brune, sensing that few were ready to die for a moribund cause, struck, offering negotiations. The two met at Theix. Brune's subordinate, Jean-François-Joseph Debelle, informed the Breton, 'I am designated by the First Consul to offer you the rank of General of Division and a command in the army of Moreau, but, if you refuse, to send him your head.'[32]

Cadoudal kept his head and made use of it when he too went to Paris. Accompanied by Achille Biget and Sol de Grisolles, and escorted by Brune's aide-de-camp, *Chef de brigade* Yves Marie Pastol, he passed through the Bons-Hommes barrier in early March. After presenting his passport at the prefecture,[33] the Chouan sought out Hyde de Neuville, collecting 2,400 livres from him, and then visited his friend the Chevalier de La Haye Saint-Hilaire, before being introduced to Napoleon on 5 March. The physical gulf between the wide-shouldered and red-faced Breton and the slim, olive-skinned Corsican was matched by that between their differing expectations. Inevitably, then, the encounter was short, and Napoleon's only conclusion was that Cadoudal was 'a huge Breton who it might be possible to have follow the interests of the country'. Following this terse encounter, Cadoudal was then largely ignored whilst his noble colleagues were wined and dined. There was a cursory meeting about disarming the rebels with General Clarke,[34] before a second meeting at the Tuileries, on 30 March. The Breton was ushered in by *Chef de brigade* Jean Rapp and stood as Napoleon paced the room and tried an emotional appeal on behalf of France and glory. When that failed, the First Consul made sport with what he supposed were Cadoudal's ambitions, offering material enticements of money and rank – he now offered to make the royalist a general of brigade – but Cadoudal perceived these as a slight, just as he saw with bitterness how Châtillon and Bourmont had been received at the Consul's table whilst he had been left out in the cold. Napoleon's fundamental misjudgement of Cadoudal was so evident and so gross that Cadoudal felt that reconciliation to the man and his regime impossible. Indeed, as that disastrous meeting drew to a close, a conspiracy was born.

Cadoudal, denied the privilege of leading armies in the field, now resolved to settle his old and new grievances with the Corsican by other means. When it came to the form of his revenge he immediately thought along Chouan lines, considering an ambush as the surest way: 'that bastard is the same as the others ... I see that he wants to slit my throat, well he won't. I shall mount up and, along with some of my best men, will take a ride along the Malmaison road.'[35]

But Cadoudal did not ride to Malmaison for a final encounter. Instead, on 8 April, informed or suspecting that Bonaparte might get to his throat first, he quit his hotel, the Maison des Ministres,[36] and, with Hyde de Neuville, fled for England and D'Artois.

They left Mercier behind them in Brittany as the western provinces were subjected to another bitter cleansing by the government's gendarmes. Few, very few, rebels took to the woods, loyal to an unknown king and a distant cause, whilst most gave up on elusive victory and slipped away, swapping their British words and muskets for ploughshares and tankards.[37]

With peace being won in the west, Napoleon was at last free to march east. After a night at the opera he quit Paris on the morning of 6 May and on 14 June shattered the Austrian army at Marengo in northern Italy. Despite the fact that it was General Moreau whose victory at Hohenlinden in September would finally force Austria to sue for peace, it was at Marengo that Napoleon conquered Paris. The Parisians were elated with their new ruler and a situation in which, having been earlier ringed by encroaching enemies, France, with an army of half a million men, was now surrounded by allies and vassals. Only London remained implacable and surly.

London and Louis XVIII, who had no other choice. The exiled king had been hopeful that Hyde, Josephine and Talleyrand might persuade the Consul to act as a General Monck and return the kingdom to its rightful monarch.[38] So it was that Louis XVIII, by the grace of God, King of France and Navarre, and Great Sovereign, had written from his cold and damp exile on 20 February:

> The victor of Lodi, of Castiglione, of Arcola, the conqueror of Italy and Egypt, could not prefer vain celebrity to glory. Nevertheless, vital time is being wasted. We, together, can assure the security of France, and I say we because I have need of Bonaparte and he cannot do it without me.[39]

But the letter had been delayed and missed Napoleon, who had left for Italy. It was only in August that the nervous bearer, the Abbé de la Montesquiou, handed it over to Consul Lebrun, having used Talleyrand as intermediary. Louis's letter had ended on a hopeful note: 'General, Europe is watching, glory is waiting and I am impatient to bring peace to my people.'[40]

It met a poor reception after the glory of Marengo. Whether Napoleon read it in Louis XVI's bed is not clear, but, having considered it for a month, he wrote back from the royal apartments of the Tuileries on 7 September 1800. His message was curt, and unwelcome: 'You should not aspire to return to France. In order to do so you would have to walk over 100,000 corpses.'

There would be no restoration. General Bonaparte's ambition was clear. He ruled France and only violence could remove him. As the royalists pondered on this obstinacy an idea was born; an idea that had already occurred to Georges Cadoudal, and which naturally appealed to D'Artois. The throne might be restored to Louis, but not through the death of a hundred thousand. The death of one man might do. The one man who stood between Louis and his throne. Killing Napoleon had never seemed such a promising endeavour.

3

AGENTS AND SPIES

On 29 March 1798 a train of coaches and wagons carrying threadbare aristocrats and furniture arrived before a baroque palace on the banks of the frozen Lielupe. This had once housed the dukes of Courland but the dukes had gone and the building now served as a military hospital, with one of the wings burnt down in a recent fire. Despite the damage it looked cheerful enough, the brightly painted plasterwork of Bartolomeo Rastrelli contrasting prettily with the snow and ice. The 100 individuals now arriving, however, found it hard to be of good cheer as they had once inhabited Versailles and were now obliged to hibernate within this Latvian palace. They had brought with them to Mitau the Comte de Lille, better known as Louis XVIII, an exiled king who had accepted the charitable gift of sanctuary – and cash – from the Czar of Russia. Whilst it put an end to Louis' nomadic existence, it hardly amounted to an improvement in his fortunes.

Those fortunes had been in slow decline and, in parallel, the cause he represented also sank to new lows. With the distant king settling further into exile, those who fought for him and who had supported him were also being chased from the field. By early 1800, as Napoleon consolidated his power, thumbing his nose at Bourbon rights, the king's loyal acolytes, who had once raised armies and conquered cities, were now mere partisans of opportunity. Despite the occasional organised raid, most royalist insurgents were now reduced to assassinating clerks and butchering gendarmes. Such a shadowy war of the knife kept garrisons on alert across Brittany, but it would be insufficient to topple a strengthening regime, however versed the royalists became in kidnap and murder. Indeed, as the final rebellion petered out in the spring of 1800, it was clear enough that rebellion alone could not unseat a Bonaparte. However, if an insurgency, however small, could shift to Paris, and combine ambush with the subversive and seditious skills of royalist agents and spies, then Napoleon and his regime might perhaps be dealt that fatal blow. The motive to kill Napoleon and destroy his regime was stronger by the day, the means to do so were shifting into the clandestine shadows of Napoleon's capital.

Espionage had always been a feature of the war on the revolution, cloaks and daggers were as much a part of the story as red bonnets and guillotines, but by the fall of the Directory the war of intrigue had been outstripped by events. The royalist agents in Paris, having worked for years to overthrow the republic, sat and watched as Napoleon did so in a day. However, if one man had overthrown a revolution, then perhaps one assassination might finish the Consulate, and with Chouans acquainted with ambush and assassination heading to Paris to settle their cases, the men of the king sensed an opportunity. Royalist sympathisers, agents and opportunists positioned themselves to continue their war in the shadows, but could now focus on just one fleshy target.

In order for such scheming to prove successful, the royalists would rely primarily on an established royalist web of secret agents. This network was centred on the French capital, and stretched thinly across Europe; taut in France but tangled around the margins. Louis XVIII was nominally at the centre of this nefarious activity, despite his distaste for such matters and for men with such skills, but he delegated such responsibilities to ageing courtiers. Besides, Louis was now in Mitau in the lands of the Czar, far away from France and reality. William Wickham, Britain's best agent on the Continent, had already informed his superior, Lord Grenville, that the king was, essentially, ignorant:

> It is a great public calamity at a moment like this that there should
> be no one person about the French king at all acquainted with the
> real state of the interior and of the public opinion in France, or
> with the secret springs and causes by which the revolution has been
> brought about and supported.[1]

Louis's advisors had over time shifted responsibility for royalist espionage within France to a group of agents known as the Swabian Agency. Hamburg and Bremen, where the British Colonel George Don helped run affairs, had been important hubs of royalist espionage, but this new collection of agents, established in southern Germany and Switzerland, soon proved itself to be the king's most able network. This was largely thanks to Wickham's support and Grenville's money, the latter being particularly welcome as Louis could not afford to be overly generous.[2] Even so, the king's agents would soon be overshadowed by a rival group run by the most active proponent of the monarchist cause, and another one sponsored by London. That flock of spies owed their allegiance to Louis's brother, the Comte D'Artois, based variously in London, which he preferred, or draughty Holyrood House in Edinburgh.

D'Artois had a high opinion of himself, and of his own abilities, one which few aside from the count's friend, the Bishop of

Arras,[3] shared. He preferred horses to people, which endeared him to his like-minded hosts, but his abiding passions were revenge and intrigue. Louis de Bouillé, an exile who orbited the exiled count, thought him 'an intriguer by nature as well as by habit, and this kind of conflict suited him more than warfare in the field, which was more honest and more dangerous.' D'Artois's energy and rank were sufficient to persuade the British into paying hefty subsidies, which the king's brother sank into developing his own parallel system of agents. At their head was Nicolas-François Dutheil de Telmont, mercifully known as Dutheil, who had initially worked on behalf of Louis in London but had gradually been tempted into the circle around D'Artois in Edinburgh. This fuelled Louis's anxiety, born of lengthy experience, that he was being marginalised and passed over, but it also posed practical difficulties because as the prince's duplicate system grew, so it weakened the common cause. Before long resources were as divided as loyalties and, with D'Artois promoting officers, briefing agents, and acting as liaison with London, the entire system seemed mired in confusion. The government in Whitehall made its contribution here too, with Wickham respectfully lending an ear to the king and his agents, whilst Grenville preferred the garrulous and generous D'Artois.

The British would have done better to impose some unity on the royalist factions, for the lessons of recent history demonstrated that they badly needed it. But unity was hard to maintain in the face of constant defeat. Indeed, the 1790s had been a long decade of dashed hope and failing endeavour for the royalists and this was particularly true of royalist attempts at espionage. The most significant disaster had been the collapse of the Factory, or Royal Agency, the first royalist network in Paris, broken in 1795 when André-Charles Brotier, a mathematician, was arrested. Despite this loss the network rumbled on, that attention-seeking journalist Fauche-Borel doing what he could to revive it, but it received another nearly mortal blow in 1797 when the spymaster d'Antraigues was caught by the French army in Italy and only allowed to escape after revealing the workings of the network.[4] Those revelations implicated General Pichegru, a soldier of the republic now exposed as a royalist agent and one brought down by the purges of Fructidor, in which the royalists and their new friends were deported or imprisoned.

This effectively destroyed the king's spies in Paris and leant those marginal agents operating out of Switzerland more significance. These were led by Antoine Balthazar Joseph D'André, once a deputy for the Third Estate at the Estates General, and ever a pragmatist and moderate. He had expended much effort pulling the constitutionalists and ultras into a makeshift league in the run-up to the failed takeover in 1797 and had spent lavishly for his king. His efforts resulted in the establishment of the Agence de Souabe, or Swabian Agency, and tempted London into supplying him with money, using Jacques de Cazalès, then resident in Marylebone High Street, as supplicant and William Wickham as patron.

Wickham had initially represented the Alien Office, originally set up to monitor the French emigrants and, almost as an afterthought, quash subversive activity by Britain's revolutionary sympathisers, but soon expanded to take the war of shadows across the Channel. By 1798 Wickham and other servants of His Majesty's Secret Service were overstretched by the demands of running a Continent-wide operation, but he made use of his new post as Under Secretary of State for the Home Department to galvanise royalism by supporting the plausible D'André.[5] But it proved an extremely difficult task to restore a functioning network within France itself. This was partly because the quality of royalist agents was sadly lacking; indeed, from Madrid, the Duc d'Havré warned Louis that 'the French don't trust your agents and they regard them as being men of poor judgement, indiscreet, lazy, imprudent and think that they have contributed to the success of our enemies through premature, partial and poorly organised insurrections, all entrusted to men who should not have been relied upon and who, once compromised, compromise all who follow them.'[6]

This dearth of effective agents was most pronounced at the heart of all intrigues, Paris. The Chouan captain, Frotté, had visited the capital in the autumn of 1798, writing 'there was no agency as such, but a crowd of agents divided into three factions, all of which loathed each other and were driven by mutual hatred.'[7] London had not only been supporting the king's agents and D'Artois, but had also been running their own cell through Abbé Louis Jean Baptiste Justin Ratel, known as The Monk, a man of 'great courage, profound insight, endless devotion and, most importantly in the current circumstances, sound judgement'. He was assisted by a woman known as Satin Skin, and his network, collaborating with the king's men, had been instrumental in rescuing Sir Sidney Smith from the Temple prison in May 1798, and spiriting him up to Le Havre.[8] D'André was happy enough to know Ratel but refused to co-operate with D'Artois and worked hard to build his own structure within Paris, a group of agents eventually coalescing into Louis's Secret Royal Agency, or Royal Council. This network was represented by the lawyer Pierre-Paul Royer-Collard and a writer, Quatremère de Quincy, although he eventually took the government's écu and retired from the fray. They were supposed to seduce the republic's leaders into turning coat. However, a different scheme took hold when the desperation of the Swabian Agency and the meddling of a British secret agent nearly led to the use of more direct methods. The agent James Talbot who, with his brother Robert, had taken over Wickham's role in Switzerland, had become willingly embroiled in a newly devised plot to assassinate key members of the French Directory, hoping to kill 'Barras and his friends'.

The Talbots worked closely with D'André and a network increasingly willing to contemplate any number of wild schemes, even assassination. D'André had initially envisaged the poetic justice of having some enraged Jacobins bring the government down, but Talbot's enthusiasms and royalist mistrust soon hatched a plan which involved funding royalist hitmen from the clandestine network of Chouans. These veterans from the wars in the west, probably 50 or so men variously said to be under a captain called Rochecotte or an adventurer called Danican, would gather in Paris to deliver the blow. D'André gave hints of the scheme to D'Avaray, the king's 'friend and, in a way, closest advisor', in a ciphered letter written on 27 May 1798:

> I'm running another operation about which I can't say a great deal, as secrecy is key to its success. It is the project to assassinate the Directory. I've asked all the Institutes for men of action. If, which I doubt given previous experience, enough can be gathered, I will go back in to the interior and attempt to land this major blow ... Vezet is establishing links with the Directory Guard and the headquarters staff at Paris but neither this agent, nor the Institute know the goal of what is being proposed.[9]

To help his Swabian faction Talbot granted £25,000 to D'André, the royalist sending it on for use in Paris where the 'body of resolute men' were planning to depose or put to death the majority of the Directory. They planned to do this either by blowing them up or by butchering them in the Luxembourg Palace, although

Talbot's account of the next stage seems rather sketchy: 'Should they succeed in making away with the Directory, it is then the intention to have the tocsin sounded to assemble the section.'

However, the summer of 1798 passed without much progress, or any sign that the 'select band of intrepid men' were doing anything. On 25 October Talbot was visited by Pierre-Paul Royer-Collard (codename Aubert), of the king's Royal Council, who told him that the plan had changed. The Council would now prefer a military coup, perhaps led by General Bernadotte, or the Breton General Moreau, to an act of murder, unless, that is, more money was forthcoming. London demurred, isolating Talbot and doubting the good faith of the plotters. This froideur led to a falling out and in March 1799 the first tranche of Talbot's money was returned by the royalists, with added interest. Lord Grenville seems to have been the one behind the change of heart and Talbot's recall, fretting that the agent had exceeded his powers and that blowing up a foreign government could not 'become the character of a civilised nation'.[10] But the change had also come about because the British had found a new scheme to back. And this scheme saw attention switch to D'Artois and his clique in London.

Wickham, his door and his purse always open to enemies of the republic, was also at the centre of this new ploy. And it had been through that door that General Pichegru had walked on 27 September 1798. Pichegru had landed in Deal the week before and, still recovering from the ordeal of American exile, he was brought up to London by Charles William Flint and allowed to recover at the Adelphi Hotel before being ushered into Whitehall to hear how the English hoped to make use of his thirst for revenge. Pichegru and his more belligerent colleague, Willot (codename Menard), who also soon returned from the Americas, would feature in British plans for the next five years. However, this initial induction involved meeting D'Artois' English Committee, the nest of royalist agents established and run by Dutheil, including William Hyde de Neuville,[11] Joseph Fiévéé, the Comte de Crénolles (Ferrand), and the Paris-based Jean Phillippe Franquetot Chevalier de Coigny. Pichegru had another meeting with Dutheil on 30 November, Dutheil not quite managing to overcome his suspicions of the general, but with options limited, rallied behind the new figurehead and promised generous support.

The promise of action even persuaded the Comte D'Artois into thinking that he might prepare to pass over to the Continent in order to lead the inevitable uprising. It was agreed that Pichegru would go on ahead and Wickham would follow to raise a small army of Swiss mercenaries, French deserters and royalist cadres, who, commanded by Pichegru, and singing *Domine, salvum fac regem*, would push into eastern France. Wickham thought that D'Artois might lead this offensive for 'if the king is placed in that position and gave out promises then those would have to be kept, whereas if it was the Comte D'Artois then that could be avoided.' D'Artois agreed, and jumped at the chance of escaping Scotland. Without informing his brother of any of this, he arrived in London,[12] that nest of intrigue, and declared himself ready to march.

To those insurgents already in the field in the second half of 1799, particularly Cadoudal and his Breton Chouans, this new plan seemed like a betrayal even though it was designed to ignite a general rebellion. However, a premature revolt around Toulouse in August 1799 showed the dangers of uncoordinated action and Cadoudal was right to be nervous. He need not have worried about hasty action, Pichegru, D'Artois and Willot were still debating when the royalists of the south were being hunted down by republican dragoons, but Cadoudal's concerns about the viability of their plans was well founded, for their schemes were increasingly peppered with fantasy.[13] They grew more unrealistic when the field armies of the Allies were defeated that autumn and when, with the Austrian and Russian armies on the French frontier, Wickham's unreliable royalist force in Switzerland also retreated, pausing long enough to send London a request for £365,000. The king's Swabian Agency also withdrew, their operations frustrated and much of their correspondence with Pichegru captured when the papers of General Korsakow fell into republican hands.[14] Louis XVIII was discouraged by this string of defeats, quite reasonably telling his brother to concentrate on operations in Brittany and Normandy before the isolated Chouans, who were still fighting that October, could claim that they too were being abandoned.

But as the Consulate was on the cusp of being established, and military campaigns were yielding disappointing results, D'Artois was still energised by intrigue. This time he opted for subterfuge over soldiers and tasked the English Committee, of which young Hyde was the most headstrong member, to take clandestine action. The Committee with their morale as high as their coffers were full, for they were now profiting from Wickham's support and £20,000 of Grenville's gold, bestirred themselves in the first months of 1800. Hyde had reached Paris in December 1799, calling himself Paul Berry, and he began working with Coigny on subverting influential forces in the capital. The British had hoped that General Massena might act as a royalist Bonaparte and organise another successful coup,[15] but Coigny thought he could do more by gaining influence through Napoleon's wife, and then seek to have her pressure Bonaparte into handing the crown back to the Bourbons. Hyde agreed and began the approach with Talleyrand (known as 1748 in the royalist cypher) and it was through Talleyrand's good offices that Hyde managed to accompany D'Andigné to Napoleon's study on 27 December. During that interview with the First Consul it became clear that Napoleon was not for turning, that he was more of a Caesar than a Cincinnatus or a General Monck. Talleyrand shrugged at this Napoleonic obstinacy, telling Hyde that if Napoleon 'survives a year, he'll go far', cleverly highlighting the predicament and the solution in one casual phrase.

Hyde, who acknowledged that he now had no scruples about overthrowing this arch-usurper, saw in his disappointment that more extreme remedies were called for. Some other royalists were also countenancing radical measures as their cause wilted before Napoleon's determination to rule. One Chouan, the Chevalier Toustain, exemplified the new approach, travelling to Paris in late January, buying daggers and white cockades, and preparing to aim a blow at the head of government. He was caught and executed on 25 January 1800, provoking outrage amongst the royalists.[16] Hyde was particularly incensed, noting 'he was my friend, his death not only filled me with sadness but also with an anger which bordered on fury.' He told London:

His death demands vengeance! They have made him a martyr and righteous. Yesterday when Bonaparte, as a member of the government, did not have the baseness of an assassin, one could have debated whether he should be struck down. Now, today, my glory lies in sticking a dagger into him.[17]

The Chevalier de La Haye Saint-Hilaire, who had accompanied Cadoudal to Paris to see Napoleon on 5 March, was similarly minded and even volunteered to return to blow Napoleon's brains out.

Hyde had come to recognise that violence might prove more effective at regime change than requests on headed notepaper. London helpfully told him that plans were underway to organise a *Chouannerie* in the capital with a guerrilla army ready to wage a war *à l'arme blanche,* killing revolutionaries, rescuing conscripts and attacking government couriers. Hyde, livid at the death of Toustain and execution of Frotté, took to the idea of doing away with Bonaparte, but also knew that a plan to make use of the ensuing chaos to engineer a royal return was also required. Hyde's scheme was communicated in a series of obscure reports to Dutheil in London,[18] the agent thinking that 'Hitting the tyrant in Siam [Paris] won't be so hard, but before knocking the foundations out from underneath that cruel construct one should first know what to replace it with.' Despite the rather cryptic phrasing - 'there's work at Siam [Paris] to trigger the execution of the Antechamber [the Consulate], particularly the Friend of the Ally [Bonaparte], done the way it should have been against Passe-Partout [Barras] and his friends before the defeat' - it was clear they were enthusiastic about assassination.[19] In the meantime, Hyde briefed Charles-Nicolas de Margadel, alias Joubert, to prepare his 'little army'[20] to actually dispose of Napoleon.

London's scheme was at odds with Louis's own plans. His more refined Royal Council in Paris had continued to work on more nuanced ideas of regime change, preferring Ancien Regime methods of corrupting the leadership of the new government, and protested that 'we cannot place our trust in the English, seeing that they only employ men who are incapable, indiscreet and who busy themselves intriguing rather than obtaining merit.'[21] They had in mind Hyde but more particularly his new associate, Louis Dupérou, entrusted with enabling the uprising. Dupérou, a dreadful windbag if he can be judged from his correspondence, was at least sufficiently ingratiating to be able to infiltrate into the French police, talking to his old friend Paul Etienne de Villiers du Terrarge, Fouché's secretary, and inducing Louis Cyprien Victor Maillefert, a 'pronounced anti-Jacobin' to bribe the desperate clerk

Philippe Joseph Clément. Through such means, and at a cost of 760 Francs, Dupérou claimed to have bought the list of 251 police informers, and also tipped off some 230 individuals about to be arrested by the Parisian police.

As Dupérou intrigued, Hyde worked on the development of his real mission, that of preparing a shadow government-in-waiting ready for the moment the Consulate, or just the Consul, would fall. His English Committee readied the coup, assigning Isaac-Étienne de La Rue, codename Isaac, who had been deported to Guiana in 1797 and who was Hyde's brother-in-law, as head of a provisional government that would emerge post-Bonaparte. It would be provisional because it was assumed that D'Artois would finally land, Hyde considering that 'his arrival with have the best effect, as will that of the money.' Stepping ashore on the Breton coast, and aided by 3,000 royalists dressed as republicans, the king's brother would seize Brest, whilst Hyde and Dupérou would take care of Paris, calling on the garrison, under Coigny's contact, General Morand, and enabling Hyde's faction to step out of the shadows. Napoleon would be killed in that confusion, with trusty Joubert doubtless taking care of those details. This would trigger a general rising across France and General Willot sent word, and a request for more funds, that he would be ready for it in Provence, and would bring in the Austrian troops then encamped in Liguria. That March, Grenville authorised Wickham, who was again at large in Germany, to draw on 12 million Francs for Willot's army of deserters.[22] Perhaps Condé[23] could even be tempted to return to the fray as his beggarly aristocrats were more amenable to London's whims since they transferred to British pay in March 1800.[24] However, all this was talk and it seemed as though everyone was waiting for a catalyst so that the action could begin.

This effectively required Cadoudal to act first to trigger the release of D'Artois from Baker Street and Covent Garden. The Chouan's commitment to the cause was not in doubt, but he was increasingly desperate, and angered by Napoleon's success, confessing to Hyde 'I so wanted to strangle him in these two arms' when he had met the First Consul in Paris.[25] Following that meeting, Cadoudal and Hyde had set off for London, hoping to persuade D'Artois to come to France for one final attempt and to extort some more money from Whitehall. Cadoudal enjoyed the attention of the government, and the luxuries of Grillon's Hotel,[26] but all this rendered him unrealistically optimistic when he met Pitt on 2 May and spoke to John Hookham Frere about the plan for 'an essential blow in Paris'. The royalists desperately offered the British Brest and its resident fleet of 25 ships in the hope that London would support D'Artois' landing with a major expedition, perhaps making use of the 6,000 Russians stranded at Jersey following the debacle in Holland in late 1799.[27] Britain's ministers seemed enthusiastic, and Bourmont was sent a letter to ready him for action whilst Willot was instructed that he should now organise his diversion in the south.[28]

The British cabinet's excitement that they might be presented with a port and a fleet chased away memories of the debacles at Toulon and Quiberon. The ministers seemed possessed, as Hyde noted, by 'the mere hope of success, all based on rumours from newspapers'. Nevertheless they formulated a plan of sorts and, on 17 May, in a meeting between those courtesans of hope – D'Artois, Pitt, Grenville and Windham – finalised the details. The scheme included a diversion against Calais and an uprising in the capital, detailed in point 6 as 'it would be convenient if the attempt [*mouvement* in the original] in Paris only takes place when the arrival of the British fleet has been confirmed and a British force or prince has been disembarked.' When Louis heard, he was delighted, telling his brother 'I see the dawn of better days after so much struggle' and urging him over to Saint Malo or Brest. D'Artois seemed just as excited, telling his brother that this might be his last letter from England, but just as he seemed ready to ride down to the Channel ports an acute attack of haemorrhoids ruined his plans and he remained sitting on his hands, or not sitting at all, in London.

Perhaps it did not matter. For the network of agents in Paris had unravelled in a way which was as sudden as it was predictable. The English Conspiracy was revealed in its entirety when Hyde's contact, Abbé Godard, was spotted handing out satirical pamphlets and followed to the third floor of 76 Rue du Faubourg Honoré, a street, ironically, just behind the Ministry of Police at Quai Voltaire. On 2 May, at six in the morning, Commissaire Julien Augustin Alletz, accompanied by Rougeot of the Ministry, hammered on the widow Anne Louise Jeannin's door. The maid opened and the police officers were inside before the widow was out of bed. Whilst looking for the incriminating pamphlets, they stumbled on a cache of letters concealed in a cupboard in the dining room. It was immediately apparent that this was a significant find; indeed, all the royalist papers relating to Hyde and Coigny's activities fell into police hands, as did a mine of information on contacts, supporters, safe houses and addresses. Dupérou, troubled by the increasing penury of the committee, had been negotiating for funds in Britain when disaster struck, but he was back in Calais, disguised as Frederick Dierhof, a German bookseller, when the police caught up with him. Agent Mengaud, Fouché's 'best hound', detained him, only to see him escape from his drunken gendarme escort.[29] Calais was thoroughly searched, rumour even had it that Mengaud employed Madame Couvert, a Tarot reader, to see whether the fugitive was still in town. The policeman denied the use of the occult to his superior, Fouché, but it was all soon forgotten when Dupérou was caught disguised as a fugitive priest and sent on to Paris with an escort of 77 men of the 35th Line.

Maillefert was also brought to the Temple and interrogated, revealing little.[30] Coigny was seized at his lodgings at 70 Rue du Faubourg-Honoré but General Morand intervened on his behalf, telling Fouché that 'Madame Bonaparte takes the greatest of interest' in his fate. Fouché was not to be overawed, and Morand was reduced to making threats, telling the minister 'if any harm should befall Monsieur de Coigny, Bonaparte and I shall be unworthy of wearing this uniform. As for you, you have never worn it.'[31] Coigny was expelled to Amsterdam. Dupérou was just as fortunate, and was exiled to Geneva.

Such generosity was testament to the elation felt in the ministry. The police had been given an opportunity to thoroughly destroy a number of networks. On 18 June 1800 Pierre-Marie Desmarest of the office of the secret police wrote to the head of the Bordeaux police: 'Citizen Commissioner, I am now sending you herewith, via courier, eight warrants for the arrest of various English agents and leaders of the royalist opposition in Bordeaux. The enclosed instructions will give you all the necessary details. The facts contained within them have been extracted from the wider scheme, paid for by the English, to institute and organise a monarchy from within the republic itself.'[32]

The destruction of the conspiracy and the defeat of the royalist agents was also a major propaganda coup, and gave the government the welcome chance to tar the royalists as being the agents of foreign powers. It was all very humiliating and the king's agent, Royer-Collard, was livid at the rival English Agency's incompetence:

If the agents of Monsieur [D'Artois] are the same as those who have fallen into the hands of the police with their correspondence, then their inexperience, the imprudence of their conduct, the extravagance of their plans, their misunderstanding of the nation's interests, their preference for intrigue, espionage and brigandage, the permanent stain of them being branded the *English* Committee, and a thousand other considerations, creates an insurmountable obstacle between the servants of the king and any of these men who have not been imprisoned or who have fled.[33]

The king's men resigned in protest that June, dissolving their council and leaving the field open to D'Artois and what remained of his incompetents. That prince was, however, pessimistic, telling his brother 'this English agency in Paris has caused me much harm; of course, all the mistakes are being laid at my door.'

There was now no hope of creating a government in waiting, ready to step in when the First Consul breathed his last, and no hope for a coup. Espionage and intrigue had failed and even the court at Mitau recognised the scale of the setback when it advised its supporters on 8 June 1800 to 'make the most of the resources at their disposal and take advantage of any opportunities that fortune brings. Their wisdom lies in recognising such and their duty lies in profiting from them.'[34]

There was just one glimmer of hope, for Cadoudal was back in France that June. He had landed at Houat with £20,000 in his pocket and, true to the original plan, made off deep into his usual haunt of the Morbihan. There he did what he could to stir up revolt. In this he was supported by his loyal subordinates, primarily Mercier, but also the Rohu brothers and Saint-Réjant who had marched over from Dinan at the end of May and who now 'commanded a band of 40 bandits in the neighbourhood of

Josselin'. Even so, Cadoudal was dismayed by the lack of recruits and realised that the taking of a port like Brest was beyond him. More worryingly, the British, seeing the republican coastal troops resolute – and the paucity of Cadoudal's forces – now seemed to lose heart. When British ships, having spent their time rolling in the bay, sailed away, Cadoudal grew increasingly bitter.

He considered his options. It seemed he had just one. The collapse of the spy network in Paris had been a setback, as had the withdrawal of the British fleet and his own inability to raise the standard of revolt sufficiently high. So Cadoudal now fixed all his hopes on that decisive act against the consul in the capital, the essential blow which could turn royalist fortunes around in a day.

Cadoudal knew that the English Committee had worked with Margadel, alias Joubert, on plans to do away with Napoleon and that Margadel was still skulking on the fringes of Paris. Cadoudal also knew that London had wanted the Marquis Pierre François Joachim Henri de Rivière to cross over to France 'to take care of the essential blow in Paris',[35] but Cadoudal's doubts as to Rivière's reliability were confirmed when the marquis failed to arrive. The Chouan therefore conferred with his lieutenants at Bignan on 6 June. He made it clear that he wanted the First Consul's death, and stated that the chivalresque idea of attacking Napoleon on the way to his weekend retreat at Malmaison, having him killed or captured in a running battle between 30 Chouans and the Consular Guard escort, was best suited to the cause he represented. Others voiced different views on the method, but not on the goal, and Cadoudal therefore asked for volunteers from amongst his officers to go to Paris and lead Margadel and his little army into action. Rohu was there and noted:

Not knowing of a quicker way to be rid of Bonaparte than to fight man to man [*corps à corps*], the general sent for four of us, Debar, Robinault de Saint-Réjeant, the Chevalier Trecesson and myself. He told us that he needed one of us for a mission in Paris. Saint-Réjeant, as the most senior of the officers present, said that he should be the one selected. The general accepted, saying 'I will furnish you with the means to reach Paris and then you will make contact with those persons whom I shall name to you, and with whom you shall liaise regarding the purchase of a number of horses, clothes, uniforms and equipment which I shall specify and which will be made use of later.'[36]

Jean-Marie Hermely, also present at the conference, recalled that the idea was to stir up Anjou and Brittany to distract the State and the police, whilst in Paris, when the consul returned from Italy, 'Saint-Réjant would try to kidnap Bonaparte, killing him if necessary, with the help of the royalists in the capital.' Saint-Réjant, who was receiving a British allowance of eight shillings a day, was to join Margadel/Joubert and effectively command them to act, as Cadoudal informed Grenville on 19 June:

It is of the utmost importance to seize that person as quickly as possible. I have sent to Paris to hear from those who are in charge of that operation. I have some 60 men ready to act and will recommend them. If they show energy then they will triumph and this great enterprise is guaranteed to succeed.[37]

Napoleon's victory at Marengo radicalised things still further. When news reached the allies,[38] London told Cadoudal he should forget a rising in Brittany, otherwise many brave men would be needlessly compromised, but said nothing about Paris. Cadoudal, seeing Napoleon more secure than ever and his own resources scattered to the winds, was more convinced than ever that killing Napoleon was their last chance, and one in which they could no longer afford to be too nice about the details. These were now desperate times and, as such, the ruthless and the reckless began to sound reasonable. Gentlemen and chivalry would have to cede the field entirely to those prepared to kill in cold blood.

Having designated a commander for operations in Paris, Cadoudal had crossed over to London that July.[39] There he was able to read a flattering letter from Louis XVIII in Mitau:

> General, I have learnt with the greatest of satisfaction that you have finally escaped from the clutches of the tyrant who so underestimated you that he even offered you a position with him. I was overcome with grief that you were forced into negotiations with him but I never once doubted you. The will of my loyal Bretons, and most particularly yours, is so well known to me. Today you are free, you are at my brother's side, and my hopes are rising. I need not say more to a true Frenchman such as yourself. Be assured, general, of my esteem, my trust and my high regard. Louis.

Such flattery could only spur Cadoudal to action, and he spent the summer talking openly to the British of what needed to be done, and how the *coup essentiel*, that essential blow, might do it. On 13 August 1800, Windham noted in his private journal that 'General Georges ... predicts that Bonaparte will be cut off before two months are over, though he professes not to know specifically of such intention, seems to think such a course of proceeding legitimate, and has thrown out the idea to Pitt as he has before to me. Not necessary to say that no countenance was given to it.'

Plausible deniability was all the rage in a London as summer turned to autumn, after all Whitehall knew that these royalists were desperate men with increasingly mad schemes, but happily continued to supply them with large amounts of money. Even the moderate General Pichegru had taken Windham to one side and 'talked of the design to cut off Bonaparte by assassination and of the general inability of the government to which latter opinion I felt inclined to assent. On the other hand, having before expressed my opinion I did not now say anything.'[40] Shortly afterwards, the Chevalier de Bruslart, Frotté's old lieutenant, also saw Windham, and alluded to a plan to kill Napoleon: 'He made wild proposals of carrying off or cutting off Bonaparte to which I pointedly declared that a British minister could give no countenance.' Nevertheless, these men and others would be sent to France, provisioned with funds by Britain, and given leeway as to how they would go about ruining Britain's most constant foe.

Across the Channel, Napoleon was at least more open about disposing of his enemies - one bears a cross for his crime, another a crown. He saw Cadoudal as someone to be destroyed, and he was past offering amnesties to his men, too, declaring on 9 May that 'nobody from Georges' band will be allowed to surrender, all will be exterminated.' Before leaving for Italy he had reminded Bernadotte, who had replaced Brune, of these measures targeting Cadoudal, his animosity born from the sense that he had personally been betrayed by the Chouan's treason. Bernadotte, who also despised 'the cargo of brigands vomited forth by England', had been enthusiastically running the few remaining royalists to ground, informing Napoleon in May that 'in a fortnight or three weeks at the latest these bands will have disappeared.'[41] However, on 4 June, Napoleon, attending La Scala in Milan to hear an opera and see Giuseppina Grassini, sent specific orders to General Bernadotte to 'take that rascal Georges dead or alive. If you get hold of him, have him shot within 24 hours for having been to England after the capitulation.' Fouché was instructed to have his agents, many of whom were former Chouans or returned emigrants seeking favour, direct their energies at hunting down Cadoudal, 'sparing nothing to capture him dead or alive'.

On 2 July, Napoleon, weary from the triumph of Marengo, and accompanied only by Duroc and Bourrienne, had returned to Paris, his Guard trailing afterwards but arriving on 14 July in time for celebrations some still regarded as being in honour of the fall of the Bastille. Back in the capital, he complimented Fouché on his destruction of the English Committee, telling his minister 'two or three successes like that of the English Committee and your honourable and handsome place in history shall be assured.' Fouché thought that perhaps the destruction of the Chouans and capture of Cadoudal might suit. On 23 July he told his men: 'The First Consul has vanquished in Italy, now he must be victorious everywhere – pursue any Chouan who tries to assert himself – shoot them without pity.'

As summer turned to autumn, the duel, the race to kill, entered a new phase.[42] The grudge between Cadoudal and Napoleon, between the royalists and Bonapartism, was coming to a head. It was not yet certain whether Napoleon and his police would be victorious or whether the Chouan gentlemen would best the state in this underhand war. The stakes could not have been higher, nor the methods more base.

4

A FERVOUR FOR REPRESSION

On Saturday 8 March Napoleon's attention was almost entirely absorbed in the preparations for a meeting with the American envoys who had been lucky enough to be sent to Paris to discuss the end of the ridiculous quasi-war. But he also found time to talk to Louis Nicolas Pierre Dubois before sending him off in his coach to his new quarters. Dubois had been appointed prefect of police for the city of Paris and as his coach trundled onto the medieval Île de la Cité, he must have felt a certain trepidation. His new office was in the prefecture building, a complex of small rooms and long corridors located in the cul-de-sac at rue de Jérusalem,[1] in the shadow of the Saint-Chapelle on its grim island in the Seine. Dubois was disappointed by his headquarters as they were small, mean and unkempt, quite the opposite of the prefect himself. He was a vain man sensitive about his appearance, but more importantly, he also wanted to be taken seriously as a professional. He would need to be, for Napoleon's police, all that stood between the Chouans and their quarry, were universally acknowledged as being very much in want of a reformer.

Napoleon's appointment as ruler, and chief magistrate, of France heralded some change for the police. He promised reform, rehabilitation and direction, but there were many wrongs to right. Indeed, as the consulate was established, and for some time afterwards, the French police force was still dominated by the moral and material disarray of the Directory. The institutions of law and order had been hollowed out before that lax regime had mishandled public affairs and were utterly corrupted during it.[2] Napoleon promised them that the general restoration of public order would elevate their role, and increased their pay[3] and settled their arrears to prepare them for the trials ahead.[4] They were grateful but this did not render them more capable. Indeed, throughout the coming years the force would be overstretched by the mere task of maintaining public order and providing a modicum of stability. They had much to do, and many to watch, Napoleon ordering them to 'keep a close eye on everybody, except me.' But the concept of a police state was beyond them all, the state of the police proving more worrisome.

Dubois could at least rely on experienced hands, especially as the existing personnel were born survivors, having made their way through the dangerous labyrinths of revolutionary ambition. They would, by and large, remain in post.[5] Of this old cadre Fouché was very much to the fore. The minister, who thought 'mercy a virtue, but weakness a vice', had found his perfect role and made sure he held on to it, for whilst none of the previous six ministers of police had lasted more than six months in office, and the most recent had served less than that, Fouché would last longer than Napoleon. The minister was energetic and rejected the limiting notion that he was there merely as an executive tasked with the 'execution of those laws pertaining to the police, and to the security and tranquillity of the republic'. Hostile to all influence save his own, he worked vigorously to undermine his rivals and frustrate the enemies of his state, whether Jacobins or royalists. As Réal put it, the minister 'gave his right hand to those people [the Jacobins] and his left to Bourmont [the royalists], all in order to know what both sides were up to.' These political aspects of state security interested him the most, a trait Talleyrand, not alone in sensing a new presence at the heart of government, noted when he quipped that 'a minister of police was someone who should involve himself in that which concerns him, but, above all, he should be involved in that which does not.' Fouché was keener to delegate routine work to others, believing that his true talents lay in the unspoken and unmentionable realm of espionage, betrayal and favours, and, inevitably, Fouché, sitting in his web at the elegant Hôtel Juigné on Quai Voltaire, developed his own extensive sources of information, making sure he had his own creatures in key positions. He hoped to be able to do so again when it came to the appointment of a prefect of police, an official charged with that routine police work the minister feigned to despise. But here, for once, he was to be disappointed.

The prefect, the head of the capital's prefecture and thus the primary magistrate of Paris, was vital for the security of that centre of power and influence. Based on the Directory's *Bureau Central*, the new prefecture had enhanced powers but it took months of wrangling to get established and to have its limitations defined.[6] Napoleon was fortunate that his candidate, Dubois, was efficient, but Fouché was less pleased and Dubois found himself having to exert himself against the competing ambitions of the ministers of the Interior, Justice and Police. He had won that contest, with Napoleon's help, by July 1800, emerging as independent and autonomous, and the subject of Fouché's abiding displeasure.

Fortunately Dubois was resilient and set to work. Having seen how not to run the capital, he began to impose his own ideas for enforcing the law in Paris, a city which, in the last ten years, had raised a revolution and, for much longer, nurtured mobs and encouraged riots. Nobody who had ever seen Dubois in his infancy could have supposed him to have been anything other than a man of law and order. He was born and raised in a family of lawyers in Lille and had gone through the lengthy and demanding apprenticeship for a legal career. His work as a prosecutor at Châtelet, in the years before the revolution, allowed him to forge friendships with fellow Masons and well-connected colleagues and this network would stand him in good stead in the turbulence to come. He was 41 when the revolution broke out and was as involved in it only as much as the good of his career would allow, joining the Club des Cordeliers, and avoiding the Terror, before rising to head of the civil tribunal of the Seine in 1795. Judged to be meticulous and loyal, he proved himself a faithful servant to whichever government was in place, serving whatever judgement was required. A former colleague and fellow bachelor, Réal, helped him up the ladder by having him appointed police commissioner for the 10th Arrondissement. From there it was a short step to prefect, but a step Dubois appreciated, as was clear in his pompous proclamation to his new charges, the citizens of Paris:

> I shall see to it that I take care of everything that hitherto has been of concern to you. Firmness, but fairness. My eye shall peer into the soul of the criminal, but my ear shall remain open to cries of innocence and even for the pleading of forgiveness.

Dubois began his new role at the prefecture in the workmanlike fashion which would so appeal to his superior; and indeed to a successor, Pasquier, who would comment that 'an absolutist power could not hope for a more docile or devoted instrument.' This, and his daily reports to Napoleon, made him indispensable to the First Consul and cemented their relationship regardless of how much the minister sniped. [7] But daily reports on life in Paris were just one of his many duties, for he took charge of an array of departments and divisions, tasked with security and an almost Ancien Régime array of responsibilities intruding into the mundane and quotidian life of the metropolis. Dubois was careful to bring in his old colleagues from the *Bureau Central*, appointing homme de lettres Monsieur Pierre-Antoine-Augustin Piis as secretary and the confusingly named Louis-Auguste Dubos as his deputy. Piis, employed to manage the voluminous correspondence, was assisted by Beauve, by the legal counsel, Julienne, and by 26 assistants. This bustling secretariat, established by one of 34 Articles Dubois had crafted that August, was the head on the shoulders of the Paris police corps.

That body was divided into eight divisions. The 1st Division was under Louis-Jacques-François de Paule Bertrand-Quinquet, an enormous individual who had begun his career as a printer in Compiègne, and had even authored a Latin grammar, but who subsequently discovered a new vocation as a spy during the Terror. After a few years in the political wilderness, he had then joined the police and was, as Barère noted, 'expert in police work, quite crafty in getting the accused to confess and the witnesses to talk'. They usually talked because Bertrand had developed the technique of breaking prisoners' fingers by putting them under the hammer of a flintlock musket and such methods, although unconstitutional,[8] won grudging respect from friends and enemies. When not listening to the screaming of prisoners, his responsibilities covered investigating conspiracies, riots, assemblies, escaped prisoners of war, fraud, forgery and the sale of gunpowder. The emphasis on conspiracies brought him into regular contact with the ministry's own Office of the Secret

Police under Pierre-Marie Desmarest, a department tasked with 'policing the state, namely investigating conspiracies or projects aimed against the constitution, the government and against the persons of senior lawmakers'. Desmarest, also from Compiègne, had been, like so many of the revolutionary offspring, destined for the Church until the Supreme Being ordained otherwise. Instead, after a stint as a soldier, he became a protégé of Fouché and used his connections[9] to climb the slippery slope of Napoleonic policing. He was well suited to the work, better suited to weighing the guilt of suspects than that of a congregation, and he worked well with Bertrand and with the minister as his section took on many of the functions that made the words Cabinet Noir infamous.[10]

Next to Bertrand's division was the 2nd Division under Citizen Jean Henry, a man of prodigious memory whose attention was devoted to Parisian low-life, investigating robberies, murders and crimes of the darkest hue, whilst also hounding tramps, escaped criminals and conscripts. The 3rd Division, run by the brusque former printer Charles Louis Limodin, moved at a grander pace, processing prosecutions, interviewing suspects and securing witnesses. Léger's 4th Division attempted to regulate the capital's visitors, issuing passports, whether the internal kind, which had been first introduced in 1792 and codified on 2 October 1795, or residency permits for foreigners. A spike in the number of vagabonds and beggars in 1798, combined with an influx of emigrants and Chouans, had nearly overwhelmed his department, to such a degree that it had become almost impossible for midwives to obtain licences to walk the streets at night.

The 5th, under Jean-Baptiste Boucheseiche, a noted geographer, concerned itself with navigating the complex shoals of moral crime, regulating prostitutes,[11] journalists and such like, whilst also censoring books and theatres, and overseeing the rites of religion and the rhetoric of political clubs. In a display of administrative completeness, rather than logic, it was also tasked with licensing swimming schools and transvestites,[12] and investigating suicides.

The 6th Division under Farmond was obliged to keep the capital moving by acting as traffic police, routinely directing the 6,000 carts and wagons coming to market each day, or imposing order on the city's most querulous taxi rank at rue du Lycée, situated by the crowds of beggars and confidence tricksters at the Palais-Egalité. This taxed *chef de division* was also obliged to oversee street lighting, building works, a rudimentary fire brigade, life-saving equipment along the Seine and to limit contagious diseases from animals and humans. The 7th was a substantial force with 115 members of staff under Chicou. It oversaw the capital's traders and merchants, rendering Inspector Margana, in charge of the market halls and markets, the most loathed man in Paris. Finally came the 8th, under Parisot, in charge of prison personnel, a role which put this division at loggerheads with Nicholas Frochot, Prefect of the Seine département, the official in charge of the upkeep of prison buildings and providing food.[13] Nobody argued over jurisdiction when it came to the task of Parisot's men to mop up blood after executions, however.

This was the rudimentary structure of the official police, but actual law enforcement had always been a thing of the streets. The city's 12 arrondissements, nine on the northern bank of the Seine, three south of the river, were divided into four divisions, later dubbed quarters, with each division receiving a local commissaire.[14] Commissaires had to pay for their own office space out of their salary of 3,000 Francs, and worked unusual hours, keeping their doors open from 8 a.m. to noon, then from 2 p.m. until nightfall, with only Sunday afternoon as a day of rest. Each commissaire, assisted by a secretary, often a member of the family, and a menial servant who dusted the office and rang bells in the street to warn shopkeepers to clean in front of their establishments, was charged with maintaining order in their own particular section. Such work was at least varied, with enquiries as to whether a neighbour's chickens were causing tension perhaps preceding a raid on the hideouts of known criminals. These were knowledgeable, practical men and, as with their colleagues further up the hierarchy, most had spent their career in office. In addition to these experienced professionals, the authorities could call upon 24 Officers of the Peace, who reported to Bertrand's division, and these men, brandishing an official cane, could direct and employ agents, serve warrants (essential for entering houses at night and advisable for the same during the day) and make arrests. Supporting them on their raids and patrols were the inspectors, less than a hundred officers for the capital, and the uniformed gendarmerie, placed within the ministry's jurisdiction and, since March 1800, commanded by Colonel Radet. Gladly avoiding the limelight was the less reliable and increasingly ridiculous National Guard, many of whom loitered at sentry posts dotted strategically throughout the capital.

This sparse apparatus of state was supplemented by a host of spies, agents and those with expertise in the more covert operations required by a modern government. Napoleon had his own resources, as did the Minister of War. Talleyrand, too, employed agents and spies from Rue du Bac, sending them abroad or making use of sympathetic Irish, Italian and German refugees. But most carrying out missions on the consul's secret service were the creatures of the Minister of Police, who had spent a decade cultivating such shadowy talent. One such man of confidence, named Lagarancière, was sent to General Hédouville on 9 December 1799, Fouché having sent him to spy on the Chouans:

This man is charged with gathering all information that you may
have regarding the sincerity of the intentions of those commanders
of the Chouans and on the results that you hope to obtain from
the armistice ... the methods of the state police are known to him
and he has proved himself in the management of affairs which are
complex and difficult, and therefore merits respect.

He had a certain Verteuil travel over to London to keep an eye
on the Chevalier de Bruslart and made regular use of others, such
as the notorious Pierre Chépy on Jersey, or agents working for
Joseph-Antoine Mengaud, about whom the minister quipped 'of
all the hounds I have on the frontiers, Mengaud is the biggest,'
deployed on the coast at Calais and Boulogne.[15]

Under, or alongside, these gentlemen from the government,
came whole squadrons of a more shadowy body of individuals.
These were spies and informers in the employ of the ministry or
the prefecture, some being given regular pay for their expertise
and others the odd reward for information just on the right
side of gossip. At the top of this hierarchy were those informers
formally entrusted with missions to infiltrate the enemies of the
government. By 1800 many were former Chouans trading on
deceit to keep penury at bay, Fouché seeming to take an especial
delight in corrupting former nobles and sending them against the
royalists: 'Our agents are being found out and compromised, I
will send you others, former gentlemen, whose names and titles
are respected by the Chouans and who will be able to win their
trust and deliver them to us at the appointed time.' One such was
Gabriel Antoine de Becdelièvre,[16] Bourmont's distant relation and
a respected officer and former emigrant who was sent to capture
Cadoudal in his retreat at an isthmus known as the Île du Bonheur
on the River Etel. Becdelièvre took with him Louis Ambrose

Laisné, a chemist, and these incongruous agents were last seen in December 1800 when they were seized and carried off into the badlands to the west.

Chemistry was an unusual qualification for a police agent, most were drawn from other elements. There was Adans, the former valet of Louis XVI, or Gérome, a cook, who had supplied information to the state for the last 18 years. The well-connected leant a hand, the officer and perhaps gentleman Chevalier Dorival keeping one eye on returning emigrants and another on his mounting debts. Then there was the charming agent employed to spy on the Prussian ambassador by bribing his Italian valet[17] or the well-bred Madame Lagrave, who spied on Josephine Bonaparte. Madame Marie-Louise Saint-Huberty, the keeper of a popular brothel in central Paris, was less worthy company but her information was better than that provided by many a more respectable citizen.[18] Such spies and informers, perhaps some 40 in all, were fortunate enough to be kept on a regular footing and paid between 1,800 to 3,600 Francs in salary, with a 100-Franc bonus for information leading to the capture of suspects. A far greater number were casual employees, providing information as it came to them, receiving recompense if the information suited the police. Fouché set the tone, making use of his former colleagues, with rumours and gossip from the likes of Barère and General Parain ensuring that he was amongst the best informed members of government.

Those they denounced, and those the police caught, could at least expect a kind of justice. The rule of law had been bent by the crass grasping of the Directory, with the government turning to courts martial and military commissions, composed of five officers, to target rebels, robbers and bandits.[19] In the first months of 1800, Napoleon partially eased this repression, but made an exception for those within the borders of France who rejected his offer of collaboration and thus continued to flirt with treason. With Napoleon now the state personified, trouble could be expected from those who viewed that state as illegal. This could be the men of the revolution, who yearned for the sovereignty of their people, or the men of the king, still agitating for their legitimate monarch. The threat of action from such factions was real in 1800, and it could come from either quarter; but the first purge was directed at the Jacobin quarters of Paris.

In order to carry out this distinctly Bonapartist reaction, the government turned to a police force which was led by men of the revolution and personnel who had been raised up by it. Yet, from the minister down to the lowliest of informers, they now proved unanimous in turning on those men who had been equally involved in forging the republic. Their victims had just been too slow to shift with the prevailing wind.

The ensuing storm would reveal the Jacobins to be less dangerous than imagined, and their movement a broken, fragmented force. The genuine radicals were too busy groaning and grumbling at their loss of influence and loss of position. Despite railing against Bonaparte the new autocrat, dubbing him Bon-à-pendre (good for hanging), they did little to actively promote resistance. This made them easy, and therefore tempting, targets for police eager to impress. Indeed, to make their work even more impressive, the police exaggerated the threat they faced from the republican old guard. In that summer of 1800, the corridors at the Quai Voltaire rang with rumours that the radical left was at work stirring up the masses, feeding off bitterness that the anniversary of the execution of the king was no longer being celebrated and that the nobility was returning to oppress the masses. Upon investigation there seemed to be no actual evidence that agitation was being transformed into action, a deficit explained away by blaming secret societies such as the Freemasons, the mysterious Company of Tyrannicides or Jacques Joseph Oudet's clandestine network of *philadelphes*. The state increased surveillance in proportion to the absence of evidence and fired a shot across republican bows, with Fouché, who kept many of his old friends close, whilst negotiating away the lives of those who had drifted away, choosing those victims who could serve as a warning. As early as 12 November there was a limited purge when orders, signed by Dubois, went out to deport 61 former deputies and a week later, on 17 November, a further 37 Jacobins were targeted for arrest.

The operation got off to a bad start. Louis Auguste Lafitte's police knocked at 1465 Rue de Bourgogne, looking for Citizen Hugues Destrem, but the porter told them he had moved out 10 days ago and he did not know where he had gone. Another call, at 554 Rue du Bac, the residence of Citizen Dessaix, was answered by a woman and when the police asked to speak to him she told them that she didn't know of such a person, but that a Monsieur Dezay lived there. The unfortunate officers, whose warrant was for Dessaix, retreated in disorder. However, a number of deputies and sympathisers, including Destrem, Aréna, Marquezy, Lepeletier, Charles Hesse (formerly Prince of Hesse-Rheinfeld) and Fournier, and many of those previously implicated in the Babeuf plot, were finally detained in order for them to be sent to Guyana whilst 24 others, including Tilly, Jean Pierre Briot and Santhonax, were designated for internal exile in Charente. Their wives, servants and secretaries were seized and questioned and a number of undesirables, including a particularly obstinate pamphleteer, Bernard Metge, were also marked as being ripe for expulsion. The process had got as far as fitting out the frigate, the *Syrène*, and a brig, the *Mutine*, for the voyage when, on 25 November, after numerous interventions, the new regime had second thoughts about creating martyrs and revoked the decree, releasing the republicans on parole.

The first purge of the new regime had, then, proved to be little more than a warning gesture, although it came across more as a declaration of incompetence. Mortified by this blow to their pride, the authorities persevered and redoubled their efforts to expose the republican agitators who posed a threat to public order. In the spring of 1800, Hugues Maret, secretary general, notified Fouché that:

> The consuls wish that within the week you send them a report on the names and places of abode of some 50 individuals who, accustomed to behave as though part of a revolutionary movement, continuously agitate public opinion; report too on the means to have these men, some of whom are in the pay of foreign powers, and who hire themselves out to disturb the tranquillity of the public, sent away from Paris.[20]

One set of 'anarchists' were found to be disturbing the tranquillity of the pubs of Paris. Louis Guibert and François Dufour, both followers of Babeuf, were overheard denouncing the government, and, as the wine loosened tongues and weakened discretion, police informers sent word that there had even been talk of a plot to kill Napoleon when reviewing a parade on the Champ de Mars on 14 July 1800. The authorities exaggerated this gossip by tying it to reports that the garrulous Thomas Avisse Desforges, a functionary whose allegiance to the sect of the Theophilanthropists, rather than to the new consulate, made him a suspect, had also been boasting of a conspiracy. He had, in late June, seemingly discussed the idea of introducing some assassins into the ranks of the 45th Line. That regiment had ostensibly proved too loyal[21] and the scheme had, if it had ever existed, floundered. Desforges, later questioned, would only confess to having been in town to buy a blue riding coat for 36 Francs, the police putting it to him that he did so in order to imitate the uniform of a gendarme and thus get close enough to Napoleon in order to stab him. This was stretching the evidence, but this was inevitable in a Paris where spies proved their worth as informants by exaggerating the value of their information. Rumours swirled that a New Brutus was preparing to stab Napoleon at a theatre, perhaps at the performance of *Britannicus*, and that August police agents were investigating whether a certain Juvenot, a former aide to Robespierre's accomplice General François Hanriot, had planned to bar the road to Malmaison and shoot Napoleon as his carriage was stuck waiting. In an embroidered version, similarly implicating poor Juvenot, the Jacobins were suspected of planning to burn down a farm on the Malmaison estate, with Juvenot killing Napoleon in the smoke and confusion.

It did not stop there. A more imaginative scheme had it that the Jacobins were seeking to get into the Tuileries cellars and there stack flammable materials. Someone had indeed broken in, and had got through the grating by the bridge, but their far from audacious effort had then been foiled by a locked door at the end of the passageway. This did not prevent the police from claiming that organised anarchists were behind these subterranean machinations. These rumours were unsatisfactory, talk was difficult to prosecute. What the authorities really needed was to catch someone red-handed. Initially, Bernard Metge, that writer of slanderous pamphlets marked for expulsion in 1799, seemed as if he might provide them with just such a possibility. His newest work, *Le Turc at le Militaire français*, published by a man belonging to the most dangerous profession in Paris, the printer Jean-Baptiste Delerue, was scurrilous enough to merit official wrath,[22] but there were no arrests as yet. Instead the police watched Metge as they considered drawing him into a wider conspiracy, the exposure of which might provide the opportunity to rid Paris of the troublesome left once and for all. It was Bertrand who suggested to Dubois 'I think it might be sensible to countermand that order issued to those officers to arrest Metge as it might spoil another scheme well under way ... and I think it better that nothing is said to the minister until complete success can be reported.'

The unsuspecting Metge led the police to a group of the disaffected clustered around Denis-Mathieu Chapelle, a humble gardener. He had come to the police's attention, and blundered into their trap, by outlining his idea that 'before long there will be a change of government' as the First Consul would be stabbed or blown up. Chapelle, the horticultural mastermind, was dubbed the ringleader, and a certain Jean-Louis Humbert, a bootmaker and another former Babouvist, was the man of action whilst other conspirators, difficult to number but including Etienne Jallabert, a wigmaker, François Dufour, the joiner from the taverns, and François Perrault, a builder, provided muscle. Informers hinted that this gang would first kill Napoleon and then assemble at Place des Victoires and attack the bank. Chapelle apparently made the mistake of talking about his secret project out loud on Saturday 13 September, bringing an interested stranger called Lavoisier into his confidence:

Chapelle thought that he had a new accomplice in Lavoisier and so shared information with him in considerable detail; he revealed that a good number of conspirators were divided into brigades; that each one had a nominated commander; that these men met in different bars, but never in groups of more than two or three at a time; that the first two to arrive asked for three glasses, turning one upside down on the table, as that is the sign.[23]

Chapelle's intention was apparently assassination:

> Chapelle added that their idea was to create some disorder at the entrance to some theatre the First Consul was attending and, in the confusion, stab him. Everything was ready and that should the cavalry forming the escort attempt to resist then they will be cut down ... On the designated day Chapelle will enter the bar where his brigade has gathered; that he will pick up a glass of wine, drink it and leave and then, on that signal, his brigade will follow him to the theatre and then instigate the disorder.[24]

Chapelle helpfully informed his new friend who was really behind the conspiracy, alleging that General Jean-Antoine Rossignol, veteran of the storming of the Bastille, noted Babouvist and thorn-in-the-side of Bonaparte, was the guiding hand. Lavoisier, pretending to be a member of the public but certainly a police informer, told his friends Leroi, a shoemaker, and a certain Jubié, also police informers, that he was desirous the First Consul be warned. He sent in his report and all three volunteered to become involved in foiling the plot. The First Consul was absent, however, so these honest citizens were taken to Adjutant Marie-François Caffarelli du Falga of the Consular Guard, Dubois reporting on what then took place:

> Three honest citizens, Jubié, Le Roy and Lavoisier, learning of these terrible plans, took pains to dissipate the danger. Two of them, Lavoisier and Le Roy were asked by General Caffarelli to infiltrate the plot and to then perform whatever acts they deemed useful to public service.

On the evening of the 15 September 1800, the two men went to the bar in the Rue de la Loi, asking for wine and three glasses. Following the agreed usage one of the glasses was upside down and the official report records what happened next.

> Then a man called Perrault arrived, went out, came back, and turned the glass over. Lavoisier offered him a drink, which he accepted. Chapelle was next to arrive. He also asked for a bottle and three glasses, and he turned one over saying to Lavoisier 'that's how it is done.' He wanted to pay for the wine which had been consumed.

He then tossed a 24-sous coin onto the table where Le Roy and Lavoisier were sitting. Chapelle insisted on paying and forcing them to accept, telling them that it wasn't his money but belonged to the Society. This mysterious cabal remained nameless, but the official implication was that it was a Jacobin club.

> He then left for 30 minutes and came back with Humbert, sitting down separately so as not to seem suspicious. Chapelle then asked Humbert if he had seen Dufour, Humbert replying in the affirmative and saying that he had only today found out about the business. Dufour had said that a reliable and audacious man was needed, and that means you.

The conspiracy didn't get any further. A police raid followed in which Humbert, Perrault, Chapelle, Le Roy and Lavoisier and a number of those who just happened to be drinking in the bar were arrested. The guilty were placed in the tender care of Louis François Fauconnier, governor of the notorious Temple prison. Citizen Jallabert, a hairdresser, was questioned but 'could not name any of those he drank with, apart from someone called Signoret, and his conduct seemed satisfactory' and so was released, as was Saulnier, 'whose frank answers proved his innocence'. The investigation, however, focussed on wearing down Chapelle and he denied everything. Metge, finally charged with acting as their propaganda arm and for whipping up hysteria in preparation for the coup, was also seized on 3 October, resisting arrest at the entrance to the Feydeau Passage. He confessed that he had been sleeping with a street girl in Rue Nicaise and there his papers were seized. Nothing to incriminate others was found, but it didn't stop the police from suggesting that some former deputies, including Felix Lepeletier, might have been behind his antics. Metge continued to deny any wrongdoing.

Fouché, who had wanted to show how indispensable he was by offering up such scapegoats precisely when Bonaparte was fearful of Jacobin sedition, was disappointed by this anti-climax. Chapelle and his ilk could not be taken too seriously and the minister would have to cast around for more worthy conspirators if he was to really prove himself a loyal Bonapartist and efficient policeman. His police therefore continued to be actively involved in creating traps, using provocateurs, and actively encouraging dissent in order to quash it. But now the minister raised the stakes a little, ready to show his master that there really was a cabal at work; that there were men presently in Paris plotting to kill Napoleon.

5

THE REVOLUTION'S REVENGE

The sickly tenant on the third floor of Mademoiselle Daigremont's shabby lodging house at 24 Rue des Moulins, was the least likely member of a political cabal. Especially as that September he was bedridden with an unpleasant ailment. Dominique Demerville's mistake had been to eat a rancid pâté and the unfortunate consequences had obliged him to never stray too far from a chamber pot. To add to his discomfort, he was treated with a purgative diet of prunes and self-pity, and spent much of the month helpless, reduced to nursing his grievances and complaining to his friends. Demerville sat up to entertain the occasional visitor, and a handful of acquaintances obliged him, including an impoverished trader called Denis Lavigne and an elderly sculptor, Arnaud Daiteg, both of whom were actually visiting to pay court to Madelaine Fumey, a former teacher who acted as Demerville's servant.

The invalid, a former secretary of the Committee of Public Safety, and a man just about managing on the poor pay of the commissariat, had once mixed in more exalted circles, even being on speaking terms with Lucien Bonaparte. However, it was his relationship with Bertrand Barère de Vieuzac, a regicide and former Jacobin, which had recently piqued police interest.[1] Barère had once been a radical, but as the Consulate began to flex its strength across the country he preferred not to be left in the wilderness and sought ways to make peace with the new regime. Indeed, in order to ingratiate himself, and placate the police and its difficult minister, he began to send Fouché regular reports denouncing many of their former comrades.

Demerville had another radical friend, one who, significantly, was also known to Barère. Giuseppe Ceracchi, an exiled Roman sculptor, was an artist who was true to his Jacobin principles, and so was having to balance finding work from the new elite with his instinctive mistrust of the regime. In this the Roman was intermittently successful and he had just finished a bust of Barère, resplendent in the toga of a tribune, and another, of Consul Bonaparte, which was stuck in Italy.[2]

The 48-year old Ceracchi was a recent arrival in Paris but he had already achieved distinction in Europe and fame in the United States. He had arrived in the French capital in the autumn of 1799 having fled from Italy where his hopes for a Jacobin republic in Rome had been dashed by Allied armies and French incompetence. Forced to live on his art alone, supplemented by a meagre allowance of 1 Franc 75 centimes a day, he now resided at 20 Rue du Mail. To improve his chances of finding employment he joined an artists' club in Rue Taranne. There he met Arnaud Daiteg and found sympathy from the club's more radical members, including young Jean-Baptiste Topino-Lebrun, a painter of enormous Roman histories, who liked to express his admiration for Babeuf long after it was fashionable, or wise, to do so. Ceracchi also had friends amongst the swarms of Italian exiles who gathered at the café de Virginie, du Caveau or Vadori's in Rue du Hasard. Ceracchi's particular friend seems to have been Giuseppe Diana, a refugee from Ceccano, aged 27, who was waiting for the situation to improve in Italy. Meanwhile, 'I read, I pay visits, I manage my own affairs.'[3] Ceracchi also seems to have met Joseph Aréna, a Corsican and an officer of gendarmes who had quit his post when Napoleon assumed power. A former member of the Club du Manège Réunion des Amis de la Liberté et de l'Égalité, he was also the brother of Barthélemy Aréna, the deputy in the Council of Five Hundred who had been brazen enough to grab Napoleon's collar during the coup in November.

The French police were generally suspicious of these Italians, and some of the Corsicans too. Napoleon had recently expressed his concern about their large numbers, the police amplifying his opinion by supplying reports on Italian subversives who clearly harboured anarchist or terrorist sympathies, and therefore posed an ultra-montane threat to security. Something needed to be done to rein in their passions, or else have them sent back from whence they came.

Ceracchi, unaware of the trouble brewing, spent his time sculpting and crafting friendships with his compatriots, and also found time to sip tisanes with the invalid Demerville and his friend Daiteg. But someone a little less welcome now joined them. The newcomer was Jacques Harel, a captain in the loyal 45th Line whose half-pay, reduced again that April, gave him cause for complaint especially as, during the revolution, he and his sister had made a small fortune supplying food and drink to the army, an activity which brought Harel into contact with Demerville in 1799. That September, Harel renewed his acquaintance and for no apparent reason became a regular visitor, walking over from Rue de la Vierge to complain that he had time on his hands due to his lack of promotion, and railing against a regime which had betrayed the army. He met Ceracchi, and saw Barère, and, on one occasion, as Demerville's wary circle discussed the state of the nation, he grew agitated, declaring, in Daiteg's hearing, that 'Bonaparte is a rascal who he would kill as he is doing France harm.'

But Harel was playing a game of double cross. He was reporting back, albeit indirectly, to police handlers and was insinuating that Demerville was the one to talk of assassination and that General Rossignol, who had moved to Paris in July 1800, was again mobilising the masses.[4] Harel had a friend, Jean-Philippe Lefebvre, a former comrade from the Regiment de la Martinique, who, conveniently, lived opposite Demerville and Harel 'confessed' his worries to Lefebvre: 'I have just come from Demerville's, your neighbour. I was there by chance with some individuals who were saying that they would do more than hang the government. They are plotting something. I don't want to get involved, I won't go back.'[5]

Lefebvre, with an eye on future court proceedings, helpfully suggested that he should indeed go back and 'note down everything they say, and if they threaten the First Consul then I shall inform the government.' Shortly afterwards Lefebvre 'introduced' Harel to key members of the government and was ushered in to see Bourrienne, Napoleon's secretary, on 8 October. Prefect Dubois stressed that Harel had merely stepped forward as a concerned citizen:

Citizen Harel ... had been with Demerville when he had been asked his political opinions and thought it possible that he could infiltrate what he thought was a conspiracy. Bonaparte was going to be stabbed and the government changed. Harel hurried to inform Citizen Lefevre [sic] of what he had discovered. Informed by the latter, Bourrienne asked Harel to stay close to Demerville and so Harel visited him again. Demerville asked him to find four men who could be relied upon.[6]

At this first conspiratorial meeting with Demerville it had been Harel who had made the suggestion, unbidden, that men of action be recruited to help change the regime. The cautious Demerville, however, perhaps sensing that matters were running away from him, informed Harel that he was against this, although Harel informed the police that Demerville 'asked me to get four other men' and that he gave him 50 écu as a bounty.

Ceracchi then arrived, fretting about an intended journey to Italy. Given the number of brigands infesting the roads, Demerville thought it wasn't safe to travel and Harel suggested he should obtain some pistols. Demerville thought he should also obtain a blunderbuss and foolishly asked Harel to procure one too, handing over 200 Francs.

On the following day, 9 October, Lefebvre arrived at Quai Voltaire at 11 a.m. and reported on progress to Fouché and Bourrienne. General Massena's name was now mentioned in connection with the developing scheme[7] and Fouché ended the meeting by impressing upon Lefebvre the need to follow the plotters closely. The minister then summarised the situation to Dubois:

It seems as though the plotting that we have broken up more than once continues to simmer. There's every indication that this is so. Let us redouble our surveillance. One of those involved tells us that everything will be in place by 23 October. One of them has urgently called for a meeting tomorrow morning and we will learn of the result. Vigilance, vigilance, I'll have this affair brought to a conclusion. If you have something on this, send it over.[8]

Galvanised by his superior's note, Dubois now called in Citizen Bertrand of the 1st Division. Under his experienced eye matters quickly came to a head and on Friday 10 October, Harel knocked on Lefebvre's door:

> On the 18th, around 10.00, Harel told me that he had bought four pistols and a pair of blunderbusses, which he showed me. He also brought me a pair of pistols, telling me one had gone to Demerville, another to Ceracchi. There were six daggers that Demerville had.[9]

Harel had made sure that he had a witness that the weapons had been delivered, and now he informed Lefebvre that the assassination attempt would be made at the performance of *Les Horaces*, a tale of fratricidal war composed by Bernardo Porta and soon to be performed at the Théâtre des Arts. Harel told his friend that all the plotters needed now were some stout young men, ideally taller than 5 foot 4 inches, to generate disorder, to clear a path for the assassins, and then to march on the arsenal and seize the lottery funds.

Lefebvre did not question whether four men would be sufficient to overthrow the state, and helpfully set about recruiting them. This was easy as he procured the volunteers directly from the police:

> I went to see the Minister of Police and there the measures I have indicated were taken to thwart this plot, namely by providing four true men to carry out the plan. That done, I liaised with Citizen Desmarais [Desmarest, secretary general of the police] of the ministry, informing him of all that had taken place.

To continue with the deception that Harel had nothing to do with the authorities, the four stout police agents were instructed to pretend to go through with the plot by meeting Harel at 13.30 that afternoon. Nicolas Blondel, Charles-Marie-François Charmont, Philippe-Joseph Spycket and Felix-Michel Langlois were briefed on the plan by Dubois and Bertrand in the morning, Blondel recalling that 'the Citizen Prefect shared with us that there was a plot afoot to attempt the assassination of the First Consul.' The agents then made their way to the rendezvous in the Tuileries gardens, where, on the main path, shaded by tubs of orange trees, and close to the statue of Papirius, they met Harel.

On the other side of the river, Dubois, having despatched these agents and sent others to the theatre, reported on developments to his superior:

> All necessary measures were taken for the security within and outside the theatre. Four reliable men, loyal, intelligent and brave, were sent to make contact with those behind the plan for this horrible crime. By this afternoon they shall have received the weapons and their instructions from the committee. They are under orders to obey whatever they are told to do, to watch carefully those individuals they have been placed amongst, to listen and to make sure they do not lose sight of them. They are being led by the citizen who first revealed the plan to the police and by a contact who is no less reliable. They will be able to communicate, secure methods having been agreed and there will be officers of the law placed around the opera for surveillance.[10]

The four police agents easily spotted Harel, his left hand tucked fashionably under the tails of his bright blue riding coat, and saw that Lefebvre was at his side. It was a Friday afternoon, and quite busy, so one of the agents suggested that the six men move somewhere quieter. Walking past the bronze statue of the dying gladiator, they exited the gardens and went for drinks in the Bar of the Rights of Man. Lefebvre hovered outside, and Harel ordered lunch before leaving on an errand. He was back in an implausibly short space of time, carrying a hessian bundle under his coat and revealing to the diners that there were weapons inside. He handed the package over to Charmont, who placed it behind his chair as Harel said 'let's eat.'

As they did so the captain briefed them on the plotters, and said there were eleven in total including the five present and Lefebvre. As for the assassination, he told his audience that the leaders would wait on the ground floor of the theatre, near the steps. Charmont then unbundled and distributed the weapons, Blondel receiving a blunderbuss, Charmont a pistol with a blade attached to the barrel, and Spycket and Langlois a pistol each. Lefebvre took a pistol and blunderbuss whilst each man also received a dagger, a poorly crafted 24-centimetre blade with a black wooden handle. One of the agents remarked that Harel should also supply them with money and fake identities to avoid suspicion. So to add the ring of truth to the whole affair, Blondel and Charmont were dubbed military veterans whilst, despite their initial objections, Spycket and Langlois agreed to act as opera-loving bargemen. The money was more problematic. Harel went out to ask for it, returning half-an-hour later with a promise of 60,000 Francs once the crime had been done.

Harel had not gone to talk to Demerville about money or anything else that afternoon. He had the opportunity, for Demerville was still at home and he had actually been receiving visitors. It was Barère, accompanied by Monsieur D'Instrem, who called upon him:

Knowing that Demerville was going to leave for the countryside, he [Barère] went to see him at around one o'clock; finding him upset, he asked him whether he was still going to leave for the country. Yes, he had replied, but I have to ask you not to go to the opera this evening to see the performance of the Horaces. He replied that he had yet to get tickets but, in any case, what was the matter? That there would be trouble, replied Demerville, and that they might close the theatre. It had to be the English trying to cause trouble in Paris.[11]

Following this obscure warning, Barère, whose account of the exchange notes that Demerville was actually too ill to get out of bed even to see his mistress,[12] then went to see his friend General Lannes, telling him 'I don't know anything for sure, but they say there is going to be trouble at the performance tonight; please warn the First Consul and take all measures necessary for his security.' He then added, for good measure, that the English would give a billion to finish off Bonaparte.

Not far away, at the Rights of Man, the meal was over and Harel arranged to meet the four men later on, suggesting the café under the colonnades of the theatre as a suitable rendezvous. He instructed them to come separately so as not to arouse suspicion, although how armed bargemen were to blend in at the opera was left unsaid. The bill was paid, Harel also giving the men 6 Francs to entertain themselves at the café later, and, to add authenticity to their performance, the men then charged their firearms with powder and shot, Blondel loading three bullets into his blunderbuss.

There was tension at the theatre too. Bernardo Porta's music was the main draw, especially amongst the Italian community, but the promise of an appearance by the ballerina Vestris also drew a passionate crowd. Inevitably, then, there was an enormous queue at the ticket office when it opened at 5 p.m. to sell off whatever tickets remained. Outside, touts were offering tickets at four times the price, and it was outside, too, that Harel sat. He had arrived

at 6 p.m. and positioned himself at a table at the café under
the portico, waiting beneath the theatre's torches for the Italian
sculptor to appear. Ceracchi was supposedly bringing tickets for
Harel and his four assistants, but the French captain nevertheless
took Langlois inside as soon as the police agents appeared. Having
purchased their tickets, Harel and Langlois then kept watch on a
bench in the foyer and it was from there that they saw Ceracchi
arrive. According to Harel he was with Giuseppe Diana, although
the Italian would later insist that they arrived separately.[13] Harel
said he immediately asked if they were armed and he alleged that
Ceracchi told him that Diana was carrying a dagger, and that
he himself would have to go and fetch his own weapons. Harel,
leaving Langlois to keep an eye on them, went to inform Adjutant
Jean-Constantin Laborde that the plotters were inside, telling the
police officer that Diana was the one who would strike the fatal
blow. It was 19.30, or thereabouts, when Laborde ran in with
his men and, climbing the stairs, encountered Ceracchi as he was
turning into the corridor leading to the Consul's box. Laborde
seized the Roman by the collar and had him searched. Diana was
next to be apprehended as he stood reading a copy of the libretto.
Taken by surprise, he was punched and had his hair pulled, acts
of violence accompanied by confused shouting as the Italian did
not speak French[14] and was at a loss to understand what was
happening. Pacified, he too was then searched. Strangely, neither
of the Italians was actually armed.

Another of the alleged plotters, Joseph Aréna, had also purchased
a ticket and climbed to the stalls, only to find there was no room.
He turned and left for home and as he came out of the theatre
'encountered the coach of the First Consul who was with his
secretary and, behind them, a little coach with the consul's young
brother, Jerome,[15] in military uniform' trundling along the Rue de

la Loi. Napoleon, Bourrienne and young Jerome Bonaparte had arrived fashionably late and now entered the theatre accompanied by an escort of 15 grenadiers of the Consular Guard. As he settled down in his Consul's lodge, General Lannes briefed him on the plot and Napoleon gave orders to find the rest of the conspirators, especially that treasonous mastermind, Demerville.

At 20.00 Commissaire Jean François Comminges, leading 12 armed agents, raided 24 Rue des Moulins. Entering Demerville's rooms, the police encountered Madeleine Fumey and Denis Lavigne, busy in a romantic tryst. At 20.30 Arnaud Daiteg, another old admirer of Madeleine, came over to see her after a game of billiards and entered the building. Seeing police agents he turned and tried to leave, but was ordered to wait. Two hours later, Comminges, who had finished with the search of the apartment and Demerville's papers, came down to see the old sculptor:

'What are you doing here?'

'Waiting for them to let me go.'

'Your identity card?'[16]

'Here is my wallet, it is in there.'

'Are you armed?'

'Not of my own. I have three small blades which I was given by an ironmonger in Rue de Thionville. Mademoiselle Fumey had asked me to go and buy a small knife, and the shopkeeper kindly gave me three for her to choose from. I have to take the other two back.'

Comminges then asked him about his relationship with Demerville.

'What kind of discussions did you have with Demerville?'

'We didn't discuss anything. He talked about his condition. We sometimes read the *Journal des Hommes Libres*. That's all.'

Despite such innocuous revelations, all three were promptly detained.

Meanwhile Ceracchi and Diana, seized at the theatre, were brought before Dubois at the prefecture. Dubois summoned Citizen Bertrand, and handed the suspects over to him for interrogation. Bertrand knew that nothing had been found on Ceracchi, and that a search of his rooms had revealed little more than two empty pistols and some correspondence in Italian. Citizen Daix, a translator in the employ of the police, combed through those letters, noting that it 'contained nothing negative about the government, indeed Bonaparte is given the honourable appellation of illustrious general and hero.'[17]

Ceracchi was forthright in denying any culpability, but, in the course of the week, as Bertrand squeezed information out of him, the Italian began to tell the police what he thought they wanted to know. He confessed to receiving money from a certain Gerard, who was working with Diana to bring about the downfall of the consul, although someone else was to strike the blow. He said that he had given Demerville the money, received daggers from Aréna, keeping three daggers for himself and distributing nine others. According to the Roman, Aréna was conspiring with Demerville and the young painter Topino-Lebrun on how the assassination of the French Caesar was to be carried out. Having written out a full confession, Bertrand rested his pen and wanted a signature, but Ceracchi refused to sign this incriminating document. Bertrand then threatened to have him shot, and he reluctantly complied.

Diana was harder to break, even though he had already been quite badly beaten. Bertrand, speaking through an interpreter, Monsieur Charles-Denis Villette, began by telling him he would be pardoned if he co-operated, but the Italian shot back that he didn't need to be pardoned as he had done nothing wrong. For good measure he added 'that it was shameful for a republic to speak of pardon, as it was a task for the law to punish the guilty or to thank honest citizens.' Diana was then subjected to menaces, an outburst which the interpreter later revealed in court: 'The interrogator, Bertrand, of the police, threatened to have Diana shot if he did not denounce those who were guilty.' But Diana protested his innocence, and reminded the police that nothing more incriminating than the opera libretto had been found on him when arrested. Dubois also interrogated the Italian, demanding to know if he was familiar with General Massena, but Diana again proved uncooperative.

On Saturday morning Fouché wrote to Dubois to urge him to greater efforts, and promising to send him Harel and Lefebvre's depositions:

> I invite you, citizen, to concentrate on pursuing those inquiries relating to the crime against the person of the First Consul. You will shortly receive the declarations made by citizens Harel and Lefevre [sic]; based on those you will have a sufficient number of facts to determine the truth and for there to be no misunderstandings when it comes to the plotters and the origin and nature of the plot.[18]

The police were nudging themselves towards the conclusion they so greatly desired, and on the way there were more opportunities to discredit opponents of the regime. When Fouché briefed Napoleon on the progress of the inquiries, the First Consul told Fouché to find out whether Salicetti, a Corsican Jacobin, had somehow been involved. The police lacked evidence but perhaps Demerville's arrest – and inevitable confession – might supply them with what they needed. Demerville handed himself in. He had been in Paris all along and now wrote a letter to the police saying he would come to the ministry.[19] From there he was sent to Dubois, along with a note from Fouché in which he told his subordinate:

All is revealed. Demerville will tell you everything: the Corsicans are behind it. Amazing foresight by the Consul, who said yesterday 'see if Salicetti isn't involved in it.' Don't arrest Massena or Salicetti yet, but get Choudieu and any others Demerville names and who aren't generals.

Dubois passed the detainee over to the tender mercies of Citizen Bertrand:

Ask Demerville whether Barère knew what Aréna and his companions were up to. If he says no, tell him that Barère was staying with him and had to know who was meeting whom, and ask him what that was about. Ask him why he, Demerville, had left home at two, and where he had gone. We need to know that. And Demerville has to talk, otherwise.[20]

Bertrand began his work, Demerville recalling that, 'The prefect of police called in someone called Bertrand, I knew him to be a horrible revolutionary.' After some minutes the interrogation intensified when Demerville was held down by two agents and told that he would be shot. Demerville replied that he was so sick that he didn't mind. Bertrand persevered and, over time, a narrative clearly implicating those who needed to be implicated emerged. Bertrand first made sure that Demerville named 'lots of former generals who had been cashiered' and then continued to probe as a rather pathetic Demerville turned on everyone he could think of:

'Was it you who first talked about a conspiracy to Ceracchi?'

'It happened by chance that we talked about it, about a month ago. Ceracchi told me that the country was lost but that we somehow had to save the republic. I replied that nothing was impossible, but that immense resources were needed. So, he told me he would consult with Aréna. It was Aréna who gave the money to Ceracchi as he himself was poor, and it was Aréna who was behind the plot.'

'So Ceracchi was Aréna's principal agent?'

'Yes, it was Ceracchi.'

'Was he the one who was going to deliver the first blow?'

'I don't know who was going to do that. Only Harel came to see me on the 10th, and he told me there were four reliable men, five if you included him. Ceracchi also had his own men and they would clear the way out for Harel.'

'Who was with you on 9 October?'

'Harel, Ceracchi, Dr Théry from Val-de-Grace, and Lacoste, a surgeon from Rue Neuve-du-Luxembourg.'

'No doubt Barère knew what Aréna and his accomplices were up to?'

'No, if he knew what was happening, then I wouldn't have needed to warn him not to go to the opera.'

'But, you aren't telling the exact truth. Barère was staying with you, and was often at your house; he must have known about the meetings, and the project that was being worked on. Even if he wasn't involved, he should have asked you what was going on.'

'He hadn't been staying at my place for the last three or four months. I barely knew him, so wouldn't confide in him in case he denounced me. Besides, I gave my word of honour to Ceracchi and to Aréna that I wouldn't tell anyone.'

'Why did you go out at two o'clock on the 10th?'

'I went out after three to get some air, besides it was closer to four.'

'Where did you go?'

'To the Tuileries, until the evening. Later on I went to a café in Rue de L'Echelle. When I came back, I discovered the police had sealed my rooms so I went to stay with a friend whom I'd rather not name.'

'Who else, apart from Ceracchi and Aréna, visited you in order to take part in the conspiracy?'

'Nobody that I haven't already mentioned. Aréna often told me that he had a lot of support, that he had people ready. He told me about a few retired generals, without naming any.'

'Really, but he should have named some of them. Did he ever mention Massena?'

'I asked him if Massena was one, but he told me those generals who were involved did not wish to be named.'

'Did they say who it should be to take over the government?'

'They talked of Massena, Choudieu, Salicetti. They wondered about Barère, but they thought that as he worked for the First Consul they could not rely on him.'

'Was Aréna connected to Massena?'

'I don't know. Aréna took advantage of the fact that I was ill and that state of weakness persists so that I can't remember everything'

'Did Ceracchi tell you where to assemble?'

'No, and I didn't ask. I was too sick. I think it was the Corsicans who were behind it all.'[21]

Napoleon would have been pleased to see that Italian and Corsican troublemakers were getting the blame he thought they deserved. General Lannes agreed and when he saw a list of those suspected of being involved with the plot, rather undiplomatically exclaimed 'All those Italians, all those fucking Corsicans, they are all scum that need to be sabred.'

'Thank you,' replied the Consul, archly. 'Not you,' replied the general hastily, 'you are one of us.'

Joseph Aréna, the only Corsican suspect to have been arrested, was also denying involvement as was the stream of Italian refugees brought in for questioning. Prince Pio Bonelli, whose house in Rue de la Loi was an incongruous meeting place for Italian revolutionaries, was detained and kept in the Temple, the police granting him the concession of a servant. Luigi Angeloni was next, then came the widow Annetta Vadori, probed to see if Salicetti had said anything during one of her midday salons at Rue du Hasard. However, she said nothing incriminating and nothing could be found in her papers. Antimo Liberati, another Roman, was caught at Bonelli's house without a passport. Questioned about whether Ceracchi, a regular visitor to the house, had spoken against the government, Liberati replied 'Ceraschy [sic] really wanted to see Rome recover its liberty and splendour, and hoped to go back there,' and then added that, if anything, he seemed a friend of Bonaparte.

Despite a lack of evidence, other than that pointing to official entrapment, Dubois and Fouché pushed this line of the Italian and Corsican threat. Convinced that the Italians posed a security risk, the police could make use of this plot to clean Paris of the foreign refugees, whilst simultaneously proving their effectiveness in matters of state security, and loyalty to Napoleon. But, even better, they also used the opportunity to blame some other foreigners, this time France's oldest enemy, as Dubois reported:

That terrible conspiracy is Italian, because Ceracchi was one; Corsican, because Aréna has been arrested; Jacobin, because

Demerville is under arrest. However much it is true that the plotters were Italian, Corsican, extremists, it was the English, and the English party of France, who were behind it.[22]

But, aside from dubious confessions, and Harel's deposition, there was still no actual evidence against anyone. Barère, who knew more than he was letting on, was even of the opinion that

There was little more to it than words, curses, threats, denunciations against the First Consul; but as for a plot, and the means of carrying it out, it was the police in the Tuileries who put it together to compromise all the patriots of Paris and to justify their expulsion or deportation.[23]

Dubois, his tidy mind hoping to clear everything up at once, suggested to Fouché that the earlier plot of the amateurs might be connected to Ceracchi's subterfuge. On 25 October he wrote:

The affair of Ceracchi and his accomplices keeps me busy. There seems to be a link with two other cases, that of Metge and that of Chapelle. You will see from my report that they were all following the same plan, had the same methods and the same goal. You will also see that all of these people knew each other and met frequently and often. So this investigation is, as you no doubt suspect, long and complicated.[24]

But for now, Fouché and Dubois used the pretext of the conspiracy to order the mass expulsion of the Italian refugees. Talleyrand had suggested that they all be expelled to barren Corsica where 'these proletarians will be too busy preserving themselves' to cause further trouble, but the object was to get them out of Paris and on 14 October, 85 Romans and 295 Neapolitans were expelled. A contemporary noted the expediency:

> They made use of the presence of Ceracchi and Diana amongst the leaders of the plot to intern, drive from Paris or even expel from France all those so-called Italian refugees cluttering up the capital and spouting their revolutionary and extremist views.[25]

Fouché had hoped that Topino-Lebrun, one of those Frenchmen on the periphery of the refugee community, might be able to throw some light on those supplying money and encouragement to those hostile to the regime. He might even reveal where the knives, key evidence for the prosecution working on this Conspiracy of the Daggers, were. But the young artist neither knew Demerville, nor was he present at the theatre on the evening in question, having spent the afternoon visiting the Salon, where his *Death of Gaius Gracchus*, who committed suicide after he had wished the people of Rome to be enslaved for the fickleness of their politics, had been on display. Unfortunately he condemned himself by going into hiding when he learnt that the police were looking for him. Only a fortuitous raid on Widow Brisset's tea parlour, a place of hospitality offering additional services, captured the fugitive.

He too was questioned, but lengthy sessions in Bertrand's office only revealed what the police already knew, namely that Ceracchi was prone to ranting, and that, in particular, he was keen on blaming 'robbers, especially those of the French administration in Italy', for the woes of Italy, something, one suspects, Napoleon would have agreed with.

Despite their best efforts and the useful confessions, the case against the plotters was still not as solid as the police had hoped. Forensics, such as they were, had also failed to reach any useful conclusions. Antoine-Arnaud Quinquet, a distinguished chemist, tested Harel's bullets for poison by boiling them in milk which was then fed to a kitten. The cat showed no signs of illness. A dog was then fed two of the balls, wrapped in meat, and the chemist collected them the next day, after nature had taken its course, again noting that the ammunition was harmless (or not poisonous, at least).

The government commissioner of the criminal tribunal, Jean-François Gaultier-Biauzat, who acted as state prosecutor saw at once that the flimsy case would rely on Harel and Lefebvre. The daggers, which were supposed to have been made in a hurry and delivered, were missing, indeed the only weapons involved were those belonging to Harel and the police. Gaultier-Biauzat, however, was experienced enough to see that the key piece of evidence was Demerville's warning to Barère, if it had really been given, that he should stay away from the opera.

So, on 30 October, 19 suspects from both cases[26] were sent from the Temple prison to the court. Gaultier-Biauzat was managing official expectations, telling Consul Cambacérès that 'the chances of a successful prosecution are slight, which might encourage enemies both within and outside France, and might even cause some derision from certain quarters, something which must be avoided at all costs.'[27]

Fortunately, alarmism intervened. Another Jacobin plot had been unmasked. This one was, if anything, even stranger as a conspiracy, especially in light of subsequent events.

The man behind it was equally eccentric, an engineer called Alexandre Joachim Chevalier who had been active in the revolutionary committees, but who had then gone on to work as an inventor for the republic, patenting an inextinguishable fuse in 1797. His new idea was for a bomb made out of a barrel, ringed with steel, and containing musket balls, which could be detonated by pulling a cord. Although Chevalier had designed this device for warships, police agents were quick to level the charge that Chevalier would use his weapon against the First Consul. His accomplices, named as Jumillard, Veycer, Bousquet, Guérault, Decreps and Martin, were supposed to have organised the renting of a cart which would then block the First Consul's route as he was being taken to the opera, the police informer providing further details:

> Six men will each launch a bomb into the carriage of the Consul and by such means shall destroy the vehicle and those inside it through poison rather than through an explosion. The conspirators would arrive in a cart and the driver would block the way so that, for a short time, they would be positioned alongside the First Consul's vehicle. It is then that they will launch their munitions. These have been made and will be delivered by means of a kind of blunderbuss. Tests have been successfully carried out.[28]

The Rue Nicaise between the Tuileries and the opera house was the intended scene for the crime. The cart was ready, and was at Rue Blancs-Manteaux where Chevalier lived. However, the idea of blocking the street was abandoned as being impractical, and Decreps apparently planned to have some iron caltrops manufactured and scattered in the road to cripple the horses, thus allowing Chevalier and Didier to launch their device. That bomb was first tested on 17 October 1800 at 10 p.m. at a place called The Station at the Salpêtrière Hospital on the fringe of the city's south east. Desforges, Didier and Juvenot were present, but Chevalier and his Greek Fire took centre stage and the initial explosion was tremendous, the roar implausibly 'lasting six minutes'.

All was ready and the attempt was to be made on 1 November. The assassination itself would signal an uprising in the Jacobin quarters where insurgents, coincidentally dressed in the uniform of the 45th Line, would seize the capital. Jumillard, a manufacturer of wallpaper and a former member of the revolutionary committee, was supposed to lead them from the faubourgs, whilst Bousquet was to bring his own mob and Thomas Avisse Desforges was again involved in some unspecified scheming.

Bousquet was discovered in a house search, sandwiched between two mattresses, two of his friends lying on top to disguise him, before any action had been taken on the part of the conspirators. It was a lead and the police pounced before their prey disappeared: 'It was then that the Minister of Police ordered the prefect to seize the plotters along with their infernal machine. The munitions were hidden at different addresses.'

On the evening of 2 November Chevalier was arrested, Madame Junot passing on details culled from her influential husband:

The device Chevalier was working on was seized from a room he shared with a man called Veycer in a house called the House of Blancs-Manteaux.[29] He had quit his normal residence in Rue Saint-Dominique, near the Invalides, because the police, and I mean the entire police force of Paris, were after him. He was working with this Veycer who was, I believe, one of those men from September '92, as was Gombaud-Lachaise and Desforges.

She thought it hadn't been an easy arrest:

When one reached the door to Chevalier's room at Blancs-Manteaux there was a special sign one had to make to gain entry. Chevalier was known to be a little mad and, should he find himself cornered he might, in a moment of despair, set alight to all the material around him and blow the house and its contents sky high.[30]

For once, however, the police report was more down to earth:

A commissaire, accompanied by armed soldiers, climbed to the second floor and knocked on the designated door. Nobody responded. A locksmith was called but the door would not open. It was barred. Precautions had been taken by Veycer and Chevalier, then in the room. The two men were arrested.[31]

Dubois reported to the First Consul:

I have the honour to inform you that, this very night, at two o'clock, I had Chevalier arrested in his current residence at Blanc-Manteaux; with him was seized an infernal machine, constructed in order to carry out a most heinous crime, as well as a basket containing other devices and some documents.[32]

It was up to the 54-year-old Gaspard Monge to examine the bomb in detail:

It was around 129cm in length and at one end was the hammer mechanism of a musket attached to a block with a trigger, all connected to an eight-inch diameter barrel; this was bound in iron rings and the whole, apart from the hammer, was covered in touch paper, canvas and putty.

A closer look at the mechanism revealed that 'the gun barrel had been replaced by a kind of channel containing a fuse wrapped in touch paper which led from the hammer mechanism at one end to inside the barrel at the other.'

Monge perhaps gave the game away when he described it as being a device for use against enemy ships rather than one designed to target an individual: 'If the inventor is not mad, then it seems to me that the machine cannot have been designed to kill a specific person without, at the same time, wounding or killing a mass of people randomly, such as, for example, would be the case when boarding a ship.' However, he added that, in his opinion, it would not do for naval service, but that it could prove fatal if it went off 'in a confined space or amongst a crowd'.[33]

Chevalier was unlikely to have been plotting to kill Napoleon, he was rather just another timely scapegoat. As for the idea of a bomb in a confined space, one like that of the Rue Nicaise, set off amongst crowds of Parisians – it still seemed like a diabolical chimera that November. But just as those arrests were being made, others were gathering with an equally infernal scheme in mind. And this time they were intent on murder.

6

FOR THE KING

With Demerville, Chevalier, and all their friends of the wrong political persuasion arrested that autumn, the authorities could congratulate themselves on having curbed any remaining Jacobin enthusiasm for unrest. Opposition to the new regime was crumbling elsewhere, too, and the government was increasingly aware that the royalists were also losing the will to resist. The more resolute rebels in Brittany and Normandy were being harried through the hedges of the west but few captains maintained their faith in the royal cause, and most of those were in London. Rare indeed were those prepared to die for it. Indeed, royalist fortunes were at such a low point that the royal war in the restive provinces had taken on new, terrible forms as informers were disappeared and government employees assassinated.[1] The royalist Louis de Bouillé lamented that 'a kind of Chouannerie more correctly known as brigandage, designed to ruin and compromise the royal cause' had replaced their once chivalrous struggle. But these were desperate times, and ruthless men were in the ascendant.

If that summer of 1800 saw some brave skirmishes as the gendarmes hunted down the remaining Chouans, the autumn saw some cowardly murders. On the evening of 19 November 1800, Bishop d'Audrein, a man who had voted the king to the scaffold and had then 'rendered unto the new Caesar the things that were Louis", was travelling from Quimper in a stagecoach. It was stopped by François Le Cat, one of Cadoudal's officers, and the regicide was recognised. He was dragged out, biting hard on Le Cat's hand, before being shot twice and dumped in the gutter. The incident had followed soon after the kidnapping of the illustrious senator, Clément de Ris, from near Tours on 23 September 1800, a man who nearly shared the same fate as the bishop. Napoleon had been forced to instigate an urgent investigation, entrusting it to his aide-de-camp, General Savary, rather than his minister of police. The senator's wife duly received a ransom note for 50,000 Francs and Savary helped her collect the ransom in silver coins before tracking the kidnappers with the gendarmes of Loches and Chinon. However, it was only when some of Bourmont's former Chouans, notably Carlos Sourdat, now working as police informers, were sent over by Fouché, that the operation was concluded successfully and the prisoner released after 10 days' confinement. It seemed as though Fouché had infiltrated even the leaders of the Chouans, and was again playing his favourite games of manipulation.

But such omnipotence was deceptive. There were other Chouans gathering in the capital that were outside of Fouché's grasp and some of them were skilled at murder and kidnap. Increasingly, the survival of their cause warranted it. Killing republicans had long been a forgivable sin, and killing tyrants pardonable.

Large numbers of Chouan officers had resorted to Paris and any one of them could have turned assassin. Republicans tutted that they were crowding the capital's parks and salons, and the collision of these two worlds at the centre of power caused some disquiet amongst the regime's more observant officials. Prefect of

Police Dubois, for one, resented that Paris had 'become a receptacle and gathering place of leading Chouans, and of royalists, the intriguers of the Ancien Regime, the cut-throats of the Midi and the counter-revolutionaries from all corners of France.' Dubois was not wrong to suspect trouble, some of the new arrivals had made their names by killing Frenchmen. Men such as François-Gaspard de La Nougarède (known as Achille Le Brun), Biget d'Achille, Roland Madiou (called Sans-Quartier) and Frotté's wounded comrade, Hilarion-Henri Hingant de Saint-Maur, had only recently been butchering conscripts and, if circumstances were right, might choose to do so again. D'Andigné and Suzannet were also recent arrivals, and Limoëlan was there too, but the police generally agreed that it was General Bourmont who deserved to be trusted the least. Following an apparently cordial meeting with Napoleon on 18 February, this royalist captain was placed under tight surveillance by Dubois's agents, most particularly Anne-Christian de Montmorency-Luxembourg, once a noble emigrant, now a creature of the police. On the surface Bourmont was busy settling into married life, having married his cousin, Juliette de Becdelièvre on 10 April, but the numerous trips to buy horses in Anjou and the nocturnal coming and going of his 'servants' fed official disquiet. Unaware of how closely he was being watched, it seemed as though Bourmont was attempting to play a double game, even at the risk of being outclassed by the expert Fouché. The Chouan did what he could to mask his deceit, offering to raise legions from his former Chouans for government service in India and even, on 26 November, signing a pledge that he would give no aid to civil war, nor succour to rebellion 'and to respect and defend the life of the First Consul, as his demise would deliver us up to anarchy.' Such outward collaboration meant he was loathed in the west as a traitor,[2] but the west did not know he had received £15,000 from Cadoudal with the blessing of London. This sum went towards protecting a knot of active royalists around the capital, feeding them information from his new friends in government, paying salaries and supplementing their income through encouraging the robbery of stagecoaches. General Hédouville informed General Girardon in Angers that Bourmont was suspected of being behind such robberies, using a valet called Fouchet and someone called Petit François, and asked him to warn the Chouan to desist. On 20 June Bernadotte, also tiring of Bourmont's duplicity, informed Napoleon:

Bourmont is tricking the government. He is paying his captains, his subordinates and a lot of rascals. I would have had him arrested but I remember that you told me that you hoped to make use of him. In any case, I wanted to warn you about his activities.[3]

Napoleon's deflective reply was: 'I fear, like you, that Bourmont and the Chouan captains are behaving badly ... Georges [Cadoudal] is one of those who is the worst. Have him seized and shot.'

Napoleon evidently wanted Bourmont to be kept close at hand, but also expected him to lend his name to the pacification, having told the royalist in February that 'should you wish to go to England, I will arrange it; but if, on the other hand, if your intention is to remain here, then you better behave for you will be closely watched. At the slightest transgression you will be shot, for you would do the same if you were in my place.'[4]

Bourmont ignored such warnings and, whether he was using the police or being used by them, he felt confident enough to help a new wave of insurgents arriving in Paris for action. These were the men being sent by Cadoudal and were funded and supported by London, for English treasure began to make an appearance and Dutheil 'who had received considerable sums in order that the conspiracy succeed' made sure, for now, that they wanted for nothing. Their intention was actually to carry out the targeted strike against the head of government. Louis Guerin de Bruslart, another of Frotté's embittered subordinates, had been asked whether he would be willing to assassinate the tyrant but the chevalier had apparently refused, declaring that he was an officer and not a murderer. It makes a nice story, but in fact Bruslart had only recently admitted to being involved in a plan to kill Napoleon having made 'wild proposals of carrying off or cutting off Bonaparte' when he met Windham in London, and to which Windham 'pointedly declared that a British minister could give no countenance.' Rebuffed, the chevalier changed his plan, now saying that he was prepared to take part in a duel of equals, declaring 'if I am given a body of determined men I can wage an insurrectionary war on the Malmaison road and attack the Consul and his escort.' Bruslart had even crossed over to Paris but, as the summer wore on, and he spent more time in the gaming dens, his declared resolved increasingly came to resemble bluster.

Charles-Nicolas de Margadel, known as Joubert, had hitherto been the only true royalist hopeful, and he thought he could kill or kidnap Napoleon, bundling him in a carriage and driving him to Boulogne, where he would be delivered to the British waiting at Fort Montorgueil in Jersey.[5] Despite the exposure of the idea when the English Conspiracy was broken in May 1800, and despite the resulting heavy police surveillance on Margadel that followed, Margadel persisted in his promises. He was then in hiding in Saint-Germain, where, with a small arsenal, and a dozen men paid 60 Francs a month for acts of robbery or the murder of heads of state, he lay waiting. His did intercept some stage coaches heading to Rouen or Caen, but as time wore on he still did nothing against traffic heading for Malmaison.

Cadoudal, sensing that this man was another who would let him down, therefore opted to replace him in command and then use his band in his preferred method of attack, sending 30 hand-picked Chouans against Napoleon and his escort. The Breton, so often disappointed by the intriguers who surrounded D'Artois and who Hyde had promised would set the capital ablaze, decided that only his own captains should be entrusted with the essential blow. However, there was a delay when London insisted that the Marquis de Rivière co-ordinate the uprising in Paris.[6] After many delays, he actually arrived in the capital in August and quickly shocked everyone with his indiscretions. The king's agents also took against this agent of D'Artois and his minions, bemoaning 'the ruffians with whom this agency is composed, and their baseness'.

The marquis left at the end of September, further contributing to Cadoudal's impatience and desire to take charge of operations. Cadoudal had hovered around Nantes in July, hoping for an English force of 20,000, but had then crossed over to see Windham and Wickham in London, only returning to Brittany on 21 August. For much of September and October he was again absent, but that November he was rumoured to be hiding, like King Alfred, in a waterlogged retreat, directing his subordinates from amongst the rushes. Following the Rivière debacle, Cadoudal thought to send Mercier to Paris to find out what Margadel was doing. Mercier, however, was stuck in the Côtes-du-Nord, although he knew what was afoot and encouraged others to rouse themselves, telling one pessimistic royalist, 'I am convinced that in a few days you shall have reason to see the true state of the republic and will then think differently.'

It was just as well that Mercier had not gone, for, on 29 October, Margadel, possibly betrayed by Bourmont, or sacrificed by other schemers to mask their own plans, was caught. The police burst in catching him in the house of his mistress's brother. He was briskly tried in November for conspiracy, robbery and conspiracy to rob. Fouché's diligent report on the affair read:

> I have just arrested Margadel, a former Chouan commander in Bourmont's division, and he is in the Temple. This man operated under the name of Joubert and was the principal agent of the English Committee. He was in Paris and was the head of a group of rebels who lived off brigandage and the robbery of public property. It was he who held up and pillaged the stagecoach to Mantes. He was preparing to carry out an even more heinous plan against the First Consul until, hemmed in from all sides by the police, he was brought in and confessed.[7]

The arch-intriguer concluded that 'it is always dangerous to grant mercy to traitors' and so, inevitably, Dutheil, in London, soon had the unhappy task of passing on news of what happened next:

> On the 19th of this month they shot Monsieur le Chevalier de Margadel, or Joubert, who was to lead that small army of insurrection in Paris which D'Artois' committee wished to mobilise.[8]

Cadoudal was finally forced into taking the initiative. He had of course written to Grenville as early as 19 June saying 'I have sent to Paris to hear from those who are in charge of that operation.' But he had left it at nominating a commander for Paris, should he need one, Rohu noting how 'Saint-Réjant, as the most senior of the officers present, said that he should be the one selected.' Cadoudal had briefed Saint-Réjant on his preference for a fight *corps à corps* and therefore told his subordinate to organise the 'purchase of a number of horses, clothes, uniforms and equipment which I shall specify and which will be made use of later.'[9] Whether Saint-Réjant would comply was another matter. The insubordinate subordinate was evidently making up his own schemes, so much so that Cadoudal, writing to Mercier, was obliged to comment: 'My most sincere compliments to Saint-Réjant; tell him to be serious and to stop daydreaming.'[10]

There had been a pause until that November when word was received of Margadel's arrest. Cadoudal's lieutenants were therefore now finally sent on their way to Paris and delegated to strike. Cadoudal might once have specified how he wanted it done, but he was sending men inured to the war of ambush, kidnap and murder[11] and he knew they must improvise. And Saint-Réjant, who was to assume command, was, after all, a man who had never shown himself to be chivalrous, preferring rather to decide his battles through the judicious employment of subterfuge and gunpowder.

Saint-Réjant would take a small clique of similarly reckless men to assist him. First to leave for Paris was the brusque Aimé-Augustin Joyaut, or Joyaux, with his hair cut short in the style of Titus, and sporting his nicely tailored riding coat. He left his native Mayenne and arrived in Paris on 4 November where a certain Jean Baudet found lodgings for him at 211 Rue d'Argenteuil and also for his friend from college, Édouard de La Haye-Saint-Hilaire. The latter, known as Dieudonné or Raoulet, who had made his desire to kill Napoleon clear to Cadoudal back in March, arrived on Saturday 8 November. The pair found it easy enough to move around as the police were busy hounding the Jacobins and unravelling Chevalier's alleged plot to set off a bomb. Even so, Fouché was sufficiently well informed to have learned that they were on their way, and of their arrival. On 17 November he received a note from one of his subordinates:

> As yet unconfirmed information came in yesterday morning that Limolan [sic] has arrived in Paris, having been sent by Georges. He arrived at Rue Hélvetius and will busy himself with organising the young men who have enrolled here in order to strike a blow when hostilities recommence. He has Joyaux and Lahaye Saint-Hilaire as seconds, the first having been here for three weeks, the other since 10 days ago. Joyaux has it that he will take care of Napoleon for 1,000 Louis. Those are the terms. The location of these two men is unknown, Limoelan's was the Hotel des Etats-Généreux but he has left there to go into private lodgings to evade police surveillance. There is apparently someone in charge of them and they call him the abbot, but they don't seem to respect him for he is a fool. I suppose it must be the Abbé Ratel judging by the description the contact gave me.[12]

Fouché later told his masters that 'since November last, I was informed that Georges, having returned from England, had brought with him new plans for murder and guineas to embolden and pay the murderers. Those who were sent to Paris to prepare the crime and carry it out, had been pointed out to me.' Such intelligence had come from his own network of agents planted in royalist ranks as he had long been of the opinion that his police 'really must introduce amongst them some reliable and intelligent agents who will become party to their secrets and who will then inform you as to their plans and projects.' One such was the loquacious Desgrées, a Breton who, for greed or a crust, had presented himself to Desmarest, head of the secret office, on 21 November. He would prove remarkably useful. Fouché also pressed Bourmont, and some of the 900 emigrants already supposed to be languishing in France's prisons, for information. The results were mixed, but hinted that trouble was likely in the weeks ahead:

> The pardoned Chouans in Paris (of whom there are few, at present, as some have left) say that at the end of next week the English will stage two landings and that this will be the signal for hostilities to reopen.

The initial intelligence on Cadoudal's men had been alarming, but the police were a little perplexed when the first arrivals seemed rudderless. The Chouan captains had limited themselves to testing out pistols in the Bois de Boulogne and then attempting to hold up stage coaches to Troyes on the Charenton road on 16 November. Most useful for such tasks was François-Joseph Carbon, who had served in the bands of the Maine and who had been kicking his heels in Paris since early June, playing billiards at the Hotel de la Mayenne and pocketing a pittance as servant to Achille Le Blond, Bourmont's former subordinate.[13] Petit François, as he was known, had been born in Paris and knew as much about the capital as he did about the ways of death. Having spurned a career as a naval surgeon, he had, with a certain Ledoux, robbed a church in Mantes in 1794 before converting to royalism and becoming 'famous for his murders, making it his profession to kill blues.' Carbon was a man of action and so too were some of the next arrivals to the royalist circle of schemers. Jean-Baptiste Coster Saint-Victor was a former deserter nicknamed the Persistent (Persévérant) who had just returned from a failed royalist settlement in Canada. As the man of confidence of the Bishop of Arras, he had been sent over from London to take part in the decisive blow. Hyde de Neuville also came over, entering Paris at the end of November, his coachman telling him that the police were no longer checking passports at the capital's gates.[14] Hyde was coy about his purpose in Paris and his role in what was to come was opaque.

The same cannot be said for the next to arrive. The new commander, Pierre Robinault de Saint-Réjant, reached the capital at the end of November and he prepared to add some impetus to the plot. The royalists had been expecting Mercier, so the arrival of this Pierrot, so called on account of his diminutive size,[15] was a surprise. Desgrées notified the police of this important development:

> Mercier has not come. An individual called Saint-Réjant, a Breton gentleman known as Pierrot, came in place of the former who will probably come later on. Pierrot, like Mercier, is an officer who had been in charge of troops in Finistere. I shall, I hope, meet him tomorrow morning [29 November] and procure his address.[16]

Much was expected of this new captain and he had particular qualities that would steer the plot as it developed. Saint-Réjant had been born in Broons, between Rennes and the sea, and was a former naval officer who had emigrated in 1794. His knowledge of ordnance and munitions had proved useful when serving under the royalist rebel Puisaye at Quiberon; and his audacity, such as when he seized 32,000 Francs in treasure at Loudéac in November 1798, was celebrated in rebel ranks. Despite a drinking problem and bouts of insubordination, he had been promoted to Commander of the Légion de la Trinité-Porhoët in the rising of 1799, attacking Saint-Brieuc on 26 October. As the insurgency waned he remained in the shadows, avoiding committing himself to Napoleon's peace, and serving Cadoudal faithfully in covert missions across Brittany. Now, in Paris, he was charged with 'carrying out military orders', but was left to his own pitiless intuition as to how he did so.

The police knew little about him but Dubois would eventually be able to draw up a physical description of the new arrival:

> Around five foot, chestnut hair and brows; long face, blue eyes, long, thin nose, average mouth, round chin, oval but narrowish face; blue riding coat, shoes and slippers lined in lambswool, hair braided and tied back.[17]

Saint-Réjant's first task was to plan his campaign, find safe houses and establish arms caches. To do so he turned to another Breton resident in Paris, Joseph Pierre Picot de Clorivière, the Chevalier de Limoëlan. This was the Limolan Fouché had already been warned about. He looked quite the aristocrat:

> 33 or 34, five feet and five inches, dark blond hair cut in the style of Titus, blue eyes, long aquiline nose, pale skin, narrow face, short-sighted, slender and slight without being too thin, well made, handsome when looked at in profile rather than from the front, well presented, well dressed, clean clothes.

He was a friend of Saint-Réjant's, and also a neighbour at a time when regional origins still trumped national identity. The short-sighted Limoëlan, sometimes known as Pourleroy, or Beaumont, was also an inveterate rebel. He had cause to be for his father, a wealthy merchant who had married the daughter of an equally wealthy Irish merchant in Nantes, had been guillotined on 18 June 1793. Even so he was a relative newcomer to the armed struggle and he had only briefly fought in Cadoudal's ranks at Broons in 1799. Following the pacifications in the spring of 1800, he had come to the capital that March and had made use of his mother at Versailles to help settle his status. The government's removal of his name from the list of sanctioned emigrants would allow him to be reintegrated into society with his relatives, and be restored to the property and rental income they declared that they needed in order to survive. Despite many fine promises, he would be frustrated. Dubois, certainly, had no reason to hold up the royalist's reintegration, noting: 'Limoëlan, an amnestied chief, at the hotel of Widow Labie, Rue du Hasard. Frequently goes to Versailles. Positive reports. He sees few people and his conduct seems unsuspicious.'[18]

Nevertheless the Chouan's dossier was not progressing and by 23 April Limoëlan was asking for an explanation for the delay, hinting at duplicity. A few weeks later, he was fulminating: 'When everyone confirms that I have contributed to the restoration of peace in my region, I might hope that I should no longer be considered as an enemy.'

General Hédouville, who had encouraged his surrender, sympathised, puzzling why he had not been removed from amongst the 40 royalists he had personally vouched for: 'with your name featuring on a specific list I personally sent to the First Consul in addition to the one sent to the Minister of Police ... I ask you not to lose hope and to pursue your course relentlessly and I will happily repeat whatever I have done to date should you judge that to be of some use.'[19]

Sensing that Fouché was behind the delay, Limoëlan's mother, who knew the minister, added her voice to the appeal. The minister, who liked to trade in the secure currency of gratitude for services rendered, sometimes extended pardons to those who might prove useful, but neither was he above playing overtly political games with their plight.[20] Limoëlan, increasingly concerned for his impoverished family and his own ability to support his intended wife, Julie d'Albert, also reached out to Fouché and hoped for special favours on account of his mother.[21] But whatever was being offered that summer was insufficient and Limoëlan was soon coming to terms with the idea of being involved in violence in Paris, enigmatically telling his family, 'When all else seems to fail, wait for the event and then judge and perhaps you will not judge me so badly.'[22]

Limoëlan briefly quit Paris on 31 August and was at Saint-Aubin des Châteaux on 16 September. There were some discussions as to whether he would take up a position in the reformed royalist bands of Brittany, or would return to Paris to help aim the blow there. It was all decided before the middle of November, and the bespectacled Limoëlan was back in the capital on the 16th, resentful but resolved. He met his fellow Chouans and was briefed on progress, even though, five days later, he made one last attempt to get his name cleared. Fouché, who had been talking to Bourmont, was, however, now suspicious of this particular case or was perhaps hoping he could turn Limoëlan into an informer, marking Limoëlan's important dossier 'for the consul' and taking no further action to exonerate him.[23] When Limoëlan found out he was livid, and took up his quill to blast Fouché:

You generously expressed your discontent with me to one of my relatives, Monsieur Boisbaudron, perhaps in order to oblige me to justify my conduct, and that you therefore regard my silence as a confession of my faults. Without knowing that of which I am accused, I nevertheless feel that I am innocent even though I have been treated in a manner which leaves me with little confidence in this government, not having been taken from the list despite many assured promises. I am not deranged enough to underestimate its power, and, consequently, to conspire against it. I am unaware of the charges you lay against me and cannot, therefore, address them, but I can assure

you, Citizen Minister, that all I wish for is peace and that I shall seek
it in Paris only because I fear I shall not find it in Brittany.[24]

So it was that the now more or less deranged Limoëlan willingly
assumed a central position in the plot to kill Napoleon, and received
the particular antipathy of the minister of police who dubbed him
a brigand amongst brigands. All this meant that he was forced into
the devious ways of conspirators, dying his hair, resorting to noms
de guerre and relying on his shadowy uncle, Pierre-Joseph Picot
de Clorivière, for alms[25] and on his uncle's ultra-Catholic support
network for shelter. The Marquise de Créquy related how she and
Mademoiselle de Cicé, elder sister of the Archbishop of Bordeaux
and a disciple of Limoëlan's uncle, took pains to hide the plotter:

> On the night of 5/6 December 1800 Mademoiselle de Cicé visited
> a young émigré, a Breton gentleman called Limoëlan. He remained
> there, hidden away, in an apartment in the Créquy household for
> three whole weeks.

Saint-Réjant summoned him from these comfortable quarters.
The commander had put an end to highway robbery and was
disinclined to pursue the notion of attacking Napoleon's heavily
escorted coach as it trundled towards Malmaison, even though his
royalists were expertly familiar with the traffic between Paris and
that country seat. Some talked of poison, but it was Desgrées who
informed the police that Limoëlan was amongst those to purchase
guns in late November for 50 Louis from a gunsmith called Bourin
at 24 Palais Egalité:

> Monsieurs Limolan, known as Beaumont, Saint-Réjant, known
> as Pierrot, and Joyaux, known as d'Assas, have purchased the

necessary weapons, manufactured at Versailles, and will test them out in the Bois de Boulogne tomorrow at noon or one o'clock.[26]

Coster-Saint-Victor, keen to be done with the murder, proposed a variation on the theme of shooting, suggesting that Napoleon be killed with a noiseless air carbine,[27] perhaps at the theatre. The police seem to have been informed of this with Desgrées having attended a meeting in which the idea of 'opening fire all at once against Bonaparte from the stalls and the boxes' was broached. A few days later, he told his masters that 'Saint-Réjant is planning something against the First Consul as I told you this morning he will use air carbines at a performance. This Pierrot is well known in this clique for all the bold acts he has carried out; indeed, that's his only merit, but he is to be feared because he desires to make himself known through some bravura act.'[28] Soon after, around 6 or 7 December, Saint-Réjant, sensing that the police knew about the carbines, made the decision to replace the silent guns with his own noisy weapon of choice.

With the conspiracy now taking shape, there was much at stake. The Parisian police were well aware that the Chouans were plotting murder but surveillance in the capital was proving difficult. Attempted raids failed to catch the government's quarry as Leclerc, Officer of the Peace, noted:

On 10 December the Citizen Prefect was informed that certain individuals linked to the Chouan faction had arrived in Paris to carry out nefarious plans. He ordered raids on a number of hotels in Rue Honoré and Rue Saint-Roch. These were unsuccessful, and we knew that such brigands changed their accommodation every 24 hours, meaning they quit as soon as they were required to register with the police that they were staying there. One of them, made known to me as Pierrot, or Régent, was five foot two, large, round faced, long nosed, tanned, blue riding coat, or sometimes a yellow one; hair in a pigtail; gesticulates when talking.[29] Following information we received this man had been present at a hotel in the Quinze-Vingts on the 8th or 9th of December. His papers were in order and he went out the next day but did not return, and was not seen again. It was thought that he had gone to the hotel Deux-Ponts in Rue Saint-Roch. Our enquiries showed there was no hotel of that name in that street but there was one in Rue du Hasard, in the Butte des Moulins, and he could easily have gone into hiding there as it is a disreputable house and the Daguerres and other brigands stay there.[30]

The Deux-Ponts at 688 Rue du Hasard was a royalist den, and Hyde certainly met the plotters there, but raids on the establishment proved fruitless and other equally frustrating attempts followed on the Hotel de Pérou and Mayenne. The prey was being driven further underground, and Desmarest's attempts to warn off the plotters by telling his Chouans that the police knew everything, whilst clever, proved of little avail.[31] Worse, Fouché was then struck a blow when one of his spies blew his cover when he was spotted entering the prefecture at midday. It was no coincidence that Desgrées then disappeared. He had been sent to Rennes by Saint-Réjant on 7 December to re-establish the connection with Brittany, as he told Desmarest:

> One of us will set out the day after tomorrow to carry the plan that is going to be carried out and to bring back his [Cadoudal's] orders. Pierrot has asked me today to take care of this. These men now have two air carbines and will shortly have more.

So off he went, carrying the correspondence for Cadoudal and with 7 Louis in his pocket for expenses. It is possible he made it beyond Rennes to Ploërmel but whatever finally happened, he was never heard of or seen again.[32]

Cadoudal was well-informed of the situation through his own channels and informants. He also recognised that the police were on high alert in the capital, and was aware that security around the First Consul had been tightened after Chevalier's explosive fiasco, as he told Dutheil:

> You have probably learned that they tried to kill our great consul. I suppose you won't believe it. In fact, from what I can gather, it seems that this gentleman put on this farce in order to make sure he remains in the public eye and in order to improve his own security, something which he has now seen to.[33]

He was, of course, partly right. Napoleon had not been unduly troubled by the Jacobin plots, remarking 'I have no fear of conspirators who get up at nine o'clock and put on a white shirt.' But Chevalier's bomb was an intriguing idea. Saint-Réjant, the artilleryman, would have seen the advantage at once of detonating such a device in a narrow street, and Saint-Réjant, the royalist, would also appreciate that imitating Chevalier's device might confuse the authorities by making it seem like a second attempt by radicalised Jacobins. Informers would surely have provided details of the plot following the arrest of the key suspects in early November, noting that they had wanted to blow Bonaparte up in Rue Nicaise, and, with some sketchy licence, attempting to set out some technical details of the barrel bomb Chevalier had devised.[34] It would give Saint-Réjant pause for thought, from which emerged a mimetic, though complex, plan. For premeditated murder on such a scale would take careful preparation, technical ability and, above all, secrecy. Desmarest, on their trail, was sure of one thing:

'No sooner had they resolved on the idea of a nocturnal explosion as their preferred method than they disappeared, enveloped in mystery.'

Joyaux had found Saint-Réjant rooms at 574 Rue des Prouvaires, where Louise Leguilloux and her husband, Jean-Baptiste, a post office courier, served as discreet landlords.[35] The Breton officer also took a second set of rooms with Madame Henriette Boufens, known as Widow Jourdan, at 1336 Rue d'Aguesseau. She charged him just 20 sous per day and he proved a welcome tenant, making a great impression on the widow and her daughter Marie Antoinette, or Toinette, so much that when Toinette found a pug in the street she presented it to the man 'on condition that he presents Citizen Toinette Jourdan with a dress.'

These two secure addresses allowed Saint-Réjant to don his white shirt and blue coat and to patrol the streets off Rue Saint Honoré, Rue des Prouvaires being a grenade's throw from the Tuileries gardens and the Jourdans' a pistol shot from the Louvre. The idea of an attack on the Consul's coach as it left the Tuileries was tempting and, again, Chevalier's plan seemed most apt. Rue Nicaise, which stretched from the palace to Paris's best theatres, was perfect especially as the plotters knew that Napoleon was likely to attend the 24 December premiere of Haydn's *Creation*, for which tickets went on sale on 10 December.

Unfortunately, not long after his arrival in his new accommodation, Saint-Réjant had fallen ill and was laid up with catarrh for over a week, a Doctor Collin treating him and recommending 'rest, and not to leave the lodgings but to stay close to the fire.' He also gave him syrup and advised him not to eat meat in the evenings.[36] So the patient remained in his room, having bland meals sent in from the Mariette restaurant, petting the pug, Mirza, now resplendent in its silver collar with green velvet lining,[37] and reading Bourdé de Villehuet's 1797 treatise on naval manoeuvres. But it was there, despite the coughing, constipation and phlegm, that Saint-Réjant calmly set out his plan to Limoëlan, who was initially troubled by the scheme, and to Carbon, who had no such scruples. Sensing the former's disquiet, Saint-Réjant told Limoëlan to look to the details of organising logistics and payments whilst he, Carbon, Joyaux and Saint-Hilaire arranged matters so that the bomb could be created on time. Time was important. The premiere of *The Creation* was in a week.

Cadoudal, hiding at Plougoumelen in Brittany, was increasingly anxious, and keen to hear of some progress, and of at least one important death, after weeks of delay. On 19 December, starved of information, he wrote under the pseudonym of Gédéon to the pseudonym assumed by Saint-Réjant of Soyer:

> Alas, two weeks have passed and events proceed in a terrifying manner. If the setbacks continue, I don't know what shall become of us. We look to you and all our confidence and our hope rests in you ... PS, we wait for your news with each courier.[38]

The courier would bring news soon enough, for the conspirators were hard at work.

On 17 December a plump Parisian walked into the courtyard of Monsieur Jean-Baptiste Nicolas Brunet in Rue de la Corderie in the Marais and asked if he could purchase one of Brunet's carts. Brunet showed the pockmarked visitor, who stood out from his usual clients in a fine blue jacket, round hat and buck breeches, what he had in stock. The stranger 'finding none to his liking' was about to leave when Brunet offered to take him to his friend Lambel, who had bought a small two-wheeled cart the day before. Brunet accompanied the affluent-looking client to 42 Rue Meslay where he met Lambel, a grain merchant, who described what happened next:

> I was in my shop and the individual was in the street looking at the cart. I said 'do you like it' He said it was exactly what he needed. And he added that was not all, for he also needed a horse.[39]

The visitor made an offer for the cart and Lambel was canny enough to include an unimpressive mare in the bargain, along with all the necessary harnessing. The final price was soon confirmed over a litre of wine and it was apparent that the plump purchaser, although pretending to be a travelling salesman, only had patience for a negligible amount of haggling. The following day, 20 December, at three in the afternoon, this suspicious salesman and Lambel arrived at Brunet's to settle the affair. Brunet recalled:

> The following day he went to Lambel's and came to fetch me to go to David's restaurant in Rue du Temple. I had a meeting with Monsieur Moriset as I had just sold him a dray. So I says to Lambel and to this individual, that I cannot come just now but that I'll be free in half-an-hour. They asked where I usually went, and I told them I am not in the habit of drinking and only rarely eat in town, although I added that there was a place at the end of the street and that I could join them there as soon as I finished.

The stranger, taking scented snuff from a box engraved with an image of Frederick the Great, then treated Lambel and Brunet to more wine at the Daufeuille restaurant in Rue du Temple, the stranger with a scar in the corner of his left eye footing the bill for 6 livres 8 sous to seal the deal.[40] Alexandre Moriset, the proud owner of the new dray, saw the man hand over 200 Francs for the horse and cart. The men talked about building a hood for the cart to keep the snow off the merchandise, the salesman saying he didn't want a new cover, but that any old cloth would do. Brunet helped build the framework for 6 Francs and, the next day, still rather incongruously dressed in his buckskin breeches tied at the knee with black cord, the newcomer arrived to collect his purchases, and seemed pleased with the adapted cart. However, he was back half-an-hour later complaining that the hood was too high, engraving himself on Brunet's and Lambel's memory as a capricious customer.

The customer made himself even more memorable by returning to Lambel's to buy and take away some sacks of lentils and peas, especially as he told Lambel to mind his own business when he asked where he lived, only saying 'around Saint Martin' when pressed. Asked whether he wanted stabling, he rudely replied that he did not need any more advice, for he had also found and rented all he needed.

That rude individual was Carbon and he had bought the cart using funds provided by Limoëlan. It would be used to shift the explosive device selected as the royalist weapon of choice. Everything needed to be prepared in secret because Fouché and Dubois, in close competition to be the first to bring good news to the First Consul, had sent parties of agents scouring the roads and alleyways north of the Rue Saint Honoré. Napoleon was no doubt growing nervous as, according to his Minister of Police, he had received warning that this time his life was very much in danger. A captain of the Chamborant Hussars had written to the First Consul on 19 December in these terms: 'I don't like you but, as assassination is against my principles I warn you that you will be attacked between 22nd and 24th December. If they fail, they'll be waiting for you on 3 January at the parade.'

Redoubled efforts were called for. Officer Leclerc, reported how: 'On 20 December we received new instructions which obliged us to search the Faubourg Poissonnière. We did all that we could but were not successful. My instructions noted that Pierrot had to be with Limoelan, known as Beaumont, and Joyau, or that he himself might make use of these names.'[41] But this fixation with the leaders meant that the busy underlings were left undisturbed for now. Carbon was busiest of them all. He had indeed found a suitable hiding place at 23 Paradis Poissonnière where, calling himself a cloth merchant specialising in Laval's robust textiles, he had initially asked to rent the place for two weeks only. The shrewd owner, Citizen, once Chevalier, Marie-Louis Baillif-Mesnager,[42] a former officer of the royal army, drove a hard bargain, however, as he himself recalled:

I'll rent it out for 20 sous a day. He told me it was expensive. I told him 'you are a fool', you would be better off renting it for a year and after three months sending in notice. 'How much would it be for a year?' I told him 100 Francs for the year and he thought about that. Very well, he said, I will rent it for three months. I told him that he was a travelling salesman and so asked that, once he, the cart and the horse had gone, who would then pay me. I would need the money in advance.[43]

Carbon, again having marked himself out as someone unfamiliar with apparently routine business practices, handed over an advance of 6 Francs, and brought the cart round that same evening, 21 December. His priority seems to have been to disguise the load, but all this coming and going piqued the professional interest of a carter who lived at Number 23, a man called Jean-François Thomas, and the concierge, Madame Albertine Ricard. Carbon and two cloaked companions had arrived in the evening and had had to ask Thomas to move his cart so their covered vehicle could be brought into the courtyard.

On the following day Thomas's wife, Catherine-Rose Duchat, saw that Carbon, the merchant in a clean blue smock and leather breeches, who seemed to know nothing about horses and carts, was back with his two friends. The concierge lit a lantern for these men, Édouard de La Haye-Saint-Hilaire and Joyaux, as they inspected the vehicle for 45 minutes and then left, arousing suspicion by painstakingly locking up the building. Carbon's next suspicious move was to obtain a 240-litre barrel, and he carelessly asked the concierge whether she could recommend a supplier. A first barrel had contained white wine but was rather small and so a second was fashioned by Alexis Baroux and reinforced with four iron rings by his apprentice and, on 22 December, the men struggled to move it into the confines of the shed. One of them then went to ask Madame Ricard for a cup to use as a scoop. The Parisian concierge obliged the men with a cup, but when they returned it to her a little later, it smelt so strongly of gunpowder that she had to rinse it several times in boiling water before she could use it again.[44] Her suspicions were further aroused when these impractical merchants asked her for a drill and tools and she nudged her husband, Monsieur Roché, into offering to help. The following morning he drilled holes in the sides and the shafts of the cart and saw that it contained at least one barrel. He was sent on his way with 8 sous.

Meanwhile, Carbon had gone out and come back with a heavy basket before spending the night in the shed with his companions and the barrels that would be used as the basis for the improvised explosive device. Saint-Réjant, now fully recovered, had also been busy. At nine on the morning of 22 December he had taken a cab from Rue Honoré to Rue des Prouvaires, paying the fare of one-and-a-half Francs and then asking the cab driver, Jacques Thierot, to return that afternoon. More reliable than many Parisian taxis, he did so:

> I was there at two and drove him to the Rue Nicaise. There, he stepped down outside the Hotel de Longueville. After seven or eight minutes he came back, and climbed back in. I took him to Rue d'Aguesseau and there he told me he would need me again that evening and I agreed. He sent a girl to fetch me and I came, taking him to Rue des Prouvaires ... the next day he had me take him to Rue Nicaise were he again climbed down for seven or eight minutes before he got back in and we went to Rue d'Aguesseau.[45]

Thierot saw him, watch in hand, pacing around the Carrousel. He was evidently measuring distances and timings from the gates of the Tuileries to various points along Rue Nicaise. At some point he conferred with Limoëlan on the best position for a lookout to warn of the approach of the First Consul's coach. Satisfied with the principles of the scheme, he then returned to his lodgings to work on the all-important fuse. With some knowledge of the properties of powder and combustible material, gleaned from years of naval service and blowing down doors, the Breton was concerned primarily about ensuring the device went off at exactly the right moment. He rejected Chevalier's design of a trigger igniting powder, and so his experiments with various lengths of fuse continued throughout Tuesday the 23rd and into the morning of Christmas Eve. It was then that Saint-Réjant was seen by Toinette, the 16-year-old daughter of his landlady, rolling out three-inch strips of textile, binding it with the highly combustible Fomes fomentarius, or amadou tinder, and, after setting it alight with phosphorous matches, timing how long it took to burn in his fireplace. He did this again and again, cutting the fuse as short as he could, and seemed so absorbed amongst his combustible materials that he made no reply when Antoinette chided him that 'one day you shall burn the entire house down.'

However, that Christmas Eve the time for further testing was over, and, taking a cab, Saint-Réjant set off to dine in his rooms at Louise Leguilloux's. Having consumed a plate of fish, he then left for an unknown destination at around five that evening. Back at Paradis Poissonnière, Carbon had harnessed up the old mare and secured the two barrels on his cart, covering them in straw, hay and kindling. As Limoëlan arrived, Carbon was adjusting his tattered and mouldy canvas sheet, thrown over the hoops to keep his precious load dry. At around half-past-five the two men, dressed alike in new carter's smocks, set off, the cart lurching forward.

The bid to kill the consul had begun.

7

CHRISTMAS EVE

The two royalists rattled out from dreary Paradis Poissonnière, leading the bay horse and cart down to the gate of Saint Denis, that monumental archway erected to honour Bourbon victories. There Carbon was abandoned to his own musings as Limoëlan rolled the largest of the barrels away, the other, already filled with powder, remaining hidden beneath its stained awning. Half-an-hour later Saint-Hilaire and Joyaux, accompanied by Limoëlan, appeared from the direction of Rue Neuve Egalité (now d'Aboukir) pushing the larger barrel on a hand cart. It was now considerably heavier, and the men struggled with the weight as it was transferred from hand cart to horse cart. As Saint-Hilaire and Joyaux wheeled the trolley back to wherever it had come from and promptly disappeared, Saint-Réjant emerged from the crowds resplendent in a blue smock. The three royalists then made their way slowly along Rue Neuve Egalité, Limoëlan, Saint-Réjant and Carbon picking up paving stones[1] and loading them onto the front of the cart to offset the weight of the barrel, and provide some additional, albeit rudimentary, shrapnel. They urged the tired jade on as far as Place des Victoires where, beneath the wooden pyramid that had replaced the equestrian statue of King Louis, Carbon left them, disappearing from the square and the plot. The vehicle then continued down Rue Croix des Petits Champs to Rue Saint Honoré and turned into the poorly lit Rue Nicaise. The plotters saw, however, that it was pulsing with life.

This street was a deliberate choice for their act of carnage, an elegant artery in the midst of a quarter known for contributing to the renewed sophistication of a capital turning its back on turmoil. Named after the now demolished Chapel of Saint-Nicaise, but shortened to Rue Nicaise in this Age of Reason, the street ran rather straight, following the course of the ancient city wall, and connecting the broad Saint Honoré to the Carrousel and the Tuileries. As with most of the capital's streets, it lacked a pavement but the mud and filth on the ground did not detract from the luxury on offer from the bars and boutiques scattered along its length. At the northern end, close to Saint Honoré, there were grocers and purveyors of fine food and wine. Further south, passing a lane named after General Hoche that ran eastwards to Rue de Marceau, Rue de Malte and the temptations of the Palais de l'Égalité, fine arts and crafts dominated. There was Madame Annette's perfumery at Number 483; Paulé's stationery at 494; Lenoir's or De Metz's hat shop at Number 497 and 511 respectively; and Mariol's leather goods, tucked conveniently under the office of Monsieur Hermand, the moneylender, at Number 505. Should all the shopping prove too much, then Doctor Sellée, who specialised in hernias, and who had a surgery on the first floor of 511, might be of use. In between all these shops were cafés, such as Menudier's or Madame Léger's Café d'Apollon, selling lemonade, and wine merchants, such as Wormé's at number 523, who were selling mulled wine to the festive crowds.

These shops ran down to the southern end of the street where various hotels and lodging houses, such as Madame Lolive's at 506 and the Hotel de Malte, looked after the city's visitors. Then the street joined the Carrousel, although it was not an especially elegant junction, Nicaise being overshadowed by the six-floor Hôtel de Nantes[2] on one side and the legal offices, assembly rooms and the office of Commissaire of Police Claude Chazot at the Hôtel de Longueville on the other.

The Carrousel continued the mean theme. True, there was Cambacérès' elegant residence in the Hôtel d'Elbeuf but it sat alongside the entrance of Consul Lebrun's stables, which backed on to Rue Nicaise, and those of the First Consul. Worse, whatever open space there was, remained covered with building materials and the scaffolding that was being removed from the renovated Tuileries. Yet even in this ugly amphitheatre, as yet unembellished by the hand of the First Architect, there were groups of tourists and citizens mingling to watch the comings and goings from the palace and who were hopeful of catching sight of Napoleon. The cold had not curbed their ardour, or that of the masses thronging the entire quarter that Christmas Eve. Indeed, the festive crowds were such that they stretched right along the length of Rue Nicaise, the heavy traffic and erratic pedestrians now slowing the two royalists as they advanced on the Tuileries, passing narrow Rue Hoche before pausing near the junction with the Carrousel. They took up an initial position by the Hotel des Quinze-Vingts and Alexandre Beirlé's glove shop at number 333 on the right of the street and went unremarked by Beirlé's pregnant wife and her servant, Marie-Géneviève Viel Barbier, who was mixing a salad. Nor did the watchmaker, Lepeautre, whose workshop was next to Lebrun's stable wall, notice them. However, a Monsieur Boubion did see them at around half-past seven and returning from his errand shortly afterwards, the observant Boubion noticed that the cart had switched sides and was now beneath the walls of Consul Lebrun's stables a little further away from the Carrousel – the high walls offering them the protection of deep shadows and the stables a reason for what seemed to be their load of hay and barrels of water.

To further cloak his movements in innocence, Saint-Réjant had ventured down to the sentry post on Pont National and asked one of two teenage girls selling bread buns whether she would be prepared to hold his horse for a while. This Marianne Peusol,[3] her red hair wrapped in a blue handkerchief, having sold all her bread, volunteered to hold on to the horse's Dutch bridle for 12 sous. Limoëlan then walked off to assume his position as lookout in the Carrousel whilst Saint-Réjant, borrowing a light from a piquet of Guardsmen at the guard post opposite the Apollon café, smoked his pipe and watched as Marianne tended the horse. Then, as eight o'clock approached, pretending to adjust his cargo, he turned the cart so that it jutted into the street, the two barrels hidden unremarked under their awning. Whilst the bomb was invisible, the cart was not and it did not escape the attention of a foreign goldsmith who noticed 'a large man who was asking a child to take care of his cart, saying "hold it steady there".' A friend of Pierre Villemenot, a certain Guillemot, also saw 'a kind of cart, drawn by a horse, and covered with a grey cloth, the horse being guarded by a young boy [sic] who was poorly dressed, and seemingly from the country, who was amusing himself by playing with his crop as he held the horse.'

Most passers-by were more intent on pleasure, many heading to Maestro Fritzeri's mandolin concert at the Hôtel de Longueville or to Piis's old haunt, the Vaudeville Theatre in Rue de Malte, but others were simply sauntering through the streets. Captain Platel of the gendarmes was escorting his mistress, Widow Lyster, back to the Rue de Lille whilst Nicolas-Alexandre Corbet was strolling through the street with his friend, Monsieur Cléreaux. Some were seeking liquid refreshment; it was, after all, Christmas Eve and the habits of a decade ago had proved remarkably resilient, with Christmas celebrated as though the interregnum of Robespierre's Supreme Being had never been. The drinkers included Jean-Frédéric Banny, assistant chef, intent on crowning his year with a festive toast, and Jeanne-Elisabeth Hugaut, a fishwife, already downing wine at De Metz the milliner. The wine merchant's at number 513 was also full but it was the Apollon that was busiest, the owner, Catherine Emas, known as Madame Léger, keeping a watchful eye on her clients. These included Jean-Baptiste Lemercier, a landlord, 'and a regular at the café Apollon for some years', Claude Barthélemy Préville, an upholsterer who was drinking half a bottle of wine with his apprentice and Louise Saint-Gilles, leaning against the window looking at the passers-by. From an upper story Gaspard Glassince also peered out, hoping to see the First Consul's carriage as it trundled to the opera house.

That opera house, or rather the Théâtre des Arts et de la République, on Rue de la Loi, just the other side of Rue Saint Honoré, was the venue for an event that had brought still more people out into the cold and contributed significantly to the atmosphere of expectation in the capital. It was there, tonight, that the Parisian premiere of Haydn's great oratorio, *The Creation*, was due to be performed.

The impresario and composer of the little-known *Hymn to the Supreme Being*, Ignaz Pleyel, had wanted to bring Haydn to Paris to conduct the Austrian's *Die Schöpfung* in person. But art and music were to be foiled by war. Haydn had first conducted his oratorio, which set the text of *Paradise Lost* to heavenly music, at Vienna on 30 April 1798, with Antonio Salieri playing the piano continuo. It had met with considerable acclaim and Paris, a little jealous of Viennese delights, expected to be next to hear the work. But war with Austria meant that Haydn could not travel to France, and the capital overreacted by announcing an enormous and grandiose production of its own. Some 150 singers and 156 musicians were booked to perform, with Jean-Baptiste Rey conducting and Daniel Steibelt, a Prussian composer who had also translated the libretto, at the piano. The Prussian's hasty version of the text had then been badly versified by Joseph Ségur, although the theatre ensured that France's finest singers were brought in to distract from the verse, with Garat singing Uriel, Chéron singing both Raphael and Adam and the magnificent Marie-Philippe-Claude de Walbonne-Barbier performing as Gabriel and Eve. The public response was also magnificent and some 1,417 people bought tickets, the seats selling out two weeks before the performance date.[4] The Parisian Jacques de Norvins noted that 'All good society, whether of the old sort or of the new, were to meet there', and indeed they did, and could be seen milling around outside that Christmas Eve. By around seven o'clock lines of coaches and carriages had clogged the right-hand sides of Rue de la Loi and Saint Honoré, increasing the congestion in neighbouring thoroughfares. A small cordon of grenadiers from the Consular Guard ringed the theatre, glaring at ticket touts and watching as nine of the theatre's ushers struggled to deal with the growing tide of traffic.

Norvins intended to be there early, and so 'following the custom of the young, a group of us ate at a restaurant, and then arrived as the gates opened. It is true that a great spectacle has two important acts, that of entering the auditorium, and that of leaving.' The public agreed and were busily seating themselves, and watching others being seated, before the performance at eight. Napoleon's secretary, Bourrienne, arrived before time, revelling in a night off from taking minutes, as did Réal and his wife Marie-Agnès. Shortly afterwards, the Russian envoy, General Sprengporten, entered and received a standing ovation, whilst Fouché, with his wife of eight years, Bonne Jeanne Coiquaud, was met with studied indifference. Then, at eight o'clock, Rey sat down before his orchestra to conduct the adagio which opened the great work. The genius of this overture, the storm and stress of Haydn's music, painting a scene of chaos before the creation, soon drowned the sound of Parisian gossip. And as God started creating Heaven and Earth in the theatre, few noticed that the First Consul was late.

As the audience was watching itself at the theatre, the son of a humble Alsatian concierge, Jean Rapp, a man who had fought his way doggedly to the position of Napoleon's primary aide-de-camp, was waiting, kicking his heels in the salon of the Tuileries Palace. With him was one of Napoleon's other ordinance officers, Anne-Charles Lebrun, son of the consul, as well as General Jean Lannes, Josephine Bonaparte, Hortense Beauharnais and Napoleon's pregnant sister Caroline Murat. As so many before and since, they were waiting for Napoleon's decision.

After having gobbled down his dinner by half-past six, largely ignoring the eleven others present at table, Napoleon was, according to Josephine's daughter Hortense, 'sat in the corner by the fire, and seemingly little disposed to going out.' Napoleon's wish to remain on his favourite divan was challenged by Hortense, who was passionately fond of music, and her mother, and they were 'all ready and impatient for him to make up his mind.' Josephine went further, remarking to her husband that 'It will distract you, you work too much.' Napoleon closed his eyes and said nothing but, after a studied pause, roused himself to say that he would not come. Hortense watched how this ordinary domestic scene in the consular household 'became a dispute between them, and it only ended when the horses were hitched to the coaches.'

After all, the agreement had always been that the Bonaparte family would attend the premiere. Napoleon was persuaded to hold true to that agreement and so, after this crescendo of irritated voices, the party rushed to leave on time. Rapp watched:

> The escort was ordered and Lannes took the responsibility of asking Napoleon whether he was now ready to leave. He was and, finding his coach ready, he took Bessières, his duty aide-de-camp, with him whilst I was tasked with escorting the ladies.

Napoleon climbed into his coach with Lannes and Bessières, with young Lebrun and Lauriston following on in a second coach, whilst gallant Rapp attended to Madame and Mademoiselle Bonaparte and Caroline Murat. But this coach was slightly delayed:

> Josephine had received a magnificent shawl from Constantinople and she put it on for the very first time. I remarked 'allow me to observe that your shawl has not quite been arranged as you would wish it'. She replied, laughing, that I should then tie it like one of the Egyptian ladies. Whilst this singular operation was being carried out we learned that Napoleon was already leaving. Madame Bonaparte, impatient to get to the theatre, called out 'Hurry up, sister, see Bonaparte is leaving.' We climbed into the coach whilst that of the First Consul was already at the Carrousel and set off in pursuit.[5]

Hortense, who says it was Napoleon who criticised her mother's dress, remarked how 'our coach, which normally followed on close after that of the Consul's was, this time, a little way behind.'

Just after eight Napoleon's vehicle had sped off, driven by the roguish coachman Germain, known as César. He would normally take the First Consul into the Carrousel, then along Rue Nicaise, turning right into Rue Saint Honoré and then left and into Rue de la Loi and to the theatre. There was another exit, a side street named after General Hoche which was halfway along and which led eastwards joining Rue de Marceau and from which a coach could go directly up Rue de la Loi. The royalists had positioned the street bomb before the turning into that side street, thus ensuring that the coach would have to pass it and, indeed, they had now positioned their cart in an attempt to block the main thoroughfare itself.

When Napoleon's coach exited the Tuileries it was preceded at a distance of 20 paces by a detachment of 12 mounted grenadiers from the Consular Guard. The short-sighted Limoëlan, standing watch and waiting to give the signal by waving his right hand, was disconcerted by this sudden movement and the nature of the square added to his discomfort, for the Carrousel was not the expansive open space it is today, but was a 'very small square, and there was a concentration of streets, little islands of houses and palaces in this space,' and this hampered visibility. So when Napoleon's mounted escort rode by, Limoëlan's line of sight, such as it was, was obscured by the grenadiers. Saint-Réjant was therefore disconcerted to see 'two coaches and the cavalry escort' bearing down, but he hoped that Napoleon would not pass. Indeed, he had barred the vehicle's passage, as one of the escort, 28-year-old Grenadier Nicolas Durand, clearly saw when he rode into the street:

On that day I was on duty for the First Consul. At eight that evening the First Consul was due at the opera. I was placed in the escort which went before the coach. As I rode into the Rue Saint-Nicaise I saw a cart that seemed to be moving across the street and which was blocking about half of the way ahead. At that point there was also a hackney carriage in front; I being 20 paces in front of the Consul's coach, had to clear the way. I pushed further ahead to have that carriage move away, had it reversed then the Consul's coach would have come to a halt as it would not have been able to pass through the gap. I drew up alongside the driver and threatened him with my sabre, then spurred my horse on and passed between the cart and the carriage, damaging my mount's leg. The horse pulling the cart was facing the wall. The carriage's driver came through the gap and we continued. I turned to look behind me and saw that the Consul's coachman had slowed his horses to a halt for a moment, because he saw that the way ahead was blocked.[6]

Rapp later heard that the escort had confronted the royalists, 'A grenadier of the escort, thinking them water carriers, hit them a couple of times with the flat of his sabre and they fell back.' But Durand was more prosaic, limiting himself to stating that he had pushed between the two vehicles. This was enough for the cart and mare to recoil sharply, momentarily disconcerting and unbalancing Saint-Réjant as he later noted in the draft of a letter to Cadoudal:

Someone had promised to warn the culprit [ie the writer himself] when the First Consul's coach set off. They did not. They said that the coach would be preceded by an escort. It was not.[7] The culprit, alone and starved of information, only became aware that the coach was on its way when he saw it. It was then that the horse of a grenadier pushed him sharply against the wall and interrupted his work. He recovered and lit the fuse but the powder was not of the usual quality and so there was a delay of one or two seconds.

Had that not been the case, the First Consul would have perished. It was the fault of the powder, not of the culprit.

Behind Durand the consul's coach, which had briefly halted, now picked up speed along Rue Nicaise. It raced past Madame Lyster and her mother, pushing them against the wall by the National Guard sentry post, and the sudden burst of speed gave Saint-Réjant just two or three seconds to light a fuse which he had only tested that morning. He did so and then hurried away, ducking into Rue Hoche and as he ran, Napoleon's coach also turned into Rue Hoche to avoid the traffic and was just turning into Rue Marceau when the bomb went off. Catherine-Julie Gaucheron, Widow Boulard, was there:

> I came out of Rue Coquillière, and was heading over to the café du Carrousel to meet a lady friend. I was passing along what was once Rue de Chartres, now Rue de Malte, and had reached Rue Marceau when I saw the First Consul going to the opera. I kept close against the wall but when I reached the corner I heard a deep boom, saw a flame and was knocked to the ground.[8]

Saint-Réjant heard that boom too and, as he was stumbling past the Vaudeville, he was hit by the debris of tiles and glass and timber. The escort travelling behind Napoleon's coach also felt some of the force of the explosion, Desmarest of the police recalling how

> The troopers of the escort felt as though they were plucked from their saddles. The shock of the explosion, the screams of the populace, the shattering of windows, the noise of falling chimneys and roofs made it feel as the entire area was collapsing on their heads.

The escort that had preceded the coach were already in Rue de la Loi when they too heard the enormous explosion. Grenadier Durand had initially been confused as to what had happened:

> We were already around 15 paces along the Rue de la Loi when there was an explosion. I told my comrades that was a round of grapeshot. Some of them said that, no, they are firing a salvo to celebrate the taking of Mantua. I told them it had to be a blunderbuss fired from a house or a round of canister. We continued on to the République theatre. There, I swerved to one side as I heard projectiles flying past and breaking glass and tiles falling from the roofs. The Consul halted there. He had our commanding officer come over and asked if anyone had been wounded. The reply was no, but that one man had been grazed on the hand by a falling roof tile. We then continued on to the opera. There, when I was inside, I heard that the Consul's coach had been tilted by the blast, lifted up on one wheel as though it was going to overturn, and that the windows had broken.[9]

Napoleon's coach was protected from the full force of the blast but was nevertheless rocked, as were its occupants. Napoleon had been jolted awake: 'The explosion woke me up, the shock resembling that when a coach is lifted up when accelerating at speed.'[10]

Lannes apparently tried to kick open the door, saying that someone had fired a cannon at them, but Napoleon restrained him and soon received the escort's report on what happened, sending a grenadier back to locate and make sure of his wife. Rapp, following on behind the Consul's coach, was just about to leave the Carrousel when the barrel exploded:

> At the sound of the explosion the ladies cried out, the blast broke the windows and Mademoiselle Beauharnais was lightly

wounded in the hand. I climbed out and walked along the Rue Nicaise, through the bodies and the rubble of the walls that the blast had blown down.

Hortense, in the same vehicle, noted:

The coach seemed to have been lifted up, the windows broke and glass fell onto us. 'It is aimed at Bonaparte,' my mother exclaimed, and fainted. Our horses, terrified by the noise, and choking on the dust, reared up, took the bit between their teeth and carried us back to the Tuileries railings.

There they were met by the member of the escort who had been sent to find them and to tell them that Napoleon had escaped unharmed; he then rode alongside them and, using an alternative route, brought them to the opera.

There Part One of *The Creation* had begun. As Haydn's music soared, God was separating the elements when there was a noise from the street. In the interval between the creation of the Earth and its peopling, rumours began that there had been an explosion and an attempt on the First Consul's life. As the singer Chéron, in a fine suit, and Walbonne-Barbier, in a plumed hat, stood to represent a dashing version of Adam and Eve, word went round that the First Consul had narrowly escaped an assassination. Norvins had seen

...Monsieur Maret, pale and breathless, having a most animated discussion with Monsieur Tourton. I approached them and learnt from them that the family of the First Consul had just escaped the explosion of an infernal machine in the Rue Saint Nicaise. That information took a second to impart, but within the minute the entire audience was repeating it, and starting to stand, agitated, worried, completely horrified.

It was then that Napoleon made his entrance. He had insisted his coachman drive on to the opera and he had quickly mounted the stairs and, to a wave of public murmuring, seated himself at the front of the box before asking Lebrun for the libretto. Norvins saw the relieved reaction of the spectators:

> Suddenly, the First Consul appeared ... the commotion was so strong, and of such energy, that the entire room shook ... the First Consul stood a few times and, with his gestures and looks, paid an emotional tribute to a public clearly relieved that he had been spared.

Shortly afterwards, Josephine entered in an emotional state and had to be calmed in another display of Napoleonic *sang froid*. He told her 'those wretches wanted to do away with me.' Then Rapp, who came later as he had walked along the length of the street, entered the box and informed the party of the bloody aftermath of the explosion and that there had been a number of fatalities. Hortense was watching:

> Rapp arrived and told us of the disaster he had witnessed as he made his way here. The Prefect of Police and Junot, Governor of Paris, came to give us their account, such as it was, of what had occurred. The Consul listened to them in silence until the point at which he heard how many people had been found dead by the cart containing the gunpowder. 'How horrible!' he exclaimed, in passionate but despairing tones, 'that they should kill so many people in order to do away with one man'.

Lauriston added to the tumult by telling Bourrienne that they had only 'escaped by 10 seconds.'

Haydn's dramatic music was now relegated to background noise and the whispering of the Parisians almost drowned out Rey's enormous orchestra. Even so the *Sturm und Drang* provided suitable accompaniment to a Napoleonic piece of political theatre for, despite the tragic events, 'the First Consul remained in the box until the curtain went down.' As silence was briefly restored, the consul and his family were taken back to the Tuileries via a circuitous route, for Rue Nicaise was blocked.

Along that unfortunate street the dead and wounded were scattered amongst the debris of the cart and fugitives were making off through the acrid smoke and dust towards safety. A number of facades and walls had collapsed, and rubble and chunks of paving stones, as well as roof tiles and broken glass, were strewn across the street. And whilst the walls still standing were all blackened with powder, the muddy street itself was red with blood. Blood, limbs and 'and also bits of trouser or coats still with flesh inside them' seemed to be everywhere. There were corpses too, perhaps seven or eight bodies; although no one could yet be sure. One of the Parisians killed by the blast, little Marianne who had led the cart, had been blown apart: one arm was later found on the roofs opposite, the other some 30 metres away. Parts of a horse were found on one of the roofs and a wheel of the cart was later discovered on top of Consul Cambacérès' residence. These pitiful sights were moving enough, but the groaning and cries of the wounded, and the thrashing of crippled horses, added to the sense of carnage. The *Gazette de France* would later list 28 wounded, but it was apparent to those who stood there on Christmas Eve that many more, perhaps even 50 or 60 civilians, had been struck down and were now unconscious or desperately pleading for help. A few of the wounded had lost fingers or hands, and legs were later amputated, but others had lost eyes, or had their faces damaged by the metal balls packed into the barrel. Still more were hit by splinters or shards of broken glass and an onlooker noticed a casualty with 'a piece of wood stuck in their chest, and another one in the arm'. Civilian onlookers, who now began to include officials hurrying over from the opera, seemed as dazed as the poor National Guardsmen manning their sentry box. Paris had been hit by a new kind of atrocity and no one knew quite how to react.

The author of the crime, however, had been quick to get away. Saint-Réjant had avoided danger, and the sight of the results of his action, but he had nevertheless been winded, bruised and partially blinded by dust and debris. He later told a confidant that

> Right after lighting the fuse, I saw nothing else, heard nothing else, felt nothing. I found myself, and I don't know how, at the offices of the Louvre where the fresh air and breeze brought me to my senses and I headed for home. I rushed towards the Pont-Royal and, making a bundle of my smock, threw it into the river.

Now dressed in a dirty russet overcoat and grey trousers he crossed the Pont Royal, passing close to the Ministry of Police at Quai Voltaire before doubling back and reaching his lodgings at 574 Rue des Prouvaires.

The police were also quick to react. Dubois at the prefecture had heard the blast and had been notified by his friend and colleague Bertrand that 'there has been an enormous explosion, and reports suggest it was outside the Vaudeville Theatre. We are on the way and are calling in the Officers of the Peace and the commissaires.' Other rumours suggested that there had been an explosion in a grocer's shop in Rue Nicaise. But Commissaire Claude-François

Chazot was the first police officer actually to arrive on the scene, his offices at 513 Rue Nicaise having been shaken by the explosion of what everyone was soon calling the Infernal Machine. Chazot, as well as being a keen amateur of Roman history, was also a diligent officer. Seeing the confusion amidst the mud and blood of what had once been the capital's most elegant street, he began to issue orders to the shell-shocked National Guard, establishing a cordon to block off the area hit by the blast, and sending the dead to the Châtelet morgue[11] whilst those who had been wounded were carried to the nearest hospitals. Those who had escaped unscathed from the street or the shops and houses, as well as those who were only lightly hurt, were collected for questioning. Then he turned his attention to what appeared to be the site of the explosion 'opposite Beirlé the culottier's, and behind the building which contained Consul Lebrun's stables'. There he found the front parts of a horse and what was left of a cart, primarily the shafts and parts of the wheels, and, with the help of some of 27 National Guardsmen, had this important evidence carefully loaded aboard a requisitioned cart and sent to the prefecture.

As a further smattering of important officials arrived from the opera, including the inquisitive Réal, who showed great interest in the horse, this diligent officer sent his first report off to Prefect Dubois. The Justice of the Peace of the Museum quarter had the more macabre task of collecting any remaining body parts and visiting the morgue to set about listing the descriptions and personal effects of the dead.

8

AN EXPLOSIVE AFTERMATH

That evening, as he closed the door on the public acclamations of relief and joy, Napoleon was livid, fuming about the Jacobins, those *drinkers of blood*, had been scheming to end his life. According to the First Consul, it was they who had placed the bomb and they who wished to destroy him and his entire family. His secretary, Bourrienne, who had also returned from the opera house, was on hand to take the First Consul's orders, and to witness the wrath:

> One had to be familiar with Bonaparte's expressions, his limited but expressive use of gestures, and to have heard his voice, to have an idea as to the scale of his anger as he spoke these words.

The growing crowd of councillors of state, ministers and senators diplomatically concurred that the Enraged (*Les Enragés*) were behind the outrage, and there were murmurs that, after all, Chevalier had tried the same method just six weeks before. Not everyone agreed, and Bourrienne was surprised when the most outspoken doubting Thomas, Joseph Fouché, arrived after inspecting the scene of the crime and made it known that he dissented: 'the minister, who came to talk to me about all this, made it clear that he did not think the Jacobins could be guilty.' Indeed, Roederer heard that the minister had gone further, telling Talleyrand that the blame for the atrocity should be directed at those taking the golden guineas of England.

Napoleon, hearing that the minister dared question his word, and the obvious, had the minister summoned, and when the First Consul demanded that 'he repeat that it was the royalists' the minister obliged, saying, with considerable sang froid, 'Yes, without doubt; I have said so and I shall prove so.'

The phlegmatic Fouché then bore the brunt of a sustained verbal barrage from his master:

> Don't try to fool me, there are no Chouans, no emigrants, no so-called nobles, no so-called priests. I know who did it. I know how to catch them and to inflict a suitable punishment upon them ... the September drinkers of blood, the assassins of Versailles, the brigands of 31 May, the plotters of Prairial, the authors of all the crimes against all the governments. If they can't be locked away, they must be crushed – France must be purged of this disgraceful sect, no mercy to the wretches.

But the minister of police was unabashed, Bourrienne marvelling:

> The most talented actor would have been at a loss to convey the utter calmness of his attitude throughout Bonaparte's rage, he was discrete, patient in the face of accusations.

Such self-assurance no doubt stemmed from the fact that, of all those gathered there in the marble halls, Fouché knew the most about the plot, and knew Napoleon knew almost as much. The minister had been following Cadoudal's agents and gathering information from his own treacherous Chouans for months. Fouché was soon to tell Bourmont 'I'm sure it was Georges' agents who were behind it, do me the service of informing the First Consul that it was Georges and the English who planned it.'[1] Such a second opinion was perhaps unnecessary, for the minister had warned the First Consul weeks before that his life might, this time, be endangered. Whilst the minister no doubt shared a sense of failure on the part of his police to prevent the crime he was equally aware that the Jacobins could not have mounted so organised a display of resistance.

Napoleon probably shared that professional opinion but his anger, so outwardly genuine, was imbued with self-interest. He saw that agreeing with his minister would rob him of a political opportunity to finish off the work begun when the Conspiracy of the Daggers had transformed the Jacobins into traitors. Napoleon had once sympathised with the radicals[2] when power was far from his grasp and the fashion had been for red bonnets and liberty, but now he was seated, almost literally, on the royal throne, he wished to purge France of the divisive notion of equality. He began to refer to the Jacobins as vermin in his clothes, his hostility being fed by the need to impose his rule, but also by daily bulletins from Dubois, and by Talleyrand and Bourrienne, aware that their loyalty to the new order required that the old be despised. The clique of those who agitated for a Napoleonic dynasty also saw this clearing away of those most vociferously in support of the republic as useful, as did many of those rising through the Council of State. A deputation from this body congratulated Napoleon on his escape on Christmas Day, and embraced this chance to smear their political rivals. So it was not difficult to colour the Infernal Machine as being the work of the diabolical Jacobins, and to yet again shape outrage into a tool of politics. Napoleon directed and drove this policy, presenting sympathetic authorities who were also eager to please with the opportunity to finally rid themselves of these political pests.

The rivals of Fouché joined this ad hoc coalition and fuelled the anger by insinuating that the man behind the atrocities at Lyon and Nantes had not only failed to stop this new insolence but that he was still actively protecting the terrorists. The new alliance saw the new minister of the interior, Chaptal, who resented his fellow minister, colluding with Prefect Dubois to arrest former revolutionaries, and thus tar Fouché by association. Dubois had particular reason to seem energetic, for he had been chastened by Napoleon. On the evening of Christmas Day, as Napoleon was sat on his favourite divan, Dubois entered the salon and made an improvised report on the casualties, considerably underestimating their number by stating that there were just five. Cambacérès contradicted him by saying that the surgeon of the Consular Guard had personally attended 22 of the wounded. Consternation followed and the First Consul stood to reprimand Dubois, telling him: 'If I were prefect of police, I would be most ashamed in such circumstances.'[3] Dubois retorted that it was impossible to see inside the minds of men but was cut short by General Bessières's outburst that 'no wonder that they didn't know what was going on, their offices are full of brigands.'

A humiliated Dubois returned to those offices and had to be seen to be doing something. He rounded up those anarchists he knew were living along Rue Nicaise, including Babeuf's friend Bertrand Lacombe, and threw in dozens of the more notorious troublemakers who had been too slow to switch sides. The vague charge of 'troublemaker, linked to every kind of wickedness' was sufficient for a suspect to be hauled in, such contempt of evidence being less important than the security of state and of salaries. Indeed, the state, and the complicit media, required 'that these hideous beings be arrested'[4] and so, that week, the bulletins featured such updates as 'Fourteen people who have featured in previous reports and who are capable of committing a crime such as the one carried out yesterday, have been arrested.' These included Chevalier's wife and brother Claude-Louis; his friend Seigneuret; the notorious Tricoteuse, Femme Chaumette; Gombeau-Lachaize, detained for having drunk to the death of tyrants back in June 1800; and Florent Guyot, who had refused a place in the Legislative Corps, and who now ran a private library. Such diligence resulted in 68 arrests by 28 December and 91 by the end of the month.

Dubois had his own blacklist of troublemakers who could be hauled in to boost such numbers but Napoleon, too, had been keeping a dictionary of political rivals. Others were added to that combined list by the minister, adept at closing up useless mouths. He told Dubois to detain Francois Bourdon, 'a man who has preached insurrection against the First Consul for some time,' but who spent his time in prison making ominous allusions from Book 12 of Daniel; or a certain Gault for singing songs against the government. Georget was brought in for having participated in the September massacres, even though he was only 13 at the time. Marat's and Babeuf's widows were hauled in for questioning, as was Alexandre Mouquet for having been involved in massacres at Nantes, atrocities similar to the minister's achievements at the same place. Therese Perignon, 'whose only crime seems to have been to belong at one time to the Jacobins', was arrested as was Charles Hacville, who, with others, had already served time or were covered by amnesties but who were now again subject to arrest.

The fate of these scapegoats looked increasingly dire. On Boxing Day Napoleon had told Méjan, deputising for Frochot, the Prefect

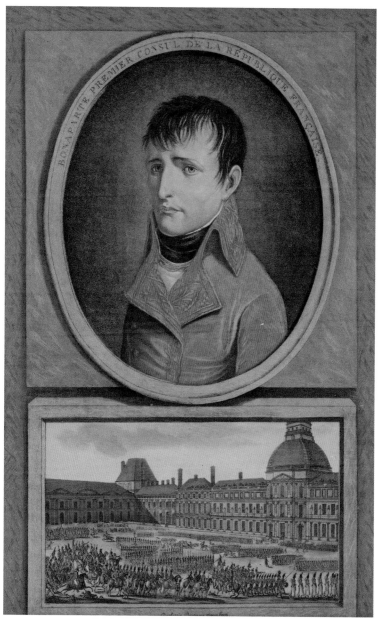

1. *A heroic image of Napoleon, First Consul of France. He wears his hair fashionably short and is in the high-collared scarlet tunic of the consuls. This is how he would have appeared in the winter of 1800.*

2. An image of Napoleon, mounted, dating from the time of the Infernal Machine. He wears the uniform of a consul of France and, oddly, does so whilst directing troops in the field.

3. *Napoleon in the uniform of a general of the republic, dating from late 1799. This heroic image is by a favoured Napoleonic artist, Andrea Appiani.*

The following text appears within the illustration:

Mounseer Beau-Napie[r]te

I read your *Parly Vouse* & have only to say I was not born Yesterday, take that as you like them am not easily humm'd, so before we Leap we look td Country men for what a Quarrel to you be not Could Gunpad by Quash YOURS as you Behave yourself Bull

Conquest of Britain an OLD Song to a New Tune

Pub[lish]d Jan[uary] 20[th] 1800 by S.W. Fores Piccadilly

The Grand-Consul of the **Great Nation** !!! Perusing **John Bulls Dispatches** !!!

4. *A far from flattering British view of the three consuls of France: Napoleon, Jean-Jacques-Régis de Cambacérès and Charles-François Lebrun.*

Fouché de Nantes

Ministre de la Police.

5. The Minister of Justice, Joseph Fouché. Here is the notorious revolutionary dressed in his imperial robes. Fouché always ensured he was well-placed to receive information from Jacobins and royalists alike.

6. The Prefecture of Police in the rue de Jérusalem. This ramshackle complex was burnt down by the revolutionaries of the Commune in 1871.

7. *The courtyard of the Prefecture of Police. Prisoners would arrive here and be brought in for interrogation.*

8. *The Tuileries Palace. Improvement works were ongoing in 1800. However the carriage gates leading to the Carrousel are easily visible.*

Above: 9. *A review before the Tuileries. There was a parade at least once a week and it soon became a popular attraction among Parisians.*

Right: 10. *A row of houses in Rue Nicaise. These were not the uniform facades imagined by Haussmann, but a more varied collection of buildings constructed over the previous two centuries.*

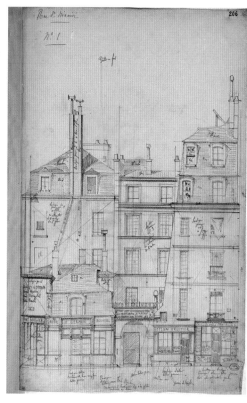

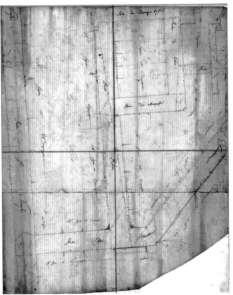

Above: 11. The street itself. This sanitised view shows regular facades and an even road service. The roads of Paris were, however, uniformly bad in 1800 and the source of numerous complaints to the prefecture of police.

Left: 12. A map of the Rue Nicaise. The bomb blast would have been at the bottom left, Napoleon's coach had just swung round the corner into the street to the right.

13. *A crowd before the theatre. This jovial street scene shows the press of people before a popular theatre. The crowd at the opera was richer but scarcely better behaved.*

14. *An artist's impression of the explosion. This is a reasonable attempt at accuracy, although the coach and escort was a little further away than suggested here.*

Left and below:
*15a & 15b.
Two contemporary
versions of
the explosion,
produced by the
French media.*

16a & 16b. Two portraits of the Comte D'Artois, arch-enemy of Napoleon and of revolution in general. D'Artois made sure that various royalist plotters in Paris were well-provided with money.

Above: 17. Georges Cadoudal, an unflattering portrait of the key royalist still fighting the revolution in France of 1800.

Left: 18. A more flattering portrait of Cadoudal, perhaps as his many supporters in Brittany saw him.

19. *The capture of Cadoudal in 1803. He was captured in Paris after a fight in which Inspector Buffet was killed and Inspector Caniolle wounded.*

Above left: *20. Saint-Réjant, the royalist who lit the fuse.*

Above right: *21. Coster-Saint-Victor, another of the conspirators and a man involved in preparing the cart.*

Above left: *22. A Breton gentleman in Paris. When not dressed in a carter's smock, Saint-Réjant would be dressed like this.*

Above right: *23. A Breton gentleman at war; one of the rebels of western France. By 1800 the risings in Brittany and Normandy were a thing of memory, more direct action was required now that Napoleon was head of government.*

Right: 24. *Louis de Frotté. The death of this royalist officer at the hands of Napoleon's troops caused outrage amongst royalist supporters and, for some, justified them in seeking Napoleon's death.*

Below: 25. *The Jacobins get the blame. Early prints, along with the Parisian press, echoed the government line that the Jacobins were behind the atrocity.*

La Machine infernale.

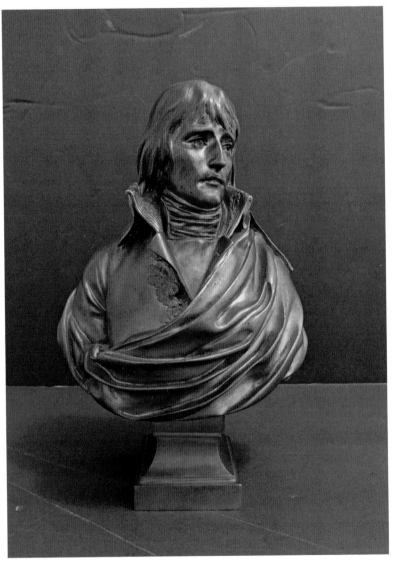

26. The bust of Napoleon by the Roman sculptor Ceracchi.

of the Seine, that 'if this band of brigands had attacked me openly, then I could have let the law deal with them; but as a crime without precedent, and one which endangered some of the population of Paris, then the punishment should be quick and terrible. Assure the people of Paris in my name that this gang of wretches, whose crimes almost dishonoured liberty, shall be punished as they deserve.'

It was no coincidence that, on the same day, the Council of State opened a session expressly convened to discuss a Bill on a law calling for the use of special tribunals to punish those plotting against the life of the consuls. This had been drafted that morning in committee, and although recourse to such measures, where transgressors were effectively placed outside the law and deprived of a jury, had been used during the Terror, this seemed a regressive step for a government wanting to be seen as respecting the rule of law. Napoleon sat listening to some nuanced deliberations which culminated in the suggestion that, through a special measure, the consuls might have conferred on them extraordinary powers to deport those threatening state security.

Napoleon was neither satisfied nor patient. He now launched into a half-an-hour rant that soon affected his voice, impatiently calling for justice to act like a bolt of lightning, and forgetting his position as first magistrate when he declared that he wished to shoot 15 or 20 Jacobins and deport 200 more, and that he was prepared to take upon himself the consequences of such a judgement. The illegal did not trouble him, but the unconstitutional would take more time and delay his quest to take immediate revenge on behalf of 'outraged human society'. Antoine-Claire Thibaudeau, who was present, was one of those who realised that this had moved beyond the issue of applying or amending existing laws in order that justice be done, and had morphed into merely 'deporting or shooting as an act of public good.' Such a tool of tyranny made some look askance, whilst the more republican-minded called to mind the similarity with Bourbon *lettres de cachet*, in which suspects were simply disappeared if they offended the state.

Admiral Truguet was one offended by the First Consul's presumption and dared to suggest that all enemies of the state, including fanatical priests and the agents of England, should be treated equally before the law, if such special measures were enacted. Napoleon burst out that the nation was pointing at the Jacobins, and it was clearly 'the *septembriseurs* and men of that ilk' who merited punishment, and then shouted the admiral down with a further 15-minute rant, which included 'don't treat me like a child ... they wouldn't spare you, so you'd be wasting your time defending them today in the Council, they'd butcher you as they would me!'

At eleven o'clock the following morning a rather calmer meeting, with more select participants including three ministers, three consuls and two legislative committees, was held at which the point was made that any new law could not be applied retroactively. Réal added that just one man could have been capable of the crime, so a mass, collective punishment was unjust, but Napoleon insisted on executing or banishing the individuals listed in his 'dictionary of men who took part in all the massacres'. This little cabal tried to reconcile these conflicting views and finally determined on a draft text, namely that 'the government is invested in the right to take extraordinary measures for state security in order to judge and to punish those who took part or were complicit in the crime of 3 Nivose and in order to prevent further such attacks.' The next day the discussion continued, without the consuls, and a final version was hammered out, Roederer bringing it over for consular approval just as Napoleon was mounting his horse to ride out of the Tuileries. The three consuls, aware that the semblance of unchecked power might seem too like autocracy, asked that the extraordinary measure be referred to the Senate to gloss it with the lustre of a constitutional act.

On 1 January the Council of State, that institution tasked with drafting laws and safeguarding the constitution, held an extraordinary session presided over once again by Napoleon. The Council agreed on the committees' text and elected not to deliberate on those who were to be selected, declaring that was a matter for others. But the point was made that the men in question were a list of suspects, none of whom had actually been tried in a court of law. In response came a justification that would become the staple of the world's security services:

> Of the men about to be named, none have been caught with a dagger in their hand, but all are known to be capable of sharpening and raising one to strike. It is no longer a question of punishing the past but of guaranteeing the social order.

Napoleon's view was a little different, declaring that they were guilty of unspecified crimes and therefore he was punishing individuals not 'for the act of 24 December, but for that of 2 September, 31 May, and for the Babeuf conspiracy', although, again, the absence of a trial should have worried friends of the constitution. Cambacérès was not one of those, supporting his fellow consul with the glib 'whoever the authors of the crime of 3 Nivose might be, the individuals who will be deported were saying every day that they planned to do the same,' Persuaded by all this official wrath, the Council asked its members to vote on just two questions:

1. Is the proposed measure necessary for the constitution and for public liberty?

2. Should the measure be carried out by the police and the government, or be incorporated into an act of law?

For the first, the Council was relieved to leave it to 'the minister of police to indicate which individuals, and whom the government designate as being part of that class of men' should be on the receiving end of that punitive measure.[5] For the second, a particular and specific government act, passed to the Senate for a ruling purely on whether it was constitutional, was deemed appropriate.

On 5 January the Senate predictably ruled that it was constitutional for action to be taken against those who 'were behind every plot, the agents of every assassination, the instrument of each external and internal enemy, the opponents of order and the scourge of society'. There would be an act of rendition in which the arrested would be deported, banished from France and from society. In one act, the grey area between discussing a crime and carrying it out had been removed by the Napoleonic security services, and equating the two had now been approved by pliant legislators. The appeasement of the lawyers to the organs of control was apparent, and the rulers of France found themselves presented with a new and despotic power. The resulting act, or *senatus consultum*, dressed an arbitrary act in the protective clothing of a measure to protect the security of the public; but it was a blow against an already broken force, and a cynical piece of opportunism that hastened the rush towards imperious absolutism. By doing away with the Jacobins, and muting dissent, the authorities made good use of the Infernal Machine, and took their first steps towards a Napoleonic empire.

Amidst the hiatus, few remembered that those on the receiving end of this legislation had not been found guilty of any crime;

indeed, by early January, the police were in headlong pursuit of the true perpetrators and knew all too well that those being readied for banishment were mere scapegoats. Napoleon, of course, was just as aware of this, confessing when he told the minister that his enquiries into the true authors of the plot should continue as 'men such as those being deported deserved what they were getting and because public security demanded it, even if they weren't guilty of the charges that have been levelled against them.'[6] Fouché tactfully agreed, noting that 'whilst none were caught red-handed, all were well known for being capable of picking up and using a dagger.'

These statements were made against the backdrop of the trial of those caught up in the Plot of the Daggers and Chevalier's bomb conspiracy. In such an atmosphere, under such a witch-hunt, it was inevitable that the military commission reporting to General Mortier made short work of Chevalier, Veycer and poor Metge. They were tried on New Year's Day, shot on 11 January and mourned by very few of a public goaded into hating the Enraged.

Demerville, Ceracchi, Aréna, Topino-Lebrun, Diana, Fumey, Daiteg and Lavigne would need to be tried with more finesse, as their Plot of the Daggers was to be put before a jury. This was assembled on 7 January and the prosecution made its case, relying on Harel and Lefebvre's testimonies. Captain Jacques Harel was to have a hard time in court, perhaps earning the 600 Francs he had claimed as expenses three days earlier.[7] The captain accused Aréna of being the one who supplied the daggers to Demerville, telling the court: 'It was Aréna who provided the money and it was Aréna who made himself responsible for acquiring the daggers.' Aréna challenged him, forcing Harel to confess that 'if that is what I said, then I made a mistake.' He grew more confused, later responding to the question 'do you recognise the pistols, the daggers?' with

'Of course I recognise them, because I was the one who bought them. I got them from the shopkeeper.' The trial was on the cusp of revealing itself to be a travesty, and Demerville, coming a little to life, added to that sense when he astutely demanded of the judge 'Citizen, I ask you to find out from this man whether he is a police informer.' He then went on to accuse the police of entrapment, wanting the identity of the four agents who had accompanied Harel to the opera to be revealed in court. Ceracchi then joined in, declaring that everything Harel said was a tissue of lies. Aréna too proved himself adept in shrugging off the accusations levelled against him, whilst Topino-Lebrun, who had not even featured in Harel's testimony, defended himself with the appearance of a man who could hardly believe that he had been dragged into this farce. But of all the accused it was Diana who fought back with the grimmest of determination, insisting he was present at the opera merely as a member of the public, and an unarmed one[8] at that. If he had confessed to anything whilst in custody, it was because he had been threatened, and Diana's interpreter helpfully supported the Italian by telling the court that 'the interrogating police officer, Bertrand, threatened to have Diana shot if he did not denounce those who were guilty.' A concerned Fouché, receiving regular updates on the process, admitted that it was tough going:

It seems as though Ceracchi, Aréna and Demerville are certain to be convicted. The evidence against Diana is not as strong. The defendants have shown great energy in refuting the statements of Captain Harel. They fought back against the prosecution and their evidence.[9]

Despite the doubts and inconsistencies, of which there were many, what seems to have persuaded the jury was Demerville's warning to Barère that he should avoid going to the theatre. Although flimsy as evidence in a trial where life and death were at stake, it proved damning for a jury eager to collaborate against enemies of state. Nobody was surprised when, on 9 January, their verdict unanimously found that:

> It is clear that in the month of October a plot existed which encompassed the death of the First Consul. The accused Demerville, Ceracchi, Aréna and Topino-Lebrun are found guilty of having taken part in that plot. The accused Diana, Fumey, Daiteg and Lavigne have been found not guilty.[10]

Harel and Barère had played their parts, and the death sentence was now pronounced, Demerville proving unco-operative to the last by shouting out that he wanted to be shot on the spot. That appeal, and the more formal test of legality at Appeal Court, proved fruitless and Ceracchi, Aréna, Demerville and Topino-Lebrun were guillotined on 31 January 1801 at 13.30 p.m. Diana was exonerated, but kept in one of Paris's teeming prisons, those institutions having being filled with radicals as well as those with minor roles in that drama of the knives and earlier police attempts to manufacture plots, men such as Jumillard, Jean-Michel Brisevin, Bousquet, Gombaud-Lachaise, Desforges, Guérault, Madame Bucquet, Laurent Burloy, Denis Chapelle, Etienne Jallabert, Guibert, François Dufour, Humbert and François Perrault. Many of these unfortunates were simply added to the official list of those being readied for banishment in the wake of the Nicaise bomb.

The key individuals on the receiving end of the senatus consultum had been taken into custody that January and were readied for expulsion beyond the frontiers of the republic. They chiefly consisted of men who had once played a role in the politics of the Terror, and who had been foolish enough to attempt to resurrect the Jacobin club as the club du Manège or become implicated in Babeuf's plot.[11] Many were men who had once counted for something but whose influence was now negligible, individuals such as René-Pierre Choudieu (who protested his innocence in a plea to the minister), Claude Fournier l'Américain, the deputy Hugues Destrem, Michel-Louis Talot, Eustache-Louis-Joseph Toulotte, Jean-Baptiste Vanheck, Jean-Louis-Marie Villain d'Aubigny, General Jean Antoine Rossignol, Felix Lepeletier and the ex-prince Charles Hesse-Rheinfeld-Rothenberg. Their significance was further diluted by the inclusion of lesser men who were known to the police, or who frequented the café Olivier, and those denounced to the authorities.[12] These unfortunates included Fougeon, a former wig maker further reduced in circumstances by the fashion for cropped hair; Andre Corchant, a veteran of the storming of the Bastille; François Millière, suspected of being been active in drowning royalists at Nantes; and Antoine Boniface and his wife, implicated in the escape of Sir Sidney Smith in 1798. There were a handful of former policeman, such as Mathurin Bourin, Jean-Joseph-Nicolas Niquille and Jacques Brabant, cast out by their colleagues for adhering to out-modish principles, and Jean-Baptiste Delerue, the man who had printed Metge's pamphlets. Also caught up in the downfall of poor Metge were Nicolas-Joseph Derval and Agricola-Louis Vitra, who had been interrogated, released, then arrested again, as well as Pépin Desgrouhette, a lawyer for the poor and, unfortunately for him, a friend of the disreputable hack.

However unjust the final list of 130 to be deported was, it was made worse by some glaring errors. Some had already been tried and acquitted, which made their subsequent punishment even more suspect. Even more strangely, Nicolas Paris had been dead six months, Gabriel was already in Cayenne, but working as a government employee, and Baudray was in Guadeloupe. René-Louis Thibault, a hairdresser, found himself arrested by a police force trying to catch Sébastien-Hubert Thiébault.

But injustice could never embarrass authorities intent on carrying out orders from above, and those readied for deportation were gathered at the notorious Saint-Pélagie and Bicêtre prisons following an order issued by Fouché:

> To the Prefect of Police, urgent and most secret
>
> You will seek to have assembled by tomorrow, citizen, a sufficient number of covered transports in order to convey to Orleans those individuals who shall be deported. Notify me as soon as they are ready and I shall forward new instructions. I believe that the transport section should be able to furnish the required vehicles.[13]

A first group of 40 was to set off on 11 January, including many of those implicated in the dubious plots of October. However, and much to the minister's consternation, the escort of Chasseurs failed to arrive at Saint-Pélagie and only showed up the following day. It was then that the convoy left for Nantes at seven in the morning with a further five prisoners, travelling by stagecoach, following on the 13th. Savary noted that at Nantes the prisoners 'would have been cut to pieces had the garrison not been called out'. Soon 83 men were held ready for deportation whilst nine remained in Paris and 36 were still being traced. Two others had been released on account of their health or intervention from friends and family.

From Nantes a first shipment of 70 set sail. The law had called for them to be sent beyond the confines of France and so they were to be transported to the island of Mahé, in the Seychelles, the status of which was in doubt after the authorities had capitulated to the British in 1794. After a 90-day voyage most were marooned there, although some were transferred on to the Ile de France.[14] In March 1802 some 33, including General Rossignol, were punished still further by being placed inside a wicker cage on the deck of Captain Hulot's *Belier* and taken to Anjouan, a desert island north of Madagascar, where they were handed over for the use of Seid Abdallah, the island's sultan.[15] Rossignol asked to be shot, but he and 20 others soon perished from disease. Only Pierre Vauversin, who escaped to Zanzibar, and Lefranc and Sonnois, who made it to the larger islands of the Comoros archipelago, survived to tell their horrific tale.[16]

Back in France, an additional group of 60, including Michel-Louis Talot and Hugues Destrem,[17] both deputies who had abused Napoleon during his attempt to harangue the Council, was taken to the Ile de Ré and Oléron and more were added over time. Some 43 of these, including René Vatar, owner of the *Journal des hommes libres* and a man to whom Fouché owed a debt of money, General Pierre Argoud, the bigamist who had made his nostalgia for the excitements of 1793 too well known, and the ubiquitous Thomas-Avisse Desforges, were sent on to Cayenne, a penal colony hacked from the jungles of South America. Only 40 survived the transit of 40 days and few survived the rigours of the hellish conditions when they reached land. Hugues Destrem, the father of 11 children, was one of the few to prove resilient, escaping to the Swedish West Indies, but finding that even that was no real sanctuary and soon succumbing to Yellow Fever.[18]

The injustice shown to these individuals, many as innocent as the bystanders blown away by the blast in the Rue Nicaise, had been enabled by public revulsion at the bomb in Paris, a revulsion cleverly nurtured by the police in collusion with the Parisian newspapers. Many of the capital's editors and journalists were excelling themselves as voluntary agents of the state, generating revulsion and anger and directing it at the regime's enemies rather than questioning some of the apparent contradictions emerging from the evidence. In that January of 1801 they were working hard to stir up opinion against the Jacobins.

It worked. Already aghast by the use of a bomb on innocent civilians, public anger was easily misdirected from the true perpetrators, the atmosphere of fear and hate being ill-conducive to reason. The police noted with satisfaction how there was

> General indignation against the authors of the atrocity. Unanimous satisfaction that providence had preserved the head of state. Everyone commented in his own way how their happiness was dependent upon his existence. Accusations against the anarchists pour in. They complain about the length of time it took to pursue those behind the first plot [Chevalier's] and say that those same people are behind the second, adding that they hoped for quick vengeance.[19]

Their informers in the streets and at the bars noted with satisfaction how the crowd was 'demanding summary executions, paying no attention to the dictates of the law' and that 'Indignation is such that, from all sides, there is a clamour that some examples be made.' Another noted how 'In the café de Foy, which is always full, they say that the First Consul has known how to vanquish both internal and external enemies' and therefore, inevitably, the perpetrators would get their due. Given the novelty of the crime, and that it had, in effect, been aimed at every Parisian, such anger was understandable, and it only increased when a full reckoning of the tragedy emerged in the weeks following the blast.

The Infernal Machine had killed nine civilians on the day or in the unhygienic but well-meaning hospitals of Paris. They included the girl who had held the bridle, variously described as Marie-Anne Puessot or Marianne Peusol. The blast had literally blown this, the youngest victim of the earliest terrorist bomb, apart; one arm, for example, being found at the door to the National Guard's sentry box, and she was so badly mutilated that her mother, Anne Alexandrine Rignier, was too distraught to identify her, sending the girl's uncle instead.[20] Then there was Jeanne-Elisabeth Hugaut, the 22-year-old fishwife;[21] Agnès Adélaide Norris, divorced wife of a Monsieur Lyster of Rue de Lille, and a teacher of the piano and English language; and Cléreaux, a grocer who died from blood loss in the street. Madame Beirlé, the pregnant wife of Alexandre the glovemaker with their shop on the corner of the street leading to Rue Malte, died on Christmas Day,[22] whilst Platel, the gendarme officer, died on 29 December as did Monsieur Barbier. Jean-Claude Leclerc, an art student, had been brought in wounded to the hospice de l'Ecole on the evening of the blast and was tended by Antoine Dubois who informed the police that he was likely to succumb. A subsequent police report on Leclerc noted the extent of his injuries:

Jean-Claude Leclerc, painter, apparently resident in the Hotel de Bretagne in Rue de la Loi and from Charmes in the Vosges, is aged 34 but says he is 36 and is one metre 70. He has chestnut hair and brows, blue eyes, average nose and mouth, round chin and an oval face. Passport issued 1 May 1799 and witnessed by Charles Imbert Mahler, Jean-Claude Arnoud and Raguel, resident in that commune. Says that he does not know what happened but that he was walking along and felt nothing. There is a significant wound and bruising half way down his thigh on the outer side of it and the prognosis is not optimistic. His identity card is in his rooms.

Jean-Claude Leclerc succumbed to this nasty wound on 29 December.

Another tragic case was that of Boyeledieu, a printer, who had gone missing in the aftermath of the bomb. His wife, the pregnant Marie Louise Elisabeth Chevalier Boyeledieu, set off on a frantic search, first inquiring at the National Guard post at the Palais-Egalité where she was told that the casualties had been taken to the 'Charité, the Hotel-Dieu and the morgue' at the Châtelet. She first spoke to the doctors at the Charité, describing her missing husband, and one of them informed her

> You have described his clothing, and we do have an unfortunate victim here who was brought in shortly after eight. He is unrecognisable, disfigured so that he can't tell who he is. Was your husband wearing trousers or breeches? Do not be alarmed, do you have papers? I want to make sure.

She asked the doctors to check his left foot where he had a burn mark about the size of a small nut. Even so, rather cruelly, the doctors insisted she come down to the mortuary to formally identify him:

> I saw my husband laid out on a table, the face entirely sliced off. I could not believe this had once been a man. I recognised a fragment of grey cloth from his trousers that had stuck to his left leg. I threw myself onto the corpse of my dead husband, crying 'it is he!'.

The public was understandably angry when it read accounts such as these, but it also showed a generous empathy to the many victims of the infernal atrocity. Although the government covered much of the material damage with a grant of 200,000 Francs, the public response matched it in spirit. Even the pupils of the military academy went without wine for a week, donating the money they had saved, whilst the officers of the 19th Dragoons and 39th Line donated a day's pay. More significantly a public subscription promoted in the press raised 77,681.19 Francs for the victims. A commission under Huguet Montaran and Commissaire Chazot established itself in Chazot's offices in Rue Nicaise to rule on how this was to be distributed to the needy. It examined those wounded or injured, collected testimony and went on to award compensation which ranged from 4,500 to 25 Francs.[23] Those who had been disabled, and were therefore unable to work, were given the most. Catherine-Julie Gaucheron, known as Widow Boulard, was a musician who had been knocked to the ground by the blast:

> I was there for half-an-hour, or three-quarters of an hour. I recovered consciousness and called for help. Some cavalrymen came to me and asked where I wanted to go and I said the café du Carrousel, they taking me there. I had lost my clothes and was half-dead.

She had 25 or 30 wounds and lost two fingers of the right hand. Being unable to play the fortepiano, she was awarded 4,000 Francs and then an additional 3,000.

Pierre-Louis-Nicolas Lion, a servant, had been

> ...walking down Rue Nicaise at about a quarter past eight when I reached Rue de Malte and was hit as though by a thunderbolt, without seeing anything and without sensing that I had been wounded. I had 22 wounds, a splinter in my chest and arm, and a piece of my trousers and riding-coat pushed into my flesh.

He was in hospital for 53 days and even then was still partially deaf.

Jean-Baptiste Lemercier, a landlord, had been

> ...in the café Apollon, having been a regular there for some years, and was one of eight or nine other people. At eight I heard the blast but was knocked unconscious. My body was badly hit, and I lost my sight. I was blind for two months. My chest was bruised, as was my body, and I had pieces of glass stuck in my legs.

His eyesight still hadn't recovered that February, and he was unable to read. For this he was awarded 4,500 Francs.

Catherine Emas, or Madame Léger, who ran the café on the corner of Rue Nicaise, and which backed on to the Rue de Malte where it met the Carrousel, had also been wounded and it took her two-and-a-half months to recover, although her leg never quite healed. Her waiters Antoine Harel and the boy Poché were also wounded, as were a number of clients including Claude Barthélemy Préville, a furniture upholsterer, who was hit by debris whilst drinking half a bottle with his apprentice, and the labourer Madame Regnault, propping up the bar. In addition, the washerwoman Louise Saint-Gilles was lacerated by the glass from the café windows. Citizen Warmé, a wine merchant, was also struck as he sat 'in the café opposite the sentry post' having been 'playing piquet between seven and eight that evening, when the explosion took place, being with an associate and drinking a bottle of cider.'

Those out in the street felt the full force of the blast. An architect, Guillaume Trépsat, who later embellished the lodge at Compiègne for Napoleon, was amongst the casualties:

> This brave man was 60 years old. He was walking down the Rue Nicaise when the infernal machine blew up and he was covered with wounds. The following day he had his leg amputated and, throughout this painful operation, he showed the utmost courage

and a firmness beyond description. He did not want them to tell his wife what had happened to him as she had been sick for four months, and wanted to inform her himself, which he did as sensitively and kindly as possible. As they were removing the bandages he said 'I am glad this has happened to me and not to the First Consul, because where would we be if Bonaparte had been killed?'

Trépsat's wounds proved that the plotters had placed metal fragments in the barrel in order to cause as much damage as possible, for Dubois noted that 'a piece of iron 7mm wide' was removed from the unfortunate man's leg.

Jean-Frédéric Banny, an assistant chef aged 19, was less philosophical about his injuries, declaring 'I was leaving work and unfortunately found myself in Rue Nicaise. I didn't see anything, but I really felt it. I hope whoever invented it, gets it in the belly. I was one of those most wounded and I have 14 wounds on my body, seven serious, and have lost my arm.'

Others simply stuck to the facts when they described their ordeal. Marie-Anne Iblot, a seamstress who received nine flesh wounds, recalled: 'I was coming along the Rue Nicaise [from the direction of Rue Honoré] when I saw the First Consul approach. I was heading for the café on the corner so, as soon as he had passed by, I crossed the street. I was struck by a blow on my right side and fell to the ground. I was wounded when I regained consciousness.'

Nicolas-Alexandre Corbet, the secretary of the 17th Division's staff, would tell a similar story: 'We were passing along the Rue Nicaise just after the First Consul, on his way to the opera, when we were hit and knocked over by an explosion which was so terrible that it caused the death of Citizen Clérot [sic], my friend.'

Marie Thérèse Larue Honoré was hospitalised for 17 days when she was hit by a falling beam in Rue Nicaise, and her daughter, Thérèse, was also wounded. Stéphanie Madeleine-Charlotte Orillard, a dressmaker, was thrown to the ground whilst out strolling in the street and spent two weeks in hospital as the doctors tried to heal 28 flesh wounds. Madame Barbier, who had been making salad in the culottier's shop, was wounded in the eye and found herself a widow. Then came others, whose stories have not survived, struck down as they went about their business. They included Madame Bataille, a grocer with a shop in Rue Nicaise; Françoise Louvrier Bourdin, concierge at number 503; Louis Buchener, a tailor in the crowded tenement at number 513; Citizen Chatelain, a porter at the Maison Longueville, and his son; Gilbert Chapuis, a former naval officer and father of nine children, wounded under the ear and on the jaw; Jean-Etienne Charles, a printer; Mademoiselle Marie Jeanne Cécile Colinet, who sold eggs, and who was knocked unconscious for three days, and left blind for five; Louis Duverne, a locksmith; Louis-Philippe Fostier, a post office worker; Alexandre-Marie-Antoine Fritzeri (or Fridzery), a blind musician on his way to a concert; Marie-Poncette Gauthier, a 13-year-old girl wounded in the bakery at number 512; Citizen Haimot, an art dealer at Palais Egalité; Louis Huguet, an unemployed chef, wounded by fragments of paving stone; Jean-Antoine Kalbert, an apprentice carpenter; Marie-Jacqueline Gillot Lambert, an abandoned woman; Simon-François Lefevre, a decorator; Nicolas Lemiere, the owner of the Hôtel de Nantes; Elisabeth Satabin Lepape, concierge at number 514; Henri Lepautre, the clockmaker at 12 Rue Nicaise; Jean François Masse, assistant in a wine shop; Jeanne-Prevost Mitaine, a 78-year-old pauper; Thérèse-Rosalie Pain, a pregnant woman on her way to Fritzeri's concert; Citizen Palluel, a porter at number 474; Antoine Proverbi,

Italian valet to Major Cattasser; Citizen Simon, a shop assistant; Citizen Varlet, a post office worker; Citizen Vitry, a wigmaker; Elisabeth Vitriée, a cook; Arnoult Wolff, a Flemish tailor, and Felix Zambrini, a Roman working in an ice-cream parlour. And there were a few more casualties, about whom we know even less: Madame Mathieu; Citizen Amiot; Jean-Marie-Joseph Boiteux; Madame Bonnet; Citizen Clement; Citizen Couteux; Julien Jardy; and Citizen Renault.

As well as these innocents, the scene of the crime had also been disfigured. Some 46 houses were damaged in the blast[24] and the cost to property was calculated at the rather precise figure of 40,845 Francs, with damage to furniture and goods costing a further 123,645 Francs. The café and Lebrun's stables were the most badly hit, unsurprising as they were the closest to the cart and the gunpowder: 'The rear wall of Consul Lebrun's stables was blown in and debris blasted 20 paces into the building' with a corporal in the stable yard being hit by part of the cart's wheel. A metal wheel rim was also found on a collapsed bed in the Hotel des Quinze-Vingts in the Rue de Malte. Louise-Marie-Ursule Annette, the perfumer at Number 484, found a more interesting artefact, a metal ball, weighing two ounces, which had been blown into her shop and which would serve as further proof that the plotters had filled their barrel with shrapnel or canister. Another shopkeeper found what seemed to be the flintlock of a pistol lodged in the wall of his premises. This led police to believe that the barrel may have been ignited by the firing of a gun into the powder, something Chevalier's bomb had experimented with. On closer examination, however, it was thought that this piece of metal was a part of one of the hops from the barrel.

As Paris groaned and fretted with each news of each new casualty, or frowned at the damage caused to one of their most attractive quarters, the police looked knowingly on. Dubois was glad to channel the consternation towards the Jacobins, but progress in the pursuit of the actual perpetrators was kept quiet. This served a political purpose, and no doubt proved popular higher up the hierarchy, but it was also practical as it lulled the plotters and their sponsors into a false sense of security. Rumour made its own contribution to this fog of war, allowing the security services to exploit word on the street to disguise their own progress.[25]

As these rumours swirled, as the Jacobins were hauled in and sent off, as the state railed against their perceived enemies and as the injured tended their wounds and the dead were buried, the pursuit for the actual perpetrators was progressing all along. Dubois, whatever he said in public, was pursuing the royalist plotters with vigour, as was Fouché, whose own judgement and abilities were, after all, on trial. After Christmas and into the new year, those who had tried to kill Napoleon, and whose short but deadly reign of terror had convulsed Paris, found themselves transformed, their status shifting from being the hunters to being the prey.

9

ON THE TRAIL OF TREASON

Pierre François Réal had come running to the Rue Nicaise shortly after half past eight on Christmas Eve. This portly lawyer, a reliable conduit for news between the First Consul and his Minister of Police, had hurried through the acrid smoke. As he ran, his increasing sense of horror was only partly alleviated by professional pride that the police were already hard at work and that clearly someone efficient was in charge as they had had the good sense to cordon off the scene of the crime:

> The Rue Nicaise and those connected to it were full of police officers and there were squads of men keeping the crowds of curious onlookers back at Saint Honoré and the Carrousel. Rue Nicaise was covered in debris, and right in the centre of it were the remains of a horse whose limbs had been torn asunder and blown away, so much so that just one leg was recognisable.[1]

This chunk of horse flesh would prove the adage that the little things are infinitely the most important, and Réal, as he examined the leg, was quick to deduce the importance of the limb as well as 'a horseshoe which was attached to the hoof and which seemed to have been newly affixed, and understanding the significance of this piece of evidence, I personally placed a sentry over it in order to secure it.'

The remains would be taken to the prefecture where Prefect Dubois was in for a sleepless night. He was already drawing up his initial report, and although he made no mention of the shoe, his text proved a remarkable initial summary:

An explosion at half past eight: there was a violent explosion of gunpowder in the Rue Nicaise, close by to the Rue de Chartres.[2] It seems certain that it happened in the street itself, the bollards were blown away and the walls on either side of the street blown in, with facades blackened by powder and knocked askew. It seems that the bomb had been transported on a cart, drawn by an old nag which then had its rear quarters blown off. The First Consul had passed by just one or two minutes beforehand and his coach was by the Theatre de la République when the bomb went off. Two people were killed and six seriously wounded. A very young girl was torn apart next to the cart, her clothes were blown off and she was unrecognisable. Nothing from the Temple [prison] suggests there were any grounds to suspect such an event and they only found out there at around ten that evening. The same with the Tower. They say that the sentries at Cambacérès's residence and the sentry post on Rue Nicaise saw a fuse burning. When they heard the explosion, the entire city seems to have thought that it was a salvo of artillery to celebrate peace or a victory.[3]

Once the horse's remains had been picked over by his officers, Dubois had Dr Jean-Baptiste Huzard, Inspector General of the Veterinary Schools of Paris, summoned to the prefecture from his

Christmas revelries. The vet, a noted authority on working horses, performed an autopsy of sorts and then had a detailed description of the animal drawn up. He concluded that it was a bay, with a mealy nose, white hair in its forelock, a plaited tail, standing 1 metre and 50 centimetres but, unfortunately, unbranded or marked with any proof of ownership.

Dubois had this description, with a vaguer one of the cart, circulated to the capital's commissaires for urgent publication. He had his men urge anyone with information to come to the prefecture to inspect the remains 'before putrefaction sets in.' Dubois also instructed his men to check the city's hospitals as it was thought that one of the perpetrators had been wounded and had been seen limping away. After being informed that the bomb seems to have been a barrel packed with powder and shot, he also told his officers to make enquiries with local barrel-makers and blacksmiths in an attempt to glean information on the horseshoe and on the hoops which had surrounded the barrel.

Meanwhile, Charles Louis Limodin of the 3rd Division was busy at the scene of the crime, interrogating the piquet of the National Guard who had been on duty at the end of Rue Nicaise, and attempting to track down the carriage driver who had momentarily blocked the street just as Napoleon's escort appeared. He failed with the driver's identity, but the guardsmen passed on the information that a man had asked for a light sometime between six and eight on the evening in question. He notified his superior, hinting that the culprits had been brazen and careless in this instance and so would probably have been at other times too, which might count in favour of the police. Dubois sent out word that each and every inhabitant of the street should be questioned. But just as this mammoth task was beginning, the police had a stroke of luck.

On 27 December, Citizen Lambel, a grain merchant, accompanied by Brunet, who said he traded in scrap metal, walked into the prefecture. Lambel had come forward to his local police officers, telling them of his and Brunet's suspicions, and they had encouraged the pair up to headquarters. Ushered in to the courtyard, Lambel easily identified the cart, harnessing and remains of the horse in the presence of Dubois, Desmarest and Dominique Garat and went on to state that he had sold the horse and cart on 20 December to a man claiming to be a market stallholder and who was then living with his sister in Paris. Brunet helpfully vouched for these facts. A blacksmith, Jean-Baptiste Legros, who came along shortly after Lambel, also confirmed it had been Lambel's horse and recognised his own handiwork on the hoof; indeed, having tended the horse for some time, he could even recognise its scars and defects. Lambel, evidently a stickler for the facts, interjected that he had bought the horse five years ago from a dealer in Rue Bleue.

Lambel, who had sold horse, cart, harness and lentils for 200 Francs, and Brunet, who had brokered the deal, were able to describe the purchaser rather well, as the transaction had only taken place the week before. It was a significant development and Dubois was glad to report:

The prefect has discovered that the horse and cart which, on 24 December, transported the infernal machine to the Rue Nicaise, was sold for 200 Francs by a grain merchant living at 42 Rue Meslay to an individual who seemed to be a servant, although well spoken, and a description has been given. He seems to be some travelling salesman living in the street close by Saint-Martin. Even after the purchase he returned to buy grain and the hay for the horse and finished by adding that he had found a place for it in the Poissonnière quarter. He had a cartwright fashion some hoops so that a canvas could be stretched over the cart and down to cover its sides, saying that he didn't want the merchandise to get wet. The grain merchant recognised the horse, the bits of harness, the halter, the girth and the collar as well as the remnants of the cart, so there is no doubt remaining there.[4]

On 29 December Thomas, who hired out vehicles and knew a thing or two about horses, also strolled into the prefecture and declared that he thought the cart had been kept and adapted at Monsieur Baillif-Mesnager's property, and recognised the additional holes that had been drilled into it at Mesnager's shed. Thomas was a tenant at that property – 23 Paradis Poissonnière – and was a sharp-eyed witness, remembering not only that the landlord had rented out his shed to a merchant for 25 Francs for three months but also recognising the horse and giving a good description of the so-called merchant. The minister reported:

> The man who bought the cart and mare from Lambel obtained a shed and stabling in the Poissonnière quarter. The wretch, along with two others, having spent the night in the shed brought out the cart and the mare on the evening of the 24th. They did not return. Nobody recognised them and some suspected them of being up to no good. We have statements from doormen, tenants and neighbours. An order is out to arrest Ménager [sic], the owner of the building.

Thomas' wife, who acted as the concierge, had also stepped forward. She had been so suspicious of men she had determined were part of a smuggling operation that she had done what any self-respecting Parisian concierge would have done and made a spyhole to keep an eye on what was going on. Her testimony was supplemented by a statement from Madame Ricard on the drill and the holes in the cart. The Minister of Police was fascinated by this revelation:

> The men working on the infernal machine had no tools, they even had to borrow a cup in order to transfer powder. They had to borrow a drill from Thomas in order to pierce the tongue of the cart and, even then, it was Thomas who made the holes. Men from the Jacobin faction would have had the tools and would have known how to use them. They would probably have also avoided the risk of working on a stranger's property as Chevalier had by working at a house owned by one of the plotters and which was therefore less exposed to the curiosity of strangers.[5]

The police were also pleased to discover that the men had purchased two barrels from a wine merchant opposite the yard, even rinsing the barrels out in the street before having Pierre Baroux, the barrel-maker, fashion iron hoops for them. But it was Madame Thomas's revelation that the men had taken the cart away between 5.30 and a 5.45 on 24 December that aroused the most interest in the prefecture offices.

That week the description of the snuff-taking merchant and his accomplices was circulated to the prefects across France and, in French and Breton, to the generals commanding the military districts in the west, with added inducements for information on those long suspected of involvement:

> Have them looked for and arrested. I will have a reward of 12,000 Francs paid out to anyone who seizes any one of the five named below.[6]

With evidence growing that the royalist faction was behind the atrocity, further orders went out on 5 January to seize Cadoudal dead or alive, General Simon being entrusted with this essential blow.[7] General Jacques Louis François Delaistre de Tilly was quick to react, sending 'spies of every class and every sex, men and women, rich and poor, smiths, tobacco merchants, etc, against him'. Fouché, having always suspected the Chouans, particularly after his own agent had been done away with, and having tracked Limoëlan and his ilk from late December, had never ceased trying to hunt them down, even if he'd been doing so on the sly. By the end of December, and no doubt with Limoëlan in mind, the minister could openly suggest that 'the courts of Mitau and London desired the success of such a crime and it was clearly in their interests ... The dress, their manner of speaking, perhaps even the youth of those behind the crime give rise to suspicion that these men sold themselves to England.'

Fouché bolstered his case by teasing out links and connections:

Independent of all the proof to be found in the documents from the English Committee, and Georges' threats, as well as the behaviour of his agents, all of which was known to the minister, there is also the question of why, when the crime had been conceived and carried out, this party was so calm, which was not the case with the anarchists. This is also the opinion of the loyal Chouans who admit that some of their party could have been behind the crime.

On 3 January he again emphasised how:

It was Georges, emissary of Pitt, who, since his return from England, had been planning this atrocity. They had to hand a number of assassins inured to murder and fearless in danger. They were the ones who killed [bishop] Audrein. The same men, or men like them were commanded by him, and provisioned with English gold brought by him, resolved to murder the First Consul.

He saw that the time was right to urge Dubois to focus on the Chouan captains, namely

Seek out with the utmost energy Limoelan (called Beaumont), Joyau (called d'Assas), Lahaye Saint-Hilaire, Saint-Réjant (called Pierrot), Dufou or Dufour and Saint-Andeol, all Georges' officers who have come to Paris in a clandestine manner and who have remained in hiding since their arrival. We should strive to get their descriptions to see if they are still in Paris.[8]

He had been working his informers and quizzing Bourmont, and a note of his records his wish 'to ask V if there is anyone amongst the Chouans who can give a description of the merchant to see if he matched the descriptions of any of these gentlemen.' He suspected that a servant of Achille Le Brun, or of Achille Le Blond, a man called Little François, who had been working for Limoëlan and hanging around the Hotel de Mayenne[9] in Rue du Four-Saint-Honoré and sometimes passing himself off as a cloth merchant, was the one he was looking for. He had somehow heard, probably from Bourmont, who was still playing a complicated double game, that this servant had bought the cart and previously supplied weapons for the robbing of stagecoaches. Fouché had initially thought the merchant might be either Biou or Chandelier, two Chouans who had refused to lay down their weapons, but these were ruled out when they were noted as still being in Brittany. Little François remained a sizable mystery until word came that changed everything.

On 11 January General Girardon sent a letter. Not from Brittany, and not from the rebellious Morbihan, but from Angers in Maine. The general passed on a note to the minister sending details of a local Chouan fitting the description of the mysterious man who had bought the cart:

> The name Petit François refers to François-Jean Corbon, a native of Saint-Sulpice, the Saint-Germain suburb of Paris. He is around 43, five foot six inches tall. He wears a grey riding coat and breeches, blue waistcoat and three-cornered hat. He has chestnut hair and brows, blue eyes, a flat nose, average mouth, round chin, blond beard, high forehead and a scar. This is the last description of him taken in April 1800. He calls himself a country surgeon and spent much time at the Port-Brillet forge, in Olivet, but he was in Paris two years before this last uprising. He lives with a wine merchant called Chevalier, Rue du Faubourg and Porte Saint-Martin, number unknown. He is not married. He carries a passport saying he is a former sailor, issued in Laval, having served on ships of the line, including the 79-gun *Saint-Esprit*, under Captain Leroux. He has a sister who has lived with Chevalier these last two years.[10]

Fouché informed Dubois on 13 January. A police raid, led by Marlier and Mercier, on Porte Martin found no trace of a Madame 'Corbon', but, instead, discovered Madame Marguerite Davignon co-habiting with a poultry salesman called Desniaux. Once she had put her clothes on, she proved a mine of information on the whereabouts of the man actually called Carbon, and cattily informed the officers that he had been living 'with his sister and lover' Vallon quite nearby and opposite the Saint-Nicolas-des-Champs church. Dubois sanitised this information for the minister and told him that through 'the care and diligence of my agents' better information had been acquired which then led to a second raid, this time on rooms rented by a Madame Catherine Jean Vallon, sister to a certain Carbon, on the sixth floor of 310 Rue Martin. There the police discovered that Carbon had been living there until recently, and had still been in residence after the assassination attempt, sometimes on a mattress on the floor, sometimes with his sister and sometimes creeping into the bed of Josephine, his 19-year-old niece. The widow had done his washing for him, as well as that of a stranger who, judging from a description given by one of the nieces, was most certainly Limoëlan. Following the blast these two men had broken and burnt a barrel, but the police raid revealed some traces of the powder around the fire and between the floorboards, as well as 12 more pounds of powder stashed away, plus some cartridges, blue shirts and, in a piece of evidence clearly linking Carbon to the shed and cart, the bushels of peas and lentils that he had bought off Lambel. But Carbon himself was absent, Catherine Vallon protecting him by calmly denying that, despite the pulses and other evidence to the contrary, she had not seen her brother in the last two months.

It had been Limoëlan who, making use of his religious connections, had spirited the coarse Chouan away. On 28 December the two had met before the Temple of Peace south of the Seine, and had walked over to Rue Cassette. There Limoëlan had entered number 11 with Carbon waiting outside in the street whilst Limoëlan spoke to Mademoiselle de Cicé, an old friend of Uncle Picot-Clos-Rivière. The canting uncle had already primed her, asking that she organise sanctuary for a persecuted royalist without papers. Cicé, a Breton and sister of the former bishop of Auxerre, was a lady of some standing and she was pleased to help, although she would prefer it if the fugitive did not reside with her. Instead, she instructed Madame Gouyon de Beaufort, a former emigrant fresh from London, to take Carbon to Rue Notre-Dame-des-Champs so he could be hidden amongst the nuns of Saint-Michel. The following morning, after spending the night in Gouyon's hallway, Carbon and his escort put on their coats and, shielded by a protective cloak of cold drizzle, hurried to the convent. There Gouyon explained to the Mother Superior, Marie Anne Duquesne, that the poor man was merely a returned emigrant waiting for papers. Once installed, he was quite comfortable in a room above the chapel, getting fat on good food and a bottle of wine a day. Limoëlan, more aware of the danger closing in, warned him to stay hidden and to keep a low profile, sending him a note telling him to 'keep your head down, on no account go out and trust no one save me; be wary of anyone else, even those who you think might be your friends or mine, they might trick you. I'll pass on any news from your sister, so stay where you are.' For a while Carbon obeyed, before temptation encouraged him to small acts of indiscretion. He was seen downstairs, incongruously attending a Te Deum in the church which gave thanks for Napoleon's escape, then on 8 January he went to see his sister, Catherine Vallon, so they could drink coffee together and so that he could bring her his dirty washing. His niece, Josephine Vallon, overheard them talking about a convent, and they had recently been seen conversing about the linen by the loquacious Marguerite Davignon. Worse, Carbon asked Josephine and Madeleine, his nieces, to bring his washing to where he was hiding with the nuns and fallen women. A few days after the police raided Vallon's rooms the nieces came forward to confess their role to Chief of Division Henry and even agreed to show him their uncle's new hiding place.

Fouché and the authorities were on Carbon's trail and indeed were making real progress on the band of royalists within Paris who had worked with Carbon. All this was happening just as the convoy of those Jacobins being banished from France was being sent over to Nantes so the arrested Jacobins could start their infernal journey. However, the minister was not minded to save them, his concerns now being entirely focused on the royalists, in particular his frustration that he was not receiving the assistance he could expect from his contacts among the Chouans. He therefore deemed it the right time to send a message to the royalist community in Paris, and having tried being nice, telling one Chouan 'Just tell me where Limoëlan and Saint-Réjant are .... They are your friends, bring them to me so they can justify their conduct, I will issue them with a safe-conduct,' now determined to be nasty. On 16 January he ordered Dubois 'to bring before you citizens Bourmont and Brulard [sic], charged with assisting enemies of the state.' Dubois cast his net wider and in an early morning raid on 17 January Bourmont was seized with a dozen Chouans including Felix Leclerc, Francois Fouchet, Hemore, Pierre Courard and Philibert Lesage. Over the coming days a further 90 well-known royalists were brought in although Bruslart, the chevalier whose 'English airs' were a giveaway, was still managing to avoid arrest: 'he is hiding carefully but his servant, Bernard, was taken last night; we are sure he knows everything about the plot, but he is a determined man and difficult to draw out.' A reward of 2,000 Francs was announced, but the police remained empty-handed and Bruslart, who had been secreted at Étienne-Denis Pasquier's, and brought with him 'a veritable arsenal of pistols and daggers, and was ready for hand-to-hand combat should things turn desperate', escaped to the Saint-Marcouf islands.[11] However, Bourmont was the bigger catch and his assistance was more important if Limoëlan was to be found. He was probed in the Temple by Judge Fardel for information on the assassination attempt but whatever was gleaned from the royalist must have been insufficient for he was soon sent off to internal exile in the Jura.[12]

Fouché was disappointed, venting some fury on Dubois through a complaint that he had arrested too many useful contacts: 'there is grumbling, Citizen Prefect, that many of the arrests are unfounded. I ask you to draw up a list of those arrested since the attack, and to note the motives for the arrest so that I can forward a report to the First Consul and rule definitively on the status of the detained.' The minister preferred subtler ways and soon heard that Anne-Christian de Montmorency-Luxembourg, Bourmont's friend and police spy, had managed to glean five names from Bourmont, all men who might aid in tracking down the true suspects. Among them were Nougarède, Aimé Louis Auguste de Boisbaudron and Biget d'Achille, and they passed on some useful information about those suspected of masterminding the atrocity:

> Those descriptions that have been published have been examined by the pardoned royalists who have remained faithful, and who share the general indignation aroused by the atrocity. They say the first strongly resembles a wretch from Georges's army, a man who had served in his artillery, famous for his murders and a man who made his living from killing blues. The second and third also seem to be known Chouans.[13]

The information nearly led to the first significant arrest of a plotter. Shortly after Bourmont was brought in, Coster Saint Victor, then hiding in the Hotel de Béarn, Rue Feydeau, narrowly escaped being caught in a police raid on his rooms at the back of the third floor. The police discovered an old pair of boots, a three-cornered hat with gold braid and an empty case, but Coster himself had left the day before. It was not all bad news that week, however, for, following a tip-off, Captain Gerard of the 54th Line ambushed a band of five travellers outside Loudéac and managed not only to kill Mercier La Vendée but also to capture Cadoudal's correspondence, which the Chouan lieutenant was carrying to England. The most incriminating letter, to Count de Chaussée, then running the royalist war department from his bedroom at 46 South Moulton Street in London, read:

> You must appreciate that our position requires something positive and quickly, for we are at each moment exposed to the blades of assassins. Duty, the instructions we have received and the hope of seeing something begin keeps us here ready. I will be forced to declare bankruptcy if I do not receive 4,000 Louis within 25 days. They promised that sum to me each month, without including the cost of Bt [sic, Bruslart?] who costs me enormous sums. You are no doubt aware that the great correspondence went off badly, although things will be done anew. I push for action but the funds are lacking ... I hope the great correspondence will soon be back on.[14]

This revelation that the conspirators might try again would soon reach Paris, and added to the pressure to secure the suspects, although the police there were keenly aware of their priorities as Napoleon was as intolerant of delay as ever, and the minister was brooking no excuses. Dubois was on the receiving end of his superiors' angst, but he had his hands full with the most decisive police operation thus far. The day after Cadoudal had written his letter, and as the Chouans of Paris were being hauled in, the prefect of police was preparing for the raid on Carbon's sanctuary at Notre-Dame-des-Champs. On the evening of that Saturday 17 January he wrote:

> Good, very good, all that work on the Chouans the other day has paid off tonight. Have the commissaires and officers of the peace ready tomorrow at five. The warrants are ready, the Temple awaits.[15]

Desmarest, who had worked closely with Bertrand throughout the investigation, was issuing similar orders:

> All the ministry's agents shall present themselves at the prefecture and be ready tomorrow, the 28th [18 January] at five precisely. There, in the office of Citizen Bertrand, they shall receive their orders and shall then carry them out.

The operation was a complete success. Carbon was caught and arrested at seven that morning. The Mother Superior saw how 'our courtyard was invaded by policemen and armed men, without us being able to understand how it had happened. It seems as though the armed men had surrounded the building whilst those who got in had made use of ladders.' The 25 'agents of the prefecture of police' searched her rooms, making a show of checking in her bed, before catching Carbon who, despite an attempt to sound the alarm, had still been asleep when the agents were breaking in. His bed was still warm to the touch, so the police knew he was close by and indeed the Chouan himself was arrested in the adjoining room. Carbon, a consummate wretch according to the minister, was brought in for interrogation at the prefecture with Dubois taking personal charge of an interrogation which lasted much of the day.[16] The police began gently enough, asking Carbon to describe his life to date. They learned he had been born in the parish of Saint-Sulpice in Paris, and that he had served in the navy. His father, the strangely named Jean-Jean Carbon, had died when he was young and his mother, Catherine Cauchois or Cauchoise, he was not sure which, had brought him up. He confessed to having served in Chouan ranks for the last seven years, serving variously under Chateauneuf, Puisaye and Bourmont. Intrigued, his interrogators asked him how many times he had seen Bourmont, and Carbon told them 'five or six times, he is a very nice and humane man, but not rich but, even so, when I told him of my own financial position, he gave me four Louis.' When they asked him where he had slept, he shrugged and told them 'here and there'. The police pressed him, telling him 'we do not think you are telling the truth, for we know you have been sleeping with your sister for the seven or eight months you have been in Paris.' Carbon was noticeably shaken, and there was little he could offer by way of explanation when he was asked why he was found hiding in a convent.

The police had listened patiently, but their real aim was to pin him to the purchase of the cart and mare. As the questioning continued, Desmarest sent a note over to the prefecture:

It is of the greatest importance that Little François is identified at once by the witnesses. You know that they will try to bribe some of them and thus ruin our chances. The minister is waiting for the results.

Henry wrote back that '15 of them have already identified him – more than we need,' mostly the carters and barrel-makers, but also those from the house and yard at Paradis Poissonnière. Fouché, reassured, then reminded his subordinates and colleagues of the importance of grinding Carbon down into confessing:

I impress upon you the need to deal with Little François rigorously, and to make sure that he is watched closely by reliable men and to ensure that he neither has the means to escape or to do away with himself.[17]

At nine in the evening a further seven-hour session of interrogation began and Carbon's resolve soon began to crumble. The previous session had finished with some general questions on the cart, the horse and the shed, and Carbon had improvised some responses, denying that he was involved in plotting against the 'Premier Consulte' and telling his interrogators that he was strolling around Porte Martin when the bomb went off. He had initially sought to deny any knowledge of the cart before admitting that he had acquired and kept one on behalf of someone he did not know. He also told the police that he had then sold everything to another stranger and that the man had thanked him and that he, Carbon, had pocketed 6 Francs. It was now, however, that Carbon's resolve began to shake, perhaps in recognition that his story was not persuading anyone.

Rather to the surprise of the hardened officers of the law, Carbon confessed that the two men he had worked with were in fact 'Limoëlan and Pierrot, the former being a major general under Georges, as far as I know, the other being a commander of a Chouan legion, also under Georges.'[18]

He proceeded to describe the two men and to inform Dubois of Saint-Réjant's address in Rue Prouvaires. He told the police that Limoëlan was going to go with him to Versailles but that when they reached the Rue Saint-Denis,

…two men took the barrel on their shoulders and went down the street, Limoëlan going with them and telling me to watch the cart. After about an hour, or three-quarters of an hour, they came back with the barrel on a hand-cart and Pierrot [Saint-Réjant] was with them and he was also wearing a blue smock. They hoisted the barrel into the cart, placing it in the centre, and placed the second barrel, which lacked a lid and was empty, next to it … the two other men disappeared the way they had come and Limoëlan, Pierrot and myself set off with the cart which had its cover pulled down so that nothing in the cart could be seen, neither from the front, the back nor from either side. As we went down towards the Place des Victoires, Limoëlan had me pick up paving slabs and cobbles and he arranged them at the front of the cart. Then when we reached Rue Neuve-Eustache, Pierrot told Limoëlan that it was time to send me off, which they did telling me to meet them the following day at the usual place. So I left them on the corner of Rue Neuve-Eustache and they carried on towards Place des Victoires without telling me where they were going.

This was co-operation of a kind, but Carbon had strung the police along until four in the morning and had, by and large, cloaked himself in innocence regarding the true purpose of the bomb. His excuses were implausible, so there was hope that he could still trip over his own strings of deceit, and the police knew that they should still press him to explain why, if innocent, he had allowed himself to be moved from one hiding place to another, eventually to seek refuge amongst the nuns.

For now, however, Carbon was returned to his cell and the police made good use of the information they had gleaned from the Parisian. Carbon had indicated that Limoëlan could often be found at the Hôtel des Deux Ponts in Rue du Hasard, and that his mother would send his shirts there from Versailles. Police surveillance on the hotel proved fruitless. However, in another early morning raid, the police paid a visit to Saint-Réjant's rooms at the Leguilloux residence at 574 Rue Prouvaires, Desmarest's warning that 'Pierrot is extremely brave and determined' and urging his officers to caution. Commissaire François Couvreur drew the short straw and climbed up to the second floor to hammer on the door opposite the staircase. Madame Leguilloux and her son appeared, and admitted they had lodged a stranger but added that he had gone and they did not know where. The police had arrived too late to catch the royalist, but there was, however, a consolation prize, unearthed following the search of the rooms the suspect had occupied. For there, under the bed, was the letter from Gédéon[19] dated 19 December with its expectant hopes for good news:

> Alas, two weeks have passed and events proceed in a terrifying manner. If the setbacks continue, I don't know what shall become of us. We look to you and all our confidence and our hope rests in you ... PS, we wait for your news with each courier.

There was also an odd account setting out his justification for the crime. The minister described it thus:

> Amongst other documents found in his room, they discovered, under his bed, the draft of a letter that he had been writing to Georges. After a few lines in which he noted that public opinion was blaming the anarchists, he described a different version of events in which a courageous man had stood next to the bomb waiting for the right moment. He should have received a signal from the palace but did not. One of the guards struck him as he rode by, but this did not prevent him from lighting the fuse. The powder was of poorer quality than he had expected and this delayed the explosion by two or three seconds, otherwise Bonaparte and his family would have perished. This is Saint-Réjant's own account of the operation. Limoelan has already confessed in his letter to his mother in which he says we should not expect any declarations against the royalists.[20]

Whilst they had some of Saint-Réjant's correspondence, the man himself had eluded them. The commissaire nevertheless brought in three of the Leguilloux and Fanny Mercier 'aged five.' A sudden descent on Widow Jourdan's at Rue d'Aguesseau was less productive, she telling the police that their suspect had left the evening before, taking his effects, and his pug Mirza, with him. They searched the house finding 153 Francs, six shirts and a pair of green slippers, but the raid proved so distressing that Widow Jourdan threw herself out of the window, landing in the courtyard and dying shortly afterwards at the Hospice du Roule.

The police now knew the ringleader, and deployed some 300 infantrymen and 25 cavalry men to support those officers tasked with hunting him. The city gates were closed so that, as an officer remarked, those men on duty 'were ordered to let nobody pass, not even one of the consuls, without first showing their passport.'

Saint-Réjant had not gone very far. On Christmas Eve, and in the wake of his bomb, shaken, bruised and half blinded, he had sought refuge in Rue des Prouvaires. His landlady, Madame Louise Leguilloux, had been playing cards with her son at their home but, after seeing the boy to bed, had been unsettled by noise in the street. She had gone out to find the cause of the tumult and was told that there had been an explosion in the Carrousel. Then, shortly afterwards, there was a knock on the door. Saint-Réjant, wearing grey trousers and a dirty russet overcoat, had gone straight up to his room and Limoëlan arrived shortly afterwards. Madame Leguilloux's account ran:

Soyer came back between eight thirty and nine o'clock. He was alone and went straight up to his room. Beaumont (Limoëlan) came a little later and asked me 'has your gentleman come back?' He then went up to Soyer's room and, a little later, came and called for me, saying that Soyer was very sick and that a confessor, an honest man, was required at once. I replied that I didn't know of any such man, but that a doctor might be better. I woke my son and he went to Bourgeois at the Red Cross. He went and fetched Doctor Collin as he knew his address. It was at 10 that Bourgeois brought the doctor and he spent the night treating Soyer ... Beaumont told me that Soyer had been run over by a horse which had trampled him on his chest and head.

Saint-Réjant's own account largely confirms this:

It is true that the explosion affected me rather badly after I got back at around a quarter past or half past eight. It is also true that Limoëlan, or Beaumont, came to see me and, seeing that I was in a bad way, went to get a doctor and confessor. I was treated for spitting blood and I told the doctor, Collin, that I had been in Rue de Malte, by the railings, when there was an explosion.

Naturally, the confessor, none other than Uncle Picot-Clos-Rivière, having heard the Breton's sins, respected his charge's secrets, but we do have an account from the doctor. This Dr Basile-Jacques-Louis Collin, the one who had treated the royalist's catarrh earlier in the month, was also a Breton and the brother of a Chouan, and so was deemed as trustworthy as the cleric. He had been attending a lecture on the delivery of babies when the bomb had gone off, dismissing it as a gunshot, before going home and preparing supper. Before he could sit to eat, Bourgeois came for him and, well before eleven, he was at the Leguilloux residence. He was kept waiting for a few moments by the confession, and told those present 'once the priest has finished his ministrations, I shall begin mine.' Perhaps the priest should stay, for the doctor found the 'patient in Rue des Prouvaires to be in a serious condition':

I removed his cap and examined his head. There were no wounds or contusions. I examined all over, the chest was unaffected as was the stomach. The limbs did not have any bruising. I saw just two symptoms, namely breathing and blood circulation. His breathing was very constrained and difficult. He was spitting blood and some blood was also exiting from the nostrils. The pulse was faint but fast. In short, he was in the condition of one who might, in two or three hours, die of a heart attack. I suggested that I bleed him and although I did not normally carry a lancet I happened to have one with me in my case. He refused ... he told me to bleed him tomorrow morning, but then changed his mind.[21]

After the bleeding, the patient seemed more at rest, despite remarking that he was partially deaf, had eye trouble and abdominal cramps, all complaints now synonymous with blast injuries. The doctor prescribed a tisane and some bouillon every four hours and left. Nobody seemed troubled by the three versions of how the patient had been injured and nor was anyone surprised by his remarkable recovery. For the patient was up and about the following morning, warming himself by his fire, and having his hair dressed by Billault, who thought him 'rather weak'. The doctor could testify to the royalist's almost complete recovery, although his Christmas greetings were negated by the recommendation that leeches be applied to the patient's anus. Limoëlan, who arrived to hand over some money, was a more welcome sight and the gift of money succeeded where the threat of leeches failed,[22] for, a few hours later, Madame Leguilloux was able to see her tenant walking off into the distance:

Soyer left on the evening of 25 December, going back to Widow Jourdan. He was so weak that I sent my daughter after him, as

I thought he might collapse. He took Rue Saint Honoré and went straight along it. My daughter left him at the end of Rue Saint-Nicaise.[23]

He spent the next three weeks quietly passing the time in his room at Rue d'Aguesseau, writing the odd letter and keeping in touch with Limoëlan who, either through generosity or because the pair were once again scheming, sent him 500 Francs. Rumour had it that he was going to try to kill again. That was if he wasn't caught.

On 18 January, as Carbon was undergoing interrogation, Saint-Réjant was deep in conversation with a man calling himself Bourgeois, an optician who had vouched for the Breton to his landlady, and who now, in a blond wig, declared that he had been concerned that his friend might be detained for not having his papers in order. Saint-Réjant reassured him by showing him his documents made out in the name of Sollier or Soyer and the two left for Rue Prouvaires, taking the dog Mirza with them, and then, apparently, went out and enjoyed the theatre. They returned to the Leguilloux residence at 10 o'clock but were surprised to find the good widow Jourdan and her daughter, Marie Antoinette, waiting for them and rather distressed, telling the Bretons that a man, most likely Saint Victor, had come to inform them that the police had just arrested 'Petit-Francois and that the wretch was likely to tell the police everything.' Marie Antoinette had heard the visitor refer to Soyer as Saint-Réjant and when her mother told this Saint-Réjant fellow about the visitor she saw a flash of anger, possibly because he sensed that he had been betrayed and not necessarily by Carbon, but by Bourmont.[24] However, the alarm faded and he seemed calm enough for 'he then dined with Bourgeois and the two female Jourdans, eating some cold veal, a few cutlets and drinking some glasses of wine.' Monsieur Leguilloux, witness to this bibulous familiarity, abstained and was able to remember that the four left shortly afterwards.

Discomforted, and aware that there had been mass arrests of royalist captains, Saint-Réjant was running out of hiding places. He quit Prouvaires, and although he had left with the Jourdans he knew that Rue d'Aguesseau was also unsafe. He therefore went to ground and either borrowed or had altered his documents, using the surname of the Chouan captain Ambroise-Marie Sougé, chiefly so he could apply for lodgings in the Hotel de Mayenne. But whoever provided him with these documents, or tampered with them, betrayed him. It was probably Sougé himself for Desmarest listed him as an agent and Fouché later declared that he had 'left an agent of Georges' at liberty as he was a man who could lead us to Saint-Réjant.' [25] On 27 January Desmarest sent a note to Bertrand:

My dear Bertrand, I ask a favour. I entrust you with an important task, but a sure one based on what I found out when I returned home at midnight. Have a search carried out very early tomorrow [28 January] at the Hotel de Mayenne. Ask for Sougé and look for him alone, but from the top of the house to the bottom. Look into each and every corner, and by looking for Sougé you will find Pierrot. Let nowhere be overlooked and seek out Sougé in each and every room.

The suspect, elegant in his blue riding coat, replete with golden buttons bearing the inscription 'Gilt Warranted' in English, was caught at the entrance to the hotel very early on the morning of Wednesday 28 January. He was brought in to the prefecture at half past three, and interrogated by Dubois himself. He first claimed he was merely Pierre Martin, an unemployed sailor from Brittany who had walked to the capital to seek work on the quays of Paris. After a lengthy session, he then revealed his true identity:

> My real name is Pierre Saint-Réjant, I am an amnestied Chouan known as Pierrot and from Saint-Réjant in the parish of Lanreslas in the canton of Broons in the departement of Côtes-du-Nord. I am aged between 32 and 33, being born in 1768 and a former volunteer in the navy having served from 1781 to 1791 first of all under the orders of Monsieur Blay, then under the captain Monsieur Kerhué, then under Captain Kergariou-Locmaria, commander of the squadron, then under the Marquis de Vallongue, then under Lieutenant Coriolis and then under the Marquis de Tilly, captain and divisional commander, when the fleet in which I was serving mutinied at Brest in 1791. It was then that a severe illness obliged me to resign, particularly as I had already been wounded three times. I was then living at Saint-Réjant or Saint Méen and I came to Paris three months ago in order to ask that my name be struck off the list of emigrants as I had never left France, although I did serve against the troops of the republic in 1793, 1794 and 1795.

He then went on to detail his role with the Chouan rebels, and saying that he was in Paris to have himself removed from the list of emigrants. The police continued to apply pressure and working backwards through his movements and aliases, and calling in Dr Collin, Madame Louise Leguilloux and Carbon, it was possible to place him near the scene of the crime. Their suspect, however, denied any association with the attempt on the First Consul's life, and when he was pressed to reveal his whereabouts on 24 December he told the police the following:

Limoëlan left me after dinner [at the Leguilloux house] but I do not know where he went. As for myself, I went for a walk down to the Pont Neuf thinking that I would go and see a play at the Elèves [theatre] in Rue Thionville but when I went into a café on the left as you turn into that street, and which I believe they call the Café de Foi, I met someone who told me that they were putting on a new play at the Français and so I determined to go there and so, in order to reach that theatre, I was passing along a street with metal fencing, it must have been the Rue de Malte, when, at eight, there was an explosion in the Rue Nicaise.

Dubois and Bertrand were eager to know whether he had noticed the First Consul's coach, and the prisoner replied that 'I saw two coaches and a cavalry escort.' Dubois and Bertrand continued to probe until some incriminating evidence began to emerge, and Saint-Réjant reacted by changing his story again, saying that, in actual fact, he had been looking for a friend called Bernard at the Hotel de Longueville. He was equally indifferent that the police had found some of his correspondence in his rooms at Prouvaires, declaring that the letter from Gédéon dated 19 December was a fake, and that the draft setting out his justification for the crime was a forgery. He told his inquisitors 'I don't know anything about this letter, it looks as though it was planted in my room to frame me. I never received any letter addressed to Soyer and nobody can ever say that they saw me with this letter in my hands. They could have put it in my room to betray me and those who searched there are wicked enough for me to suppose that they planted it in an attempt to frame me. In any case, I had only just started renting that room.'[26]

He was equally disdainful about the experiments with fuses and matches that had been witnessed, declaring that it had only been because he wanted to smoke in the American way and had made two cigars. The police persisted in their argument that he had made the fuse for the barrel in order to kill the First Consul. Saint-Réjant, his exasperation at the relentless questioning now showing, surprised everyone by declaring: 'If I had wanted to put an end to the First Magistrate of the Republic then I would have blown his brains out and then blown mine out too.'

Following this outburst, Dubois sent the suspect down to the Conciergerie prison, along with Carbon, warning the warder that they should be deprived of the means to kill themselves. He then drew up the formal charges for the tribunal so that the legal process could begin. In the coming days Saint-Réjant was allowed the luxury of dictating and sending a letter to Thérèse Mélanie Ropert, the wife of his half-brother and a noted partisan of the royal cause. The police, perhaps hoping that it might contain incriminating confession that had hitherto eluded them, agreed to see it delivered. It ran:

I assure you that ever since I was arrested I have suffered like a martyr and have said nothing against either my comrades nor against the party, despite being submitted twice to secret interrogation. You can't imagine what kind of torture that is. I shall tell you when I see you. After all that suffering they offered me the rank of general of brigade and 50,000 Francs if I would inform them that it was the persons known to you who had ordered the affair. I told them that I did not know who was behind it and thus saved myself from such a cowardly lie. I hope that you know me well enough to believe that I am worthy of being your friend and that of my former comrades.[27]

It had been dictated because the Chouan had been subjected to Bertrand's favoured means of extracting confessions, the breaking of fingers under a musket's hammer, and was therefore incapable of holding a quill. Fearing that none of her replies had reached the prisoner, Ropert reacted by coming to Paris, arriving at the Hotel de Mayenne on 19 March. Rather innocently she then wrote to Fouché asking that she be permitted to send in some documents or certificates which might attest to the Chouan's good character. Fouché was impassive, placing her under arrest and happily confiscating the 258 Francs she had been able to raise for the defence.[28]

Dubois also had reasons to be cheerful. He had some convincing evidence to implicate the plotters, documentary as well as more circumstantial material, and a battalion of witnesses prepared to testify. And he held two of the key conspirators, indeed only Limoëlan, and some of the lesser Chouans, remained at large. The police had discovered that Limoëlan had stayed at a patissier's called Leclerc, and that a certain Micault Lavieuville had arranged this. Lavieuville's property was searched, and trunks containing weapons were found, but the Breton was missing. This was because he was then hiding in the cellars of the Saint-Laurent church, kept hidden by his uncle Picot-Clos-Rivière, a man who 'runs risks for himself, but I have no doubt that he places his friends at risk in order to advance his projects, and without any remorse, for he thinks that they should be happy to die for the good cause.' Working for the good cause had, however, left Limoëlan bitter, confessing to an acquaintance, with whom he discussed the matter on 27 December, that the conspirators had proved incompetent, burning a fuse rather than lighting a trail of powder with a torch. Fouché had evidently contacted Bourmont to find him and lure him in, but the fugitive told his former comrade in early January that 'The minister can do what he likes; he made me declare war on him and the government. That's the way it has been for ten years, and it can be like that for the rest of my life.'

Fouché then turned to his old acquaintance Limoëlan's mother, Renée-Jeanne-Roche Picot Limoëlan, seemingly probing her for information as early as 4 January:

One individual, whose name features on the list of emigrants wished to be removed from it. His mother and sister, fearing that this would now be impossible, said that they would stop at nothing to seek him out and beg him to show himself, even to have him confess if he knew anything about the plot if he had taken part in it.

Limoëlan's mother and the minister had renewed acquaintance in the autumn of 1800 when the mother was trying to get her son removed from the list of emigrants, and the minister now seems to have held out an offer of amnesty in exchange for information. The mother seems to have communicated this on to her son but, as we can see from his letter of 8 January, this was declined:

Limoëlan has just written to his mother that he will not place any trust in the promises of the minister as he is determined not to put his name to anything which might damage the royalist cause and that he had warned the servant of Monsieur de Saint-Réjant not to show himself.[29]

The mother refused to do more, declaring that 'all you need do if you wish not to find him is to involve me' and the minister was livid that this potentially profitable channel had proved so disappointing:

All those who know the audacity of Limoëlan think that he is capable of such a crime. And if he was not involved, why, then, if he is not guilty, has he not shown himself at the ministry, for he has been offered immunity and removal from the list if he reveals his accomplices?

The police were instructed to mount a series of raids, including a surprise dawn raid on the mother at her residence at 32 Rue de Publicola in Versailles. On 19 January 1801 the Commissioner of Police for Versailles informed Prefect Dubois that:

> Citoyenne Picot Limoëlan lives at Versailles. She has two sons, one at Nantes, the other she believes to be dead, killed in the past war in the Vendée. Her daughters, the sisters of the deceased, wear mourning. The mother, who is very honest, idolises the First Consul. Whenever the weather is good she goes to watch the parades held at the end of the week. She has nothing but praise for the current government. As for the son who is a suspect, his mother hates him and will not offer him shelter. However, given your views, we shall carry out a raid tomorrow at dawn and make a thorough search. I shall inform you if we find anything.[30]

The lady of the house declared that her son Michel lived in Nantes whilst her other, Joseph, had gone to Saint-Brieuc but that she had had nothing to do with him directly or indirectly. Nothing was found that suggested otherwise. A large number of female companions were quizzed, but nobody was detained, the house being placed under surveillance. Commissioner Pile duly reported, rather enigmatically, that 'you will see that we discovered nothing. The next time I'm in Paris I beg that you'll allow me an audience for two minutes, for I have something to tell you that cannot be written down.' But someone in the police was minded to be tough and, on 23 January, Madame de Limoëlan was arrested and brought to the Madelonnettes prison in Paris and interviewed by Dubois on suspicion of 'having given shelter to one of her sons ... suspected of having carried out the mass murder of citizens by means of the detonation of the Infernal Machine.'

Limoëlan was vital as he had been the link between Cadoudal and the plot, with Limoëlan in charge of the money, organising safe houses, overseeing tactics. But he eluded capture and even the arrest of Mademoiselle de Cicé and her retinue of former nuns following a raid on 11 Rue Casette on 20 January lead to no important new leads. Efforts were made to track down the uncle, the minister instructing Dubois that 'the man is probably not in a hotel, he was the director of the institution where Madame de Gouyon lived, so he probably has quarters there.' The former Jesuit was not found, and, before long, it was apparent that his nephew had escaped too.

Limoëlan's fate seemed destined to remain a mystery. However, when Charles, an employee of the Bains Vigier on Quai de la Tournelle, came forward to state that he had unsuccessfully tried to save a young man who had thrown himself from the bridge on the night of the crime, it was generally assumed, in that age of sense and sensibility, that Limoëlan had committed suicide. Such an explanation also suited the police and, after weeks of intense work, the investigation now seemed closed.

10

TRIAL AND PUNISHMENT

Limoëlan was, however, hiding in the crypt of the Saint-Laurent church, the protective embrace of his uncle ensuring sanctuary and the provision of alms. Before long he was smuggled out to the family lands at Sevignac, in Brittany, less a fugitive than a man convinced he had carried out God's will and prepared to wait for the deity's judgement in the afterlife. Meanwhile, the other conspirators had to face their accusers in Paris.

Fouché had wanted a court martial to try the felons, but Julienne of the prefecture had noted that this would be contrary to all laws and so a court convened to try them was presided over by Judge Claude Nicolas Louis Hémart, sombre in his black gowns and imposing in his plumed hat. He was a man whose loyalty as a servant of Bonapartism[1] ensured he would go on to play a key role in some of the regime's more controversial trials and here he was on firm ground, ably supported by judges Rigault and Laguillaumye. These dignitaries now presided over a jury of the good citizens of Paris, the final panel consisting of a grocer, a paver, a cutler, five landlords, an art dealer, a merchant, an architect, an ironmonger, two lawyers and a carpenter.

Some 62 witnesses were going to be produced before this jury of 15. Some, such as Jean Lambel, the man who had sold the cart, and Alexis Baroux, the man who had supplied the barrel, were central to the case. But 10-year-old Nicolas Thomas, son of the man who hired out carts, and 69-year-old Marie-Catherine Toulousse, a former nun, would also have their say. So too would some of the victims, including Guillaume Trépsat, Marie-Louise-Elisabeth Chevalier and the mother of the unfortunate redhead who had held the cart horse's bridle, Anne-Alexandre Rignier (Madame Peusol). To act as counterpoint to the pathos of the maimed, the learned and precise men of science, including the handwriting experts Augustin Oudart and Jean-François Legros, also appeared.

This was a sizable mass of human evidence and testimony, and it was exploited to the full by an experienced prosecution. Their task was eased because the accused, principally Pierre Robinault de Saint-Réjant and François-Joseph Carbon, represented by the lawyers Roussialle and Louis Dommanget, had already fallen out, with Carbon trying to save himself by blaming the unco-operative Saint-Réjant. Many of the others, including Limoëlan, Édouard de La Haye-Saint-Hilaire, Jean-Baptiste Coster Saint-Victor, Bourgeois and Joyau, were being tried in absentia, which further strengthened the case for the prosecution as these Chouans had proved their guilt by absconding.

The trial opened at 10 o'clock on the morning of 1 April 1801 at the Palace of Justice in the shadows of Notre-Dame. The accused were brought before the judge, the shackled Carbon staggering in first. He had attempted to barter his way out of this ordeal, offering information in return for an amnesty, and Piis had been sent to his cell to hear how the Chouan 'was utterly convinced that it was General Georges who had sent them

[Limoëlan and Saint-Réjant] to Paris in order to assassinate the First Consul in order to overthrow the current state of affairs, but that he could not swear to it as he had no proof.' Carbon offered to track Cadoudal down in exchange for forgiveness, but Piis and his colleagues had learned to mistrust Petit François so he found himself before the judge.

Carbon was a relatively easy case for the government as he had confessed to his role in materially assisting the plot, but Saint-Réjant was a more stubborn proposition. He would spend the proceedings in denial, haughtily demanding that more or better evidence be presented and insisting on his innocence. The prosecution had tried hard to find someone who had witnessed the Chouan lighting the fuse but had failed and hoped that circumstantial evidence, and suspicious activity, would be enough to condemn this key suspect. Both Saint-Réjant and Carbon were to be tried for having conspired and plotted against the legitimate government, contravening Article 612 of the Criminal Code of October 1795, which set out that

> ...all conspiracies and plots designed to harm the republic through civil war, by arming citizens one against the other or against the legitimate government, shall be punished by death should that sentence be in force, or by 24 years in irons should it have been abolished.

But as well as these principals, there also came an extended procession of prisoners accused of complicity in the crime. There was Catherine Vallon, Carbon's sister, and her two daughters Madeleine and Josephine, arrested for having hidden the fugitive. Louise Leguilloux and Jean-Baptiste Leguilloux, aged '65 or 66' according to his own account, were similarly accused, having lodged Saint-Réjant throughout his stay in the capital, even following the atrocity. The holy women around Adelaide-Marie-Champion de Cicé, Mother Marie-Anne Duquesne and the Widow Aubin-Louise Gouyon de Beaufort with her daughters, Angélique and Reine-Marie, were accused of the misdemeanour of having sheltered Carbon without, after 24 hours, notifying his presence to the police. Doctor Collin also appeared, for not having informed the police that he had treated a wounded man, as did Jean Baudet, culottier, for having hidden Joyau and seemingly for being friends with Saint-Hilaire. Finally came Mathurin-Jules Micault-Lavieuville, a military veteran living at Rue de la Sourdière with Louise-Catherine Cudel-Villeneuve, present in court for having hidden some weapons on behalf of Carbon. The secondary participants lengthened and complicated the process but they were there not only to contribute to the guilt of the ringleaders but also because the women who had played host to the plotters, and the men who had been drawn into acting as accessories in the crime, could serve as a warning to ordinary citizens. Their lack of vigilance had imperilled the lives of those around them and should be punished, and with that chastisement would come the implication that citizens would do better to turn informer and collaborate in the safety of their state, the liberty of the many residing in the efficient policing by the majority.

With the accused having heard the charges, the law set to weighing the sins of the individuals before it, and here the prosecution excelled itself. The government's ire and eloquence were directed against those who had contrived this premeditated attempt at assassination through the use of an Infernal Machine at three minutes past eight on 24 December. Through the cynical choice of their method they had also caused the death of several individuals and torn the heart out of the capital, the prosecution going on to paint a scene of devastation: 'amidst the shadows of the night, faintly illuminated by a few isolated torches, one of the most beautiful districts of this superb city was seen transformed into a picture of complete desolation.' But the government lawyers also underlined the risk to the welfare of the state; indeed, the First Consul had escaped death, and France anarchy, by three seconds. Cowardly assassins had nearly deprived France of the man who had braved death 'on the arid rock of Malta' and who had 'overcome a thousand obstacles in the wide expanses of Egypt and amidst the burning sands of the desert and the celebrated plains of Syria.'

As for the accused, they were evidently committed rebels steeped in the blood of their fellow citizens, and therefore men accustomed to murder. But the government wanted to highlight that there was another motive for their execrable designs and here the English Conspiracy raised its brutish head. The court therefore sought to emphasise the link between the Chouans and the republic's eternal enemy, perfidious Albion, and Cadoudal, whose role made him little better than a bandit chief and whose language 'made use of expressions used by brigands,' was that link between terrorism and England. His machinations were aided by Limoëlan, a man of ferocious character, and abetted by Saint-Réjant, 'bold only when attacking his fellow citizens', and both these subordinates were painted as being Cadoudal's underlings, and all as London's hirelings.

Having set an emotive scene, and emphasised the dead hand of D'Artois and London for public consumption, the court then established its version of events. It noted how Carbon had purchased the cart and horse and acquired the barrel; how Limoëlan had overseen the work, paid for it from the proceeds of highway robbery and escorted Carbon on the fateful day; and how Saint-Réjant had met these two royalists on 24 December near Porte Saint-Denis, helping load the heavy barrel on to the back of the cart whilst the others added some paving stones to add to the devastating impact of the vehicle-borne device. Saint-Réjant, who had been seen experimenting with fuses and matches, had evidently been at the site of the carnage, and had been badly injured and temporarily rendered deaf by the explosion that evening. From this it was clear he had been the one to detonate the bomb. The police supported their narrative with witness testimony, confessions and statements made during interrogation, and from correspondence seized from Saint-Réjant. Accompanying this recitative were details of efforts to track down the culprits. The telling of their determined hunt reflected well on the forces of order but it also implied that men who move from one address to another, or go into hiding to evade the authorities had, by implication, something to hide.

Now, in support of what was already a substantial case against the accused, came a mass of witnesses, promising to speak without hatred and without fear, and to tell the truth, the whole truth and nothing but the truth. First was Jean Lambel, who, along with Thomas, his wife, his 10-year-old son Nicolas, and many of the tenants in Rue de Paradis, would identify Carbon as the man who had bought the cart and the horse. They testified that he had excited curiosity and suspicion by being too well dressed and flash with his money to be a true merchant and too secretive as to where he lived to be honestly employed. Hearing their evidence Carbon, to the relief of the court, admitted to all this, but declared, in another attempt to shift blame, that he had done so on behalf of Limoëlan and knew nothing about the intended purpose of his purchases. The court suspected he knew the reason as he had only wanted to rent the shed for such a short space of time, and that Saint-Réjant had inspected the location and the cart with a specific purpose in mind. Carbon was on even more shaky ground when the president of the court asked him about the barrel, how it related to his plans to trade in cloth and why he had gone to such lengths to hide what was, according to his own testimony, an empty receptacle. Carbon was fully implicated in the purchase of the barrels, cart, powder and horse. The court poured scorn on his disguise of a merchant needing a cart for his merchandise, after all, why would a merchant without cloth and money of his own be laying out large sums only to let others lead his purchases away towards the Tuileries? And why was he transporting barrels and disguising them with straw? Nor could Carbon explain why it was that, after the explosion, he had allowed himself to be taken from his sister's and hidden in a convent. This was suspicious behaviour which, in the eyes of the court, indicated guilt, as did the note from Limoëlan telling him to remain hidden and to trust nobody. All this and the fact that the powder found at Carbon's sister's was identical to that found in the shed and in traces in Rue Nicaise was damning.

The prosecution rested its case against Carbon, and turned on Saint-Réjant, wanting to know what he had been doing in the shed. He denied having been there, having seen the cart, or having known that a cart was being used as a vehicle for the explosive device. Reminded that Carbon had implicated him by saying that he had visited, the royalist accused his comrade of lying. Carbon protested, and when he revealed that Saint-Réjant had been dressed in a blue smock Saint-Réjant grew agitated, declaring that 'I persist in declaring that I was not, and defy anyone to come forward and say that they saw me attired thus and with the cart.' The president noted that it was dark at the time, so the witnesses might not be able to make an unequivocal identification, but that Carbon's testimony alone would stand. Then the president changed tack, asking the accused whether he had seen Carbon or Limoëlan on 24 December. Saint-Réjant declared that he had been sick for more than a month, and that he had come to Paris for a cure, but admitted that he knew Limoëlan and that this individual had been to his lodgings. Asked when and how he had come to the capital, he declared that it had been four or five months ago via the Evreux coach. When the court pointed out that this contradicted his statement to the police, and asked for details, he grew vague, declaring that his illness prevented him from remembering. Sensing confusion, the president then asked about Cadoudal and Saint-Réjant declared that he had fallen out with the Chouan and had not seen him for 10 months. The court informed him that a letter from Cadoudal had been found in his lodgings, a fact Augustin Oudart, the handwriting expert, was brought in to verify, but the royalist denied knowing anything about any letters before suggesting they were forged. Smelling blood, the prosecution wondered why he had been warned of Carbon's arrest and subsequently had not returned to sleep at his lodgings. Saint-Réjant admitted going into hiding because he did not wish to be arrested as a suspect, but again this seemed like an admission of guilt. Just as incriminating was the evidence of him experimenting with amadou tinder at Widow Jourdan's. His attempt to explain this away by saying that he was fond of smoking 'the American way', i.e. with cigars, and needed combustible material to obtain a good flame, met with scepticism, especially as he had told Widow Jourdan's daughter that good amadou takes two seconds to catch, and that he had been seen timing and testing a fuse combining amadou and powder at least three times in his fireplace. The Breton denied this, and when the prosecution demanded to know why the suspect kept a barrel of powder at home and whether it had been of government manufacture, he rather nonchalantly explained it all away by saying that it wasn't his.

The prosecution, irritated by this phlegmatic stance, returned to the charge, demanding that the Breton account for his movements on the fatal day. Here Saint-Réjant launched into a rather too lengthy account of his pilgrimage from one theatre to another, and declared that 'I was next to a railing in Rue de Malte that ran towards the Palais-Royal when the explosion went off and I was wounded, as were many others who happened to be in the vicinity.' The court asked whether he had been hit by a tile, and Saint-Réjant limited himself to agreeing that he had been hit by debris. This allowed the prosecution to make use of the doctor's testimony that one of the Breton's injuries seemed to be deafness in one ear. Saint-Réjant weakly shot back that he had always been deaf in that ear, but the prosecution was able to crow that the damage came from him being close to the blast.

Having made their point, a chastened Saint-Réjant stood down whilst some of the secondary characters took his place and sought to prove their innocence or shift blame by accusing those who masterminded the crime. Catherine Vallon, having denied everything about her brother, now admitted that he and Limoëlan had brought the barrel and shirts to her lodgings, but distanced herself from any involvement in the alleged plot. Dr Collin limited himself to saying that he had only sought to assist a wounded individual, a professional responsibility. That afternoon the widow Gouyon Beaufort and Duquesne also gave evidence, Cicé's reputation as an honourable and ethical pillar of the community winning her credibility as she denied involvement with or knowledge of those whom she had helped hide. Her friend, the Marquise de Créquy, revealed some of the melodrama:

> Can you imagine our distress, seeing Mademoiselle de Cicé, innocent as a lamb, delivered up to Bonaparte and the judges of his ruthless court in a process in which normal justice would not apply. She was ably defended by Monsieur Bellard, who managed to reduce that irreligious and gutless mob to tears by talking about his client's piety and works of charity. He softened the judges' hearts.[2]

Cicé proved expert at disguising the involvement of Limoëlan's uncle and her own role in the apparel of injured virtue, so much so that the jury seemed won over. The president's insinuations against, and abrupt tone with, Widow Gouyon-Beaufort also won her sympathisers and it was the same with Duquesne, the public throwing oranges to the Mother Superior so she could refresh herself. The defence counsel persuaded the court that the women were innocent of Carbon's true identity, but were forced to concede that they were indeed guilty of the lesser crime of breaching the law about notifying the police about lodgers.

The prosecution, slightly taken aback by this show of innocence abused, and ripples of understanding for some of the accused, now recovered lost ground with its own dramatic flourish. The courts of the Consulate were given to more melodrama than would be allowed in the deliberately dispassionate processes of today, and so there was now a moment of engineered outrage as the unfortunate victims of the atrocity were brought forward to present their stories. There was Claude-Barthelemi Préville, who was sat in a café sharing half a bottle with his apprentice when the bomb went off 'at a quarter past eight', crushing his right hand. He showed the court the remnants and his other wounds, caused by debris and fragments tearing into his chest. Madame Boyeledieu was then brought forward to recount how she had identified the mangled remains of her faceless husband, testimony which affected the court but before which Carbon and Saint-Réjant managed to remain impassive. Tightening the tension, Anne-Alexander Rignier, the mother of the teenage Marianne Peusol, was next to be ushered forward to testify that her daughter's limbs had been scattered across the street, and that she had been so overcome that she had asked her brother to identify the remains. It made for an afflicting sight and the president took the opportunity to remind those present that: 'the tribunal, by presenting the victims of this act of perfidy to you, does not wish to influence your opinion; it only does so because the law requires it to do so.' Carbon was evidently shaken and spoke out in the hope of making it clear that he hadn't been present at the site of the atrocity, denying any part in the carnage that had caused such loss. Saint-Réjant, less plausibly, also denied using and paying the girl, and demanded witnesses who could actually link him to her. The parade of victims had been cathartic for those traumatised by the blast, but it had also damaged the accused in the eyes of the jury, making Carbon's denials before the victims seem callous and Saint-Réjant's obstinacy free from atonement. Their conduct, as much as the case against them, was condemning them but at least on the next day, 3 April, they would have a chance to claim innocence, with their defence counsel due to speak up on their behalf.

This wasn't quite the revolutionary tribunal, although many of those present would have been familiar with the workings of that court, and so Carbon and Saint-Réjant enjoyed the privilege of experienced defence lawyers to plead their case. Citizen Roussialle spoke for Carbon, and opened with another rhetorical flourish, contrasting the present epoch with the recent past when 'the ship of state, sailing under the most stormy of skies, without masts, without sails, without a pilot at the wheel, but battered by contrary winds, had for some time been afloat on the sea of misfortune.' It was a nice trick, to raise the emotion of the courtroom, only to direct it against the Jacobins, who, just two months before, had after all been working on an identical conspiracy. But his brave rhetoric then petered out when it came to evidence and, in the absence of any sympathetic facts, he attempted to win some sympathy for a man who had lost his way – after all, Carbon was an orphan, and therefore easily manipulated by others. Sensing that this was winning Carbon few friends, he then went too far and informed the court that if they dealt too harshly with the defendant, a man who had denounced his fellow conspirators, then France could never expect to foil another plot. It was an unusual approach, but it indicated to the prosecution that the defence had admitted defeat and was now only bargaining over the sentence. It might have worked had not the court, in a timely intervention, then destroyed any potential sympathy for Carbon the orphan with a brazen piece of character assassination, informing the jury that Carbon had robbed a church in Mantes in 1791 and should have served 16 years in irons if he had not absconded and disappeared into the royalist cause.

With whatever remained of Carbon's integrity destroyed before his eyes, Louis Dommanget had, if anything, an even more difficult task, to plead for Saint-Réjant who had been consistently unco-operative and easily incriminated. He made a valiant effort, highlighting the defendant's war record which, although he was a rebel, showed that he was at least a gentleman. After the implication that gentlemen do not conduct assassinations, he then contradicted himself by seeking to denounce that absent chevalier, Limoëlan, as the true murderer. With little evidence to support this assertion, Dommanget made a final attempt to exonerate Saint-Réjant by reminding the court that his client had been a victim of unconstitutional proceedings, having being tortured in attempts to make him confess.[3] It was, necessarily, a short intervention and Dommanget sat down whilst others spoke for Vallon, Dr Collin and the women who had played an important role in hiding the plotters.

Then, on 4 April, the final summing up began.

No mention was made of Napoleon's plan to eject the Jacobins of Paris, or to recall those who had been sent into exile in the colonies and indeed more were being sent and more expelled.[4] But here and now the court was clear that the authorities viewed the royalists as culpable, with London and the court of Saint James again designated as the masterminds, directing the royalist cabal and, whilst holding their noses at the methods, made sure all the necessary expenses were duly compensated. Their chosen intermediary was loyal Cadoudal 'and the gang of brigands associated with him' who would act as pawns in the diabolical plot. Many were absent, and English guilt left unexplained, so the court restricted itself to serving justice on those actually present. The summing up began and this time with less emphasis on rhetorical flourishes:

On 24 December last year, at around eight in the evening, an explosion was heard in this immense capital. Those some distance from it imagined that it was a celebration of the signing of a peace whilst those a little closer were more troubled. Those at the site of the explosion became its victims. The police, to whom the attack was as shocking as it was unexpected, arrived at Rue Nicaise, the scene of the explosion, and learnt that the First Consul had, most fortunately, escaped, but saw that mutilated corpses, their clothes torn to shreds, and the grievously wounded, were scattered about along with the debris of the infernal machine, the cart and what remained of the horse that had drawn it.[5]

The police were praised for their diligence and each one of the accused was allotted a role in the crime, although Marie Antoinette Jourdan was treated with some leniency as her mother, Widow Jourdan had thrown herself out of a window to avoid arrest on 19 February. However, Carbon and Saint-Réjant, 'more astute, more capable, braver' than his fellow accused, had to listen to a detailed repetition of their crimes, and Limoëlan, always elevated to the status of arch-villain, was similarly denounced. Then the judge in his republican majesty called upon the jury to pronounce the verdict 'with the calm and impartiality of which you are possessed' and without being called upon to justify their decision. It was a difficult task, not because the prosecution or the police had failed to make their case, but because the jurors would have to rule on 92 charges, which covered the whole gamut of crimes from lighting the fuse to failing to inform the authorities that a room was being sublet. Then, on Monday 6 April 1801, after more than 24 hours of discussion, the head of the jury informed the president that the jury had not reached a unanimous verdict on all counts. The jury was then asked to reach majority decisions on the controversial questions and, four hours later, they were back.

Carbon and Saint-Réjant were indicted of being involved in a plot designed to murder the First Consul, and Vallon was found guilty as an accessory. Then came the indictment for the deaths caused by the explosion of the infernal machine and again Carbon and Saint-Réjant were culpable. Adelaide-Marie-Champion de Cicé, Widow Gouyon de Beaufort's girls, and those of Vallon, were acquitted as were Baudet and Monsieur and Madame de Lavieuville, all of whom had played a negligible role in housing the Chouans. However, Widow Vallon, the Leguillouxs, Widow Gouyon de Beaufort, Mother Superior Duquesne and Dr Collin were found to have been more directly implicated. Madame Leguilloux served three months before being sent to Alsace and placed under surveillance. She fell ill at Vaucouleurs and returned to Paris and was promptly sent to the Madelonnettes prison. Despite being mother to 24 children, she was not finally released until February 1804.

Widow Vallon was also despatched to Alsace after her three-month term in prison, and she was reduced to begging in Strasburg to keep hunger from the door. Mother Superior Duquesne was released in November 1801 but, enjoying some powerful protection from someone in a position of authority, was rehabilitated and restored to her position. Widow Gouyon de Beaufort also served her term before asking for permission to return to her family in the country.

Dr Collin was more unlucky, even though he was only fined 300 Livres. Indeed, he was remanded in custody for the next 18 months, being detained at the First Consul's pleasure, before being appointed to a position as medical officer and sent to the West Indies.[6] Widow Gouyon de Beaufort's defence insisted on a literal application of the law and a reprieve as Carbon had lodged with her less than 24 hours, and the court partially accepted this plea, and also seemed to heed the Mother Superior's complaint that she had already suffered sufficiently in pre-trial detention. The Leguilloux couple also hoped to be treated leniently as Saint-Réjant had shown them a residence permit, albeit in a false name. There was to be no leniency for the Chouans and Limoëlan, Édouard de La Haye-Saint-Hilaire, Jean-Baptiste Coster

Saint-Victor, Bourgeois and Joyau were condemned to death in absentia. But it was the shackled Carbon and Saint-Réjant who now felt the full force of the law as they were summoned before the president and sentenced to death.

The judge set out the macabre details, namely that they would be taken to the place of execution and done to death, and their estates charged for legal costs and costs associated with their execution, and then asked if they had anything to say. Saint-Réjant spoke up, merely demanding an officer's right to be shot within 24 hours. He was not accorded this last request. Carbon kept quiet but later, back in his cell, made one last attempt to save himself, asking Secretary Piis to Bicêtre prison to take down a revelation in which he blamed Cadoudal. Piis took down the following confession:

We, the secretary general of the prefecture of police, were tasked by the criminal court to hear at his own request the prisoner named François-Jean Carbon, or Little François, or Constant. We arrived at 11.30 this morning and he was brought before us so that he could communicate what it was he wished to tell us. He told us that he was convinced it was Georges, former Commander-in-Chief of the Royal and Catholic Army of Vannes, who supplied Limoelan and Saint-Réjant, known as Soyer, or Pierrot, with the money they made use of in getting to Paris and in their stay there last December. That he was equally convinced, and very much so, that it was Georges, to whom these men served as Major General and divisional commander, who sent them to Paris to kill the First Consul in order to reverse the course of events. However, he could not swear it was so, having no proof. He added that he presumed that Georges had remained in the Morbihan in order to keep up hope and spirits and hold them to the resistance they had previously shown and that he, Carbon, would be able to discover his whereabouts if he were to be sent into that province with a strong escort, for he would obtain information from a certain Monsieur de la Haye who once ran a forge in Saint-Brieuc, he knowing Georges who is a local of the area. He said he thought Saint-Victor could be found around Vitré as he had commanded a legion in that area.[7]

Carbon was not granted his wish to lead the manhunt against Georges, so he wrote a final plea – this time to Napoleon himself:

Citizen Consul, despite being given a sentence I think I do not merit, and hoping that my innocence will be recognised, I nevertheless remain attached to the French government and to your person and I therefore wish to render a particular service [to you]. I can, if you wish it, deliver the following to you: Georges, Limoelan and Saint-Victor, the leaders and the only ones involved in this abominable plot against your person which took place in December last. Only I know where they are hiding, what resources they command and what they are planning against the French government and against the security of your person. I demand nothing more than a safe-conduct and the means with which to arrest these men who are the secret agents of England who have been seduced by gold and promises in order to act against all good citizens. If you will confide this mission to me I shall answer with my life for its success and it will give me great joy to carry out my revenge and increase your safety. I beg you, Citizen First Consul, to look with pity on an unfortunate who has strayed and done wrong, but whose repentance is sincere. I await your orders, Citizen Consul.[8]

These heartfelt attempts to escape justice did not, in the end, save him. Saint-Réjant was of a more sadistic turn, and chose to tease the police. He asked Henry of the police to send him a shirt and a handkerchief and then told the police he had information. Citizen Desmarest duly arrived to hear the prisoner, only for him to inform them that on 24 December, as he was in 'the toilets of the Café Foy, he heard two individuals talking, saying that a certain Francois could not have been guilty as he was just a tool being used by others.' Asked by a puzzled Desmarest whether he actually 'had any revelations which might be significant for the security of the nation', he replied 'no'.

So it was that the tragedy and farce of condemnation lurched towards its inevitable conclusion. On the morning of 21 April the prisoners had a last confession, administered by a priest from Notre-Dame, and put on the red shirts and black hoods of the condemned. The gaoler tied their hands and cut their hair and they were lead out to their execution:

> The odious nature of the crime committed by these two had attracted a huge crowd and they endured the curses of the mob every step of the way to their execution. Saint-Réjant tried to keep his head up when faced by such exasperation but, little by little, his conscience got the better of him, and his head sank, stammering some replies to the invective. When he caught sight of the scaffold his legs gave way and he began to wheeze and lose focus; he had to be propped up as he climbed the stairs to where Carbon was waiting. On the platform he attempted to shout at the crowd but he could not find his voice and only a strange rasping sound came from his lips.[9]

There, on the stained boards of the scaffold at Place de Grève, Carbon apparently shouted out 'it was for the king,' then kept his silence, as his companion did throughout. The crowd too was quiet, watching as the guillotine noiselessly despatched them, before the onlookers came to life and celebrated their death with a noisy cheer.

On 21 April at one in the afternoon, state prosecutor Jean-François Gaultier-Biauzat informed minister of the police Fouché:

> Citizen Minister, the judgement on the condemned men Carbon and Saint-Réjant has just been carried out. I have expressed on a number of occasions my desire to keep you informed on the particulars of this case, however, your duties have not allowed time for this. Nevertheless, I do have some confidential information which you would be interested to learn. I would insist on doing this in a personal interview. Please, therefore, inform me as to the date and time you might be available for a two-minute conversation.

We do not know what information Gaultier-Biauzat had for the minister, but it made little difference. Carbon and Saint-Réjant went to the scaffold as guilty men and the only unknown that remained was the extent to which the pair were following orders to detonate a bomb or had done so of their own volition. This controversy rumbled on beyond the lives of those who had carried out the crime, and those who had participated in its investigation.

Cadoudal had of course conspired against the state, and was still doing so in December 1800, and his role in preparing the ground and selecting the men to carry out the crime is beyond dispute. In his letter signed Gédéon he acknowledged that he was working closely with Saint-Réjant, whilst his 16 January letter to the Count de Chaussée, a key member of D'Artois's circle, largely confirmed his influence by talking openly of an attempt on Napoleon's life, disappointment with its failure and of plans to renew it.

Cadoudal was clearly intending to kill Napoleon and sent his subordinates to carry out the deed, but following the outrage provoked by the choice of weapon – a barbaric bomb in the street – he subsequently seems to have tried to shift the blame onto the shoulders of the decapitated assassins:

> I sent a few of my officers to Paris to be rid of Bonaparte as I thought it necessary, but I never gave orders as to which method to employ. They chose to detonate a device, which is criminal as innocent people were killed. But my idea had been to attack the First Consul in the open and equipped with weapons of the same kind as used by his escort.

There is some truth in this as Cadoudal had originally wanted his men to attack Napoleon on the road to Malmaison and his argument is confirmed by at least one eyewitness who saw him react to news of the atrocity when it reached him in Brittany on 30 December. Receiving a missive from Paris, his lieutenant heard him exclaim 'that bastard Saint-Réjeant wanted to prove to us that he could get rid of Bonaparte all by himself. He has ruined all our plans.'[10] However, even this statement of Cadoudal's innocence can be challenged. Rivoire, who had planned to help the Chouans hand Brest over to the English, states that the giant Breton told him on 28 December that 'That whore's son won't escape. If Saint-Réjeant comes here he'll be shot for not having carried out his instructions. There were supposed to be two carts and when one blew up it was supposed to ignite the other.' His letter to Chaussée also reveals that he had no qualms about bombs in streets. By the time of his trial in 1804, Cadoudal merely indicated that plans were changing and that Saint-Réjant and others had been discussing various ideas, declaring 'many officers present talked about different means that might be employed in such a situation but this was in conversation and was not a fixed plan.'

Although in his own words it would be 'difficult to prove' that Cadoudal encouraged the bomb plot, still Cadoudal has to bear responsibility for much of the crime. He selected and sent subordinates to Paris, furnishing men he knew to be wild and ferocious with instructions to do away with Bonaparte, and to have the deed done quickly. He had not been too particular regarding the methods, telling the assassin that 'in you alone we place our confidence and all our hope', and if he made excuses and distanced himself from the crime after the event it was not just because of public revulsion, but because he found that many on his own side, the exiled king included, were horrified.

Carbon might have declared that his act of terrorism was for the king, but the king himself disapproved. This stands in contrast to D'Artois who was less squeamish and who had surrounded himself with a retinue intent on striking a blow regardless of the cost in blood, gold and good opinion. His circle and his agents in France had worked closely with Cadoudal making sure that his conspirators had men, money and encouragement and that his essential blow would be landed at a time when they themselves were ready to act. The princely support of D'Artois, and that of those ministers in Whitehall who had closed their eyes as they opened their purses, enabled Cadoudal to push forward with his scheme which, they hoped, would transform their fortunes and return them to Paris in triumph.[11] When the plot failed they were disappointed, but for themselves, and did not condemn it for its cruelty. Indeed the prince's reaction is instructive, for when his secretary Belville told an assembled gathering that the methods employed 'were atrocious, and never should have been used,' the Bishop D'Arras, Dutheil and the Count de Chaussée were seen to maintain an awkward silence and so too did D'Artois, biting his tongue rather than taking the opportunity to speak out in condemnation at the loss of innocent lives.

This should not come as a surprise for everyone connected to anyone in London knew the circle around the prince had been actively running conspiracies in Paris, and Louis de Bouillé noted that the general sentiment amongst the exiles was that, 'they suspected that the royalists sent from London, namely those around the Comte D'Artois and in English pay, may have been equally responsible; this opinion is with merit and I heard confirmation myself from the less than discreet chatter of Hyde de Neuville who was then in London and who had come over from France a short time before the plot had been carried out.'[12]

It is clear that D'Artois had long hoped to decapitate the republic and had encouraged his agents and received funding from Whitehall to further that aim. Only failure subsequently led them to question the methods, and even then the reaction was muted. These men in London, mouthing morality and integrity in public but planning murder in hushed tones, would not go to the scaffold. Only two men would pay for the first act of urban terrorism, and, having killed and wounded indiscriminately, only these two bent before the egalitarian blade of the guillotine. As they did so they were, rightly, condemned as inhuman by their victims and, with less justification, dismissed as isolated fanatics by those who had recently urged them on.

Napoleon knew an opportunity and the moral high ground when he saw it, adept as he was at seizing heights on the battlefield as well as in the cut-throat political theatre of France, and he moved quickly to exploit the anger and confusion in the aftermath of the bomb. It helped him secure his hold on Paris, and by extension, the rest of France. The country, reeling at this early act of urban terrorism, supported him as he cleared away the opposition, allowing him to impose his version of their security and watching with complacency as he drove the left and the right from the field whilst telling France that now there was no safe alternative to Bonaparte. Napoleonic ambition and French blood would keep him on the throne for the next 15 years but the atrocity designed to do away with him played its part, too, in strengthening his grip on power. Cadoudal's plot and the actions of the desperate gang of assassins had not only failed, it had backfired. Indeed, this bungled attempt at killing Napoleon, by failing to blow him away, played an important role in catapulting him to the heights of empire.

POSTSCRIPT

Madrid is unbearably hot in summer and it was in that stifling capital, in August 1804, that a tall, sunburnt Frenchman made his way to the French embassy, the spacious hotel of the Comte de Campo Alange at the Calle de Alcala near Madrid's own arc de triomphe. He was dressed in the blue uniform of the Rutiman Regiment, a Swiss unit in Spanish service, and his attire enabled him to penetrate beyond the footmen and to be ushered into the presence of General Pierre Riel de Beurnonville, the portly ambassador. Beurnonville, another Frenchman who had rejected the priesthood in favour of a career in the revolutionary armies, sat to hear the man's confession. He told the envoy that he was Limoëlan and that, four years after the detonation of the infernal machine, he wished to hand himself in and make his peace with God.

Beurnonville had been in the diplomatic corps long enough to know that facts require confirmation, so he noted down a description of this strange visitor and sent a despatch off to Paris, hoping that the police might have information on French officers in Spanish service, and on Limoëlan. The police were diligent enough and, after checking through various dossiers, informed the ambassador that far from being Limoëlan this man was from the Eure region and had been accused, and arrested, for fraud in 1801. He had then been released from prison in May 1803 and, despite evidently being deranged after his spell in the Consulate's prisons, had made his way to Spain. On 9 September 1804 his identity was confirmed as being that of the so-called Comte de Comminges.

The real Limoëlan had disappeared. He had not drowned in the Seine, nor had he fled to Spain. After going to ground in a Parisian crypt in the aftermath of the explosion he had then retreated to the safety of the fortified manor house at Sevignac in Brittany. He remained there, hiding in contempt of the authorities, until April 1802 when the Treaty of Amiens, and the death of a distant relative in the United States, presented him with an avenue of escape. Boarding Captain Leblanc's *Richemont* and disguised as Granville, the servant of his younger sister, Madame Marie-Thérèse de Chappedelaine and brother-in-law Jean-Baptiste, he sailed from Saint Malo for Savannah. His in-laws held land there on Jekyll Island, but the ship deposited its strange passenger at Norfolk on 5 June and, disguised as Guitry, he first made his way to Baltimore. On 31 January 1805 word, probably from one of the French merchants operating in the south, reached the authorities in Paris that Limoëlan was residing in Savannah. A few months later, in June 1805, the French envoy, General Turreau, was asked to make enquiries but, busy with more pressing matters, he let the matter drop.

Turreau was probably right to concede. The royalist fugitive had, after all, now turned his back on political violence, and was seeking the consolation of religion to shield him from the stings of remorse. After a brief career as a miniaturist, he sought a more worthy vocation and in July 1808 he wrote and told his sister he had entered a seminary in Baltimore and was learning Latin.

Just over four years later, on 1 August 1812, he was ordained as a priest. Inspired by the spirit of his uncle, and encouraged by another exile, Simon Bruté, Bishop of Vincennes, he set to work administering to the congregations of Charleston before attaching himself to a convent of the Order of Visitation in Georgetown (the Monastère des Visitandines de Georgetown). This refuge for the saintly and dispossessed had been founded by Miss Alice Lalor with the support of two wealthy Irish benefactors, and Limoëlan, now known as Father Joseph de Clorivière, found a measure of peace there. He was elevated to aumonier in March 1818 and continued to serve as confessor and moral adviser for another nine years, despite, in 1825, benefiting financially from the Bourbon compensation for property confiscated during the revolution.[1]

His good work came to an abrupt end on 6 May 1826 when he collapsed after mass, possibly after a stroke. He died on 29 September 1826, and was buried just a short distance from the remarkable altar piece which graced the order's little Chapel of the Sacred Heart. It portrayed the scene when Christ entered the home of Martha and Mary and reassured Mary that although she might be 'careful and troubled my many things' listening to his word was all that was needed to soothe an anguished soul. No doubt the thought had consoled Limoëlan, just as much as the gift of the painting had flattered him. After all, it had been donated by the Comte D'Artois following his coronation as King Charles X of France.

CODA

Artois, Charles Philippe, Comte D'

After a further 12 years of exile in Baker Street, D'Artois left for the south of France in 1814. There, as Lieutenant General, he joined Wellington's troops as they restored Bourbon rule in the south of France. Following Napoleon's abdication, he arrived in Paris on 12 April, acting as regent until his obese brother crossed the Channel and assumed the throne as Louis XVIII. Following his brother's death in 1824, the count became king and was crowned Charles X. He provoked a second revolution, fled from Paris to Versailles and abdicated in favour of Louis-Philippe. By 1831 he was back in Holyrood Palace in Edinburgh. He died of cholera in sunnier Gorizia, now in Italy, in 1836.

Bertrand-Quinquet, Louis-Jacques-François de Paule

Bertrand, that expert in interrogation at the prefecture, had managed to put his past behind him by 1800 (in 1794 he had been instrumental in changing the name of his birthplace, Compiègne, to Marat-sur-Oise), but never quite lost sight of his interest in printing. The author of a famous treatise on printing in 1799, he continued as managing director of a print workshop in Rue Saint-Germain-l'Auxerrois despite his onerous duties at the prefecture, until 1802. He then handed responsibility over to his son, Bertrand-Pottier, and continued in his police duties until forced to retire through illness. He died on 12 June 1808.

Bonaparte, Napoleon

On 2 August 1802 Napoleon was voted Consul for life, 3,653,600 voting yes and 8,272 no. On 18 May 1804 Napoleon I was proclaimed Emperor of the French. A plebiscite on 2 August 1804 saw 2,579 objections, and these did not prevent his coronation from taking place on 2 December 1804. He ruled for less than a decade, and died, in exile, on Saint Helena in 1821.

Bourmont, Louis Auguste Victor de Ghaisne, Comte de

Bourmont was kept prisoner in Besançon until he managed to escape in 1804, fleeing to Portugal. There he managed to join the French army of occupation, eventually being promoted to general of brigade in Napoleon's armies. Bourmont celebrated the return of the Bourbons in 1814 but when Napoleon escaped from Elba he once again pledged allegiance to the returning emperor. He served in the final campaign, commanding the 4th Division, but, on the night of 14 June, a few days before Waterloo, he deserted to the Allies along with his aide-de-camp Captain D'Andigné.

Cadoudal, Georges

After fleeing for Britain in September 1801, and considering exile in Canada with 50 companions, this rebel spent much of the next 23 months in lodgings in Broad Street and then Gerard Street, London. On 9 August 1803 he left Hastings for France. He was captured in Paris after a fight in which Inspector Buffet was killed and Inspector

Caniolle wounded. When Dubois chided Cadoudal for having killed a married man, the Chouan shot back that Dubois 'should have sent a bachelor.' Tried, Cadoudal excused the plot to blow up Napoleon with 'many officers present talked about different means that might be employed in such a situation but this was in conversation and was not a fixed plan.' He was executed, along with Aimé-Augustin Joyaux and Jean-Baptiste Coster de Saint-Victor, on 25 June 1804 and Napoleon donated his body to science, with the Chouan's skeleton kept on display in the School of Medicine until 1814.

Desmarest, Pierre-Marie

Desmarest, or Desmaret, from Compiègne, continued as head of the office of the secret police where he sought to foil all the conspiracies and plots against the constitution, the government and the persons who act as first magistrate. He also placed bookshops under surveillance, investigated counterfeit money and forgeries which might be of significance to the government. He was responsible for policing the prison of the Temple and for running secret agents across France and abroad. He nominated individuals suspected of conspiracy for arrest and contributed to editing the daily bulletins on the political situation in Paris and events abroad, which were of significant interest to the government. This was quite a task under Napoleon, and he was rewarded with the title of knight of the empire in 1811. He retired when the Bourbons were restored, briefly returning to the police in 1815, and was then placed under surveillance by Fouché, the Bourbon minister of police. However, Desmarest had disappeared into the shadows and nothing more was heard of him.

Dubois, Louis Nicolas

Dubois was rewarded with a payment of 30,000 Francs, was later nominated to the Council of State and was granted the title of count and the chateau of Vitry-sur-Seine. His fortune lasted until October 1810 when he was dismissed following a fire at the Austrian embassy, which damaged his credibility as head of Parisian security and supervisor of the Parisian fire brigade. He was demoted to serve in the Council of State and as a prison inspector until the restoration of the Bourbons allowed him to retire, gracefully, to count his fortune.

Fouché, Joseph

The minister briefly lost his job when he attempted to stand in the way of making Napoleon consul for life, but he soon returned from the wilderness and remained at the centre of power until 1809 when continual intrigue forced Napoleon to place some distance between the Oratorian and France. Fouché was appointed to govern the Roman states for a while, and spent some time in internal exile at Aix, before being sent to govern the Illyrian provinces in what is now Slovenia and Croatia. From there he went to that nest of intrigue, Naples, before returning to Paris at the first restoration of the Bourbons in April 1814. Snubbed, he was then restored to minister of police when Napoleon returned from Elba and was instrumental in getting Napoleon to abdicate following the disaster at Waterloo. Following the second restoration of the Bourbons in 1815 he was, bizarrely, retained in that position. He proved his loyalty by an active participation in the White Terror, or the settling of scores with Bonapartists who had remained in France. Even this could not save the royalist regicide and, after a brief period as ambassador to Saxony, he was dismissed and sent into exile. He died in exile, in Trieste, on Boxing Day 1826. His son, Athanase, took up service with Charles XIV of Sweden, a man who had once been the Jacobin General Bernadotte, and Fouché's descendants, working their way through the Swedish aristocracy from a country seat in Södermanland province, have married into many of the royal houses of Europe. The second duke of Otranto, Joseph Liberté Fouché, died in 1824 and it is the eighth duke who currently resides at Elghammar castle.

Harel, Jacques

The star witness in the trial of the Conspiracy of the Daggers was promoted *chef de bataillon* on 12 December 1800, having recently received 1,200 Francs for his expenses during the entrapment of the Jacobins accused of plotting Napoleon's death. He was made commandant of the château de Vincennes in March 1801. His wife moved into the grocers shop at number 485 of the elegant Rue Nicaise. On 12 February 1803 after the Legion of Honour was established Harel and Lefebvre wrote to Napoleon stating that 'We broke up the armed conspiracy against the First Magistrate in October 1800. We ask that you reward our conduct by including us in the Legion of Honour.'

Louis XVIII, King

Louis escaped from the long winter at Mitau to take up residence at Warsaw in March 1801, a journey marked by the pain of gout and the band welcoming him by playing *La Marseillaise*. He eventually sought refuge in England, landing in Yarmouth in 1807 and finding, when his wife joined him in 1808, that Goswell Hall was too small for him and his family. He moved on to Hartwell Hall in April, renting it for £500 per year, only returning to France when it was safe to do so in May 1814. He fled to Ghent when Napoleon escaped from Elba in 1814 but was restored to his throne by Wellington's victory at Waterloo in June 1815. Louis ruled until gangrene, gout and complications brought on by his obesity killed him in 1824. He was buried in Saint Denis and his ingenious wheelchair is on display at the Chateau de Breteuil.

Neuville, Jean-Guillaume Hyde de

Hyde and his wife were in Rue Faubourg Saint-Honoré, staying with Aglaé de Damas, when the bomb went off. Hyde went to ground in the provinces and La Rochelle before managing to quit France for New York. There, teaching and practising medicine, he saved enough to purchase an estate on the Raritan River in Somerset County, New Brunswick, he breeding sheep whilst his wife showed a vocation for sketching. There he waited until the Bourbons returned to France and, back in Paris, he found himself promoted to French ambassador to Washington.

Picot de Clorivière, Pierre-Joseph

The elderly uncle of Limoëlan did not entirely escape from the clutches of the Parisian police. They had failed to find him during their searches following the explosion, but, in April 1804, Napoleon seems to have remembered the former Jesuit and urged General Moncey of the gendarmerie to find the old man. He had last been seen in the Archbishop of Aix's house and so the gendarmes were charged with proceeding with caution and to take account of the respect due to that personage. However, Picot de Clorivière had left for Paris with his old friend, Mademoiselle de Cicé. The police traced him to Rue Notre-Dame-des-Champs and arrested him on 6 May 1804. The former Jesuit, 'tall, with grey hair, brown eyebrows and a plain face, grey-blue eyes, small mouth and pointed chin', was asked where he was on the night of the explosion. He told his interrogators that he had been amongst the pious, but would not compromise anyone by naming them. Probed for more information as to whether he tended the man who had set off the bomb, the holy man replied 'I will only tell you when I believe I may do so without compromising anyone. It is not a crime to minister to an individual who is unknown to me or who I have never met and, if there is a risk in doing so then that makes such ministrations resemble more an act of heroism rather than something I should be reproached for.' Picot de Clorivière did not co-operate and was taken to the Force prison before being transferred to the Temple in July 1804 where he lived in some comfort, ordering meals from a local restaurant owner for 20 sous per head. He found time to finish his *Commentary on the Apocalypse* and was eventually released in April 1809. He lived to see the restoration of his beloved Bourbons and died on 9 January 1820.

Piis, Augustin de

The poetic chevalier of the police force continued to work as secretary at the prefecture, and welcomed the Bourbon restoration in 1814. For that hasty commitment to the royal cause he was demoted to archivist during the Hundred Days. Following the fall of Napoleon he went into retirement. Throughout his career and his enforced retirement he continued to compose songs, ballads and poems. He died in 1832.

Réal, Pierre-François

Réal, who had promoted Dubois to prefect of police, had made good use of the contacts he had made as a lawyer then a journalist under the revolution. His closeness to Barras made him close to Josephine, and therefore indispensable to Napoleon. The First Consul made him a councillor of state, using him as a counterweight to Fouché and a man who knew how to fill the gap between the law and public opinion. He went on to be showered with honours and titles, being created count of the empire in 1808 and taking up residence at the exquisite country seat of Boulogne-Billancourt. This contrast with his Jacobin roots singled him out as a hypocrite, a detractor noting that 'the highway assassin is preferable to the fearful and hypocritical Réal; you are on your guard against the former, whilst the second, with all the appearance of virtue, makes you fall into his traps.' Réal was appointed prefect of police in Paris following Napoleon's return from Elba in March 1815 but he was expelled by the returning Bourbons after Waterloo and went into exile in Belgium. Shortly afterwards he emigrated to New York, buying land next to Joseph Bonaparte at Cape Vincent. In 1819 he was pardoned and Hyde de Neuville, then French ambassador, issued his passport. However, he only returned to France in 1827, becoming adviser to the new prefect of police following the revolution of 1830. He died in 1834.

ANNEX

A list of those wounded by the blast, taken from Dubois's report of 30 October 1801 (Arch. préf. Pol. AA 273). This informed the Minister of the Interior how the sums raised by public subscription were spent.

Name	Address	Amount received in Francs	Comments
Banny, Jean-Frédéric	33 Rue des Grands-Augustins	1000P* plus 400 per year	19 years old, married, without children, a cripple and no longer capable of physical work
Barbier, Marie-Géneviève Viel	1383 Rue Saint Honoré	1000P* plus 100 Francs per year and a place in a hospice	Lost an eye and the use of a hand
Bataille, Madame,	481 Rue Nicaise	100	A grocer, wife of Francois-Gilles

Name	Address	Amount received in Francs	Comments
Beirlé, Alexandre	333 Rue Nicaise	800P* plus 500 per year	Wounded and left with a two-year-old child to raise
Boiteux, Jean-Marie-Joseph	4 Rue Clopin	50	A former cleric
Bonnet, Madame	513 Rue Nicaise	200	Affected by the explosion
Catherine-Julie Gaucheron, known as Widow Boulard	Rue Jean-Jacques Rousseau	4000 and a further 3000	Tendons in the right hand damaged, unable to play the pianoforte
Bourdin, Françoise Louvrier	503 Rue Nicaise	50	Lightly wounded
Buchener, Louis	513 Rue Nicaise	25	Lightly wounded
Chapuis, Gilbert	253 Rue du Bacq	800	Wounded by flying glass, his right arm still painful
Charles, Jean-Etienne	513 Rue Nicaise	400	A printer
Clement, Citizen	Rue du Petit Carousel [sic]	50	Blacksmith's assistant
Cléreaux, Marie-Joséphine-Rosalie Lehodey	333 Rue Neuve Egalité	3800	Widowed by the blast, mother of an 18-month baby
Colinet, Marie Jeanne Cécile	551 Marché des Innocens	200	Wounded in the head
Corbet, Nicolas-Alexandre	Rue Saint Honoré	240	Spat blood and had blood coming out of his ears, took a month to recover
Couteux, Citizen	510 Rue des Prouvaires	150	Pasta maker wounded in the head

Name	Address	Amount received in Francs	Comments
Duverne, Louis	4 Rue du Harlay	1000	Locksmith still troubled by a chest wound which was refusing to heal
Fleury, Catherine Lenoir	6 Rue Batave	50	Was sent to a hospice for a month due to state of shock
Fostier, Louis-Philippe	449 Rue Marceau	25	Lightly wounded postal worker
Fritzeri, Alexandre-Marie-Antoine	Rue Nicaise (unknown number)	750	Italian mandolin player and composer
Gauthier, Marie-Poncette	39 Rue de Chaillot	100	Wounded with abscess in the head
Harel, Antoine	375 Rue de Malte	3000	Waiter, lost his right eye and damaged his left
Iblot (or Hiblot), Marie Anne	377 Rue de Malte	240	Clothes shredded and wounded in the chest and leg
Honoré, Marie Thérèse Larue	62 Rue Marceau	100	Wounded in the neck
Honoré, Thérèse	62 Rue Marceau	50	Wounded whilst walking with her mother
Huguet, Louis	Allée des Veuves aux Champs Elysées	50	Wounded by fragments of paving stone
Jardy, Julien	80 Rue Saint Honoré	100	Lightly wounded
Kalbert, Jean-Antoine	Maison Conti, 238 Rue Saint Dominique	100	Injured in the right hand
Lambert, Marie-Jacqueline Gillot	203 Rue Froidmanteau	100	Knee damaged as she was blown over by the blast

Name	Address	Amount received in Francs	Comments
Lefevre, Simon-François	127 Rue de la Verrerie	200	Lightly wounded
Léger, Catherine	Café d'Apollon	1500	Wounded badly and still finds it difficult to walk
Lepape, Elisabeth Satabin	514 Rue Nicaise	300	Wounded in the head, hospitalised for 43 days
Lemiere, Nicolas	474 Rue de Malte	400	Wounded in the face
Lion, Pierre-Louis-Nicolas	Allée d'Antin	600	Treated in the Roule hospital, foreign matter forced into his wounds had caused infections
Masse, Jean François	77 Rue des Saints-Pères	150	Wounded on the crown of the head
Mitaine, Jeanne-Prevost	491 or 493 [sic] Rue de Malte	450 plus 100 Francs per year and a place in a hospice	A 78-year-old pauper, hit in the head, and asking to be placed in a hospice as she is unable to support herself
Lemercier (or Mercier), Jean-Baptiste	1351 Rue Saint Honoré	4500	Heavily wounded, with many wounds on the chest, face and back, and loss of the right eye
Orillard, Stéphanie Madeleine-Charlotte	646 Rue de Lille	900	Generally mutilated
Palluel, Citizen	474 Rue Nicaise	50	A porter, lightly wounded
Préville, Claude Barthélemy	1234 Rue des Saints-Pères	4500	Disfigured, loss of right eye, numerous teeth and use of right hand

Name	Address	Amount received in Francs	Comments
Proverbi, Antoine	Hotel Angleterre, Rue des Filles Thomas	750	Wounded in the head, shoulder and knee; returned to Milan
Regnault, Madame	Rue de Grenelle Saint Honoré	200	Head wounds and contusions
Saint-Gilles, Louise	6 Galerie des Innocens	400	Cut by glass and wounded by collapsing ceiling
Selleque, Widow	Rue Denis	200	Her invalid husband died from the effects of shock
Thirion, Jean	513 Rue Nicaise	25	Tailor, suffering from symptoms of shock
Trépsat, Citizen	395 Rue de Bourgogne	4500	Left leg amputated and seven more wounds of a serious nature
Varlet, Citizen	552 Rue Saint Louis	25	Lightly wounded
Vitriée, Elisabeth	334 Rue Nicaise	100	Citizen Ricard's pregnant cook was lightly wounded
Vitry, Citizen	513 Rue Nicaise	50	Wounded in the leg
Warmé, Citizen	514 Rue Nicaise	100	Lightly wounded
Warmé, Madame	514 Rue Nicaise	Share of the above	Lightly wounded
Wolff, Arnoult	Rue de Malte	150	Was knocked over whilst standing by the window, his wife also lost four teeth
Zambrini, Felix	Place de la Concorde	150	Wounded when fragments blown into his body

P* = Provisional award

Other awards

Agnès Adélaide Norris of 680 Rue de Lille left three orphaned children. Two boys (aged 14 and 9) were found places as a midshipman and military cadet, and the girl (aged 7) was granted fees to allow her to attend school. Grandmother Norris, aged 78, and who maintained herself through work, was granted 1200 Francs and a place in a hospice. Widow Boyeledieu was granted a one-off sum of 1500 Francs and 400 per year to support her children whilst the widow of Citizen Platel, Jeanne Smith, of Place des Americains in Lille, was granted 1000 Francs and 300 per year so she could look after her son (aged 5) and daughter (aged 10).

BIBLIOGRAPHY

Manuscripts
British Library Additional Manuscripts
Add MS 37851; Add Ms 37869; Add Ms 37903 (Windham's notes);
   Add Ms 37904; Add Ms 38769 (Huskisson Papers, payments to
   royalists); Add Ms 51463; Add Ms 51465.

Unfortunately, or fortunately depending on one's point of view, many
   of the Parisian police records were burnt when the prefecture
   was destroyed in 1871. Only some documents survived. Most
   relevant are the criminal records held in Series A, sub-series AA
   271–361. Prison records can be found in the sub-series AB. Of
   relevance to this work are Arch. préf. Pol. AA 273 (Dubois on
   the subscription opened for victims) and 276 (7 nivôse an IX); as
   well as Arch. préf. Pol. AA 281 (8 nivôse an IX) and 282.

At the Archives nationales, series Arch. nat. F⁷ includes much
   material which was preserved from ministerial files, particularly
   in sub-series 104 to 167 on the emigrants and 6139 to 6997 on
   political affairs. The dossier on the Nicaise plot is in cartons

6271 to 6276, dossier 5588 being particularly relevant. The *conspiration anglaise* is in cartons 6245 to 6251, the Ceracchi affair in 6267, and that of many Chouans in Paris in 6228 to 6236 and 6284, 6285 and 6300.

Published sources

Allen, Robert. *Les tribunaux criminels sous la Révolution et l'Empire 1792–1811*. Rennes, 2005.

Almanach du commerce de Paris pour l'An IX. Paris, 1801.

Anon. 'L'attentat de la rue Saint-Nicaise, Liaisons', in *Bulletin d'information de la Préfecture de police*, 161, 1969.

Aulard, A. *L'Etat de la France en L'An VIII et en L'An IX*. Paris, 1897.

Aulard, A. *Paris sous le Consulat*. Two volumes. Paris, 1904.

Arvengas J. 'Le Comte Dubois, premier Préfet de Police (1758–1847)', in *Revue du Nord*, 39/154, 1957.

Blanc, O. *Les Espions de la Révolution et de l'Empire*. Paris, 1995.

Bouillé, F C A, Marquis de. *Souvenirs et fragments pour servir aux Mémoires de ma vie*. Paris, 1911.

Broers, Michael. *Napoleon: Soldier of Destiny*. London, 2014.

Bruyant, Pierre. 'Trois innocents guillotinés. Episode du ministère Fouché sous le Consulat', in *Bulletin de la Société percheronne d'histoire et d'archéologie*, 3, 1904.

Cadoudal, G de. *Georges de Cadoudal et la Chouannerie*. Paris, 1887.

Caudrillier, G. *La trahison de Pichegru*. Paris, 1908.

Caudrillier, G. 'Le complot de l'An XII', in *Revue historique*, 75/76, 1901 and 1902.

Clauss, Charles. *Le jury sous le Consulat et le Premier Empire*. Thesis, Paris, 1905.

Clayton, Tim. *This Dark Business: The Secret War against Napoleon*. London, 2018.

Cobb, R. Death in Paris. Oxford, 1978.

Condamnation à mort de douze brigands qui étaient venus d'Angleterre en France pour assassiner le premier consul. Détails des crimes commis par eux. Leur projet de mettre Paris à feu et à sang. Noms de ces brigands, auteurs et complices de la machine infernale du trois nivôse. Récit des massacres et des assassinats commis par eux dans les départements de l'Ouest. Paris, c. 1801.

Conspiration Anglaise. Paris, 1801.

D'Abrantès, L. *Mémoires de Madame la duchesse d'Abrantès, ou Souvenirs historiques sur Napoléon.* Paris, 1833.

D'Andigné, L. *Mémoires du général d'Andigné.* Volume 1. Paris, 1900.

D'Hauterive, E. *La police secrète du Premier Empire.* Paris, 1913.

Darrah, D. *Conspiracy in Paris: The Strange Career of Joseph Picot de Limoelan.* New York, 1953.

Daudet, E. *Histoire de l'émigration. Les émigrés et la seconde coalition, 1797–1800.* Paris, 1886.

Daudet, E. *Histoire de l'émigration pendant la Révolution française.* Paris, 1904.

Daudet, E. *La Police et les Chouans sous le Consulat et l'Empire.* Paris, 1885.

Deladouespe, Jacques-Étienne-Louis. *Papiers et correspondance de J.-É.-L. Deladouespe.* Paris, 1904.

Denis, V. 'L'épuration de la police parisienne et les 'origines tragiques' du dossier individuel sous la Restauration', in *Revue d'histoire moderne et contemporaine*, 59/1, 2012.

Desmarest, Pierre Marie. *Témoignages historiques ou Quinze ans de Haute Police sous Napoleon.* Paris, 1833.

Destrem, Jean. *Le Dossier d'un Déporté de 1804.* Paris, 1904.

Destrem, Jean. *Les déportations du Consulat,* Paris, 1878.

Détails de l'événement malheureux arrivé hier soir au coin de la rue de Malte et Nicaise, un moment après le passage du Consul Bonaparte. Paris, 1801.

Duncan, K. 'A Blast from the Past: Lessons from a Largely Forgotten Incident of State-Sponsored Terrorism', in *Perspectives on Terrorism*, 5/1, 2011.

Durey, M. 'Lord Grenville and the "Smoking Gun": The Plot to Assassinate the French Directory in 1798–1799 Reconsidered', in *The Historical Journal*, 45/3, 2002.

Dwyer, Philip. *Citizen Emperor: Napoleon in Power*. London, 2013.

Fauriel, C. *Les derniers jours du consulat.* Paris, 1886.

Fescourt, *Histoire de la double conspiration de 1800 contre le gouvernement consulaire.* Paris, 1819.

Gaubert, H. *Conspirateurs au temps de Napoléon Ier.* Paris, 1962.

Gavoty, Georges. 'Les lettres de cachet sous le Consulat et l'Empire', in *Revue hebdomadaire*, 1, 1907.

Godechot, J. *The Counterrevolution: Doctrine and Action, 1789–1804.* London, 1972.

Guillot, J. *Révolution et chouannerie en Morbihan.* Gourin, 2014.

Hall, J R. *General Pichegru's Treason.* London, 1915.

Forneron, H. *Histoire générale des émigrés pendant la révolution française.* Paris, 1884.

Hue, G. *Un complot de police sous le consulat. La conspiration de Ceracchi et Aréna (Vendémiaire an IX).* Paris, 1909.

Huerta, Carlos de la. *The Great Conspiracy: Britain's Secret War against Revolutionary France.* Stroud, 2016.

Hyde de Neuville, J G. *Mémoires et souvenirs du Baron Hyde de Neuville.* Volume 1. Paris, 1892.

Lanzac de Laborie, L de. *Paris sous Napoleon.* Paris, 1905.

Le Turc et le militaire français, dialogue sur l'expédition d'Égypte et analyse des dépêches de Menou, relatives à l'assassinat du général Kléber, commandant en chef de l'armée d'Orient. Paris, 1800.

Lebon, A. *L'Angleterre et l'émigration française de 1794 à 1801.* Paris, 1882.

Lentz, Thierry. *Nouvelle Histoire du Premier Empire.* Paris, 2007.

Lettre du Ministre de la police générale au général Meynier, commandant la 18° division militaire, donnant les signalements de quatre criminels mêlés au complot du 3 nivôse contre le Premier Consul. Paris, 1801.

Lignereux, A. 'Le moment terroriste de la chouannerie: des atteintes à l'ordre public aux attentats contre le Premier Consul', in *La Révolution française*, 1, 2012.

Lorédan, J. *La machine infernale de la rue Nicaise (3 nivôse, an IX).* Paris, 1924.

Martel, M A de. *Étude sur l'affaire de la machine infernale du 3 nivôse an IX.* Paris, 1870.

Martel, M A de. *Les Historiens fantaisistes. M Thiers. Conspiration de Cadoudal.* Paris, 1887.

Martel, M A de. *Les Historiens fantaisistes. M Thiers. La pacification de l'ouest. La machine infernale.* Paris, 1885.

Masson, F. 'Les complots Jacobins au lendemain de Brumaire', in *Revue des études napoléoniennes*, 18, 1922.

Mitchell, H. *The Underground War against Revolutionary France: the Missions of William Wickham, 1794–1800.* Oxford, 1965.

Monney, Denise. 'Un complot contre Bonaparte sous le Consulat, Liaisons', in *Bulletin d'information de la Préfecture de police*, 252, 1981.

Napoleon. *Correspondance.* Volume III. Paris, 2006.

Nodier, Charles. *Les prisons de Paris sous le Consulat*, in Volume VIII of Œuvres complètes, Paris, 1833.

Papiers saisis à Bareuth et à Mende, département de la Lozère. Publié par ordre du gouvernement. Paris, 1802.

Paris et ses curiosités ou Nouveau guide du voyageur à Paris. Paris, 1802.

Pasquier, E-D. *Mémoires du chancelier Pasquier: histoire de mon temps*. Paris, 1893.

Peuchet, J. *Mémoires tirés des archives de la police de Paris: pour servir à l'histoire de la morale et de la police, depuis Louis XIV jusqu'à nos jours*. Paris, 1838.

Pocock, Tom. *The Terror before Trafalgar: Nelson, Napoleon and the Secret War*. London, 2003.

Polnay, P de. *Napoleon's Police*. London, 1970.

Pommeret, Hervé. *La Troisième Chouannerie*. Saint-Brieuc, 1935.

Procès instruit par le tribunal criminel du Départément de la Seine, contre Demerville, Ceracchi, etc. Paris, 1801.

Procès instruit par le tribunal criminel du Départément de la Seine, contre les nommés Saint-Réjant, Carbon, et autres, prévenus de conspiration contre la personne du Premier Consul; suivi du jugement du Tribunal de cassation qui a rejeté le pourvoi des condamnés. Two volumes. Paris, 1801.

Rao, A M. *L'emigrazione politica italiane in Francia (1792–1802)*. Naples, 1992.

Rapp, J. *Mémoires du général Rapp*. Paris, 1823.

Rapports officiels et complets faits au gouvernement par le préfet de police de Paris [Dubois] sur la conspiration tramée depuis six mois contre le premier consul Bonaparte et l'explosion de la machine infernale. Paris, 1801.

Réal. P F. *Indiscrétions: Souvenirs anecdotiques et politiques*. Paris, 1835.

Remacle, Comte de. *Bonaparte et les Bourbons. Relations secrètes des agents de Louis XVIII à Paris sous le Consulat.* Paris, 1899.

Rigotard, Jean. *Les commissaires de police de Paris sous le Consulat et l'Empire.* Thesis, Paris, 1995.

Rohu, J. 'Mémoires autographes de Jean Rohu', in *Revue de Bretagne et de Vendée*, 2, 1857 and 3 1858.

Salomé, K. 'L'attentat de la rue Nicaise en 1800: l'irruption d'une violence inédite?', in *Revue d'histoire du XIXe siècle*, 40, 2010.

Sanson, H. *Sept générations d'exécuteurs, 1688–1847: mémoires des Sanson.* Paris, 1862.

Schmidt, A. *Paris sous la Révolution d'après les rapports de la police secrète, 1789–1800.* Paris, 1867.

Sewrin, C A B. *Hilaire et Berthille ou la machine infernale de la rue S. Nicaise.* Paris, 1802.

Signalements de plusieurs individus dont la recherche et l'arrestation sont ordonnées par le gouvernement. Paris, 1804.

Sparrow, E. 'The Alien Office, 1792–1806', in *The Historical Journal*, 33, 1990.

Sparrow, E. 'The Swiss and Swabian Agencies, 1795–1801', in *The Historical Journal*, 35, 1992.

Sydenham, Michael J. *The crime of 3 nivôse (24 décembre 1800)*, in Boscher (J. F.), ed. *French Government and Society, 1500–1850. Essays in Memory of Alfred Cobban.* London, 1973.

Taws, Richard. 'Infernal Machines in Nineteenth-Century France', in Dethloff D, ed., *Burning Bright: Essays in Honour of David Bindman.* London, 2015.

Thibaudeau, A-C. *Mémoires sur le Consulat, 1799 à 1804, par un ancien conseiller d'État.* Paris, 1827.

Thiry, J. *La machine infernale.* Paris, 1952.

Vandal, A. *L'avènement de Bonaparte.* Paris, 1911.

Vaudreuil, H. F. *Correspondance intime du comte de Vaudreuil et du comte D'Artois, 1789–1815.* Paris, 1889.

Villeneuve, P L B de. *Le vrai Limoëlan: de la machine infernale à la visitation.* Paris, 1984.

Waresquiel, E de. 'Joseph Fouché et la question de l'amnistie des émigrés (1799–1802)', in *Annales historiques de la Révolution française*, 372, 2013.

Wickham, W. *The Correspondence of the Right Honourable William Wickham.* Volume II. London, 1870.

Windham, William. The Windham Papers. London, 1913.

NOTES

Introduction
1. Brutal deaths which pale next to the murder of King Alexander I of Serbia who was shot, stabbed and then thrown from a window in 1903.

Revolutionary Fever
1. A young lawyer from Flanders, Maximilien Robespierre, even spoke out for the abolition of the death penalty in May 1791.
2. Liberty, equality, fraternity was only made the official slogan of the republic after 1794, previously 'liberty, equality, fraternity, or death' had found favour. The original phrase was perhaps coloured by Chamfort's bon mot that the republicans were essentially saying 'be my brother, or I shall kill you.'
3. The Association bretonne of the Marquis de La Rouërie was an early network of resistance to the new regime in Paris.
4. Napoleon had come up to Paris in May and had taken sick leave in the capital. Nominated to command a brigade in the west he sent his baggage on (it was captured by the Chouans in July) but remained in the capital. He was soon appointed to the Army of the Interior instead.
5. Forcing Louis XVIII to flee from Verona. The king eventually established his bitter little court at Mitau, now Jelgava, in Latvia.
6. Pichegru managed to escape to Dutch Suriname and from there to the United States. He was in London by June 1798.
7. Lorédan, p. 12. Itemised in the Huskisson Papers, Add Ms 38769.
8. Jean Rohu, one of Cadoudal's lieutenants, even heard that George III was offering 200 Guineas and a voyage to Canada for those who could no longer stomach the fight or live in a republic.

A Coup of Grace

1. The deputy Riffard Saint-Martin declared that this was a myth, that no one threatened Napoleon with either daggers or pistols. But the Napoleonic legend of this new Caesar this time escaping the daggers of Brutus was too good to resist.

2. What a difference a few years make. In December 1797 Louis Bro 'was so close that I was able to reach out and touch his hand. He fixed me with a menacing stare and I cried out "Long Live Bonaparte!" "Young man," he declared, "you better shout Long Live the Republic" and, saying that, he smiled.'

3. Madame de Chastenay, who was intimate with Napoleon's circle in 1800, wrote 'he considered the republican edifice to be flawed, the great slogans discredited if not empty of meaning.'

4. A royalist agent noted that Napoleon himself was made up of factions: 'a third philosopher, a third Jacobin, a third aristocrat, but not an atom which was royalist'.

5. To prepare the palace for its new resident the revolutionary slogans above the palace doors were removed. Only one was overlooked, bearing the refrain 'the monarchy has been abolished in France, never to return.'

6. He would later tell Abrial 'I cannot keep you as a minister, you are too honest a man to be that of the police'.

7. Talleyrand's bon mot was that the three consuls were Hic, Haec, Hoc (masculine, for Napoleon, feminine, for Cambacérès and neuter for Lebrun). An anonymous wit thought that the Consulate was 100 times better than the revolution, as it had one consul followed by two zeros.

8. On 20 October 1800 measures against the many categories of emigrants were boldly dropped. Some 52,000 royalists, including deported priests, the wives and the children of those who had fled the revolution, now found themselves reinstated back into French society following a simple oath of loyalty to the constitution. The list was reduced to 3,373 names, and now mostly comprising nobles serving in foreign armies.

9. Limoëlan's father had been executed on 18 June 1793 after having been denounced as a royalist by an informer. His wife had tried to persuade the representative on mission in Nantes to intervene and win a reprieve. But to no avail. That official's name was Joseph Fouché.

10. The British, with 13,000 men led by the Grand Old Duke of York, and a Russian contingent, had landed in the Netherlands in August

1799 leading to ignominy when on 18 October the allies evacuated the Low Countries. The French also beat the Russians and Austrians at Zurich that September, and pursued the allies through treacherous mountain paths with such élan that, on 22 October, Russia pulled out of the coalition altogether, slamming the door as it left.

11. Napoleon's comment was 'tell him to be careful that he is not being messed about and to conclude negotiations quickly, given that the consuls wish for all this to be concluded in December.' Fouché would prove even more dubious, sending in report after report listing royalist breaches of the truce.

12. Châtillon had already written to Windham on 7 November saying that 'unless money was sent promptly, along with arms and munitions then I, along with the other captains, shall be obliged to treat.'

13. Cadoudal, p. 211. Cadoudal had told Sir John Warren that Bonaparte would try to offer them favourable terms, but that he, Cadoudal, would not accept them so long as England supported the Chouans.

14. The British had landed a huge supply of arms on 27 and 28 November. Six artillery pieces, thousands of muskets and 60 carts of powder were delivered to the royal armies.

15. Napoleon, rather archly, would later counter that Louis XVIII could be made king of a unified Poland. Louis was furious, writing 'And what crown does he offer me? That of a country ruled by the three most powerful sovereigns of Europe, one of whom is my benefactor ... My silence and contempt shall be my only answer to his insolent and insidious proposal.'

16. The connection was probably engineered by the Bishop of Arras, D'Artois's confessor, who had sent La Tour du Pin-Gouvernet to sound the minister out on a future compromise.

17. D'Andigné, p. 416-7.

18. D'Andigné, p. 418.

19. D'Andigné, p. 422.

20. London was deluded about Napoleon's intentions. On 31 December 1799 Canning had told Windham 'I am persuaded that the whole game is in our hands now, and that it wants little more than patience to play it well, to the end.'

21. D'Andigné, p. 428.

22. D'Artois had written to Châtillon saying that he had heard how 'you have come to a temporary arrangement with the tyrants of our country' and promising to send money and arms, and to appear himself to lead those true Frenchmen, loyal to their God and king, against the republic.

23. The timing was important as Napoleon wished to transfer his soldiers eastwards against the recalcitrant Austrians in time for a spring offensive.

24. Correspondance, 4872, 14 January 1799.

25. Correspondance, 4976, 13 February 1799.

26. Later Bishop of Orleans. Napoleon's view of him was that 'I know he is a scoundrel, but I need him.'

27. Martel, 1885, p. 104. On 19 January Captain William Lukin in Quiberon Bay informed Windham that Georges had been onboard the *Boudica* to collect the monies and oversee the landing of supplies.

28. Bourmont knew the game was up, and even London was realizing that the royalist armies were beaten. Windham wrote that 'poor Georges' situation having become so exceedingly critical from the conduct of the other chiefs who have absolutely made peace. Again, whatever might have induced the leaders of this party to make a peace, the name of which is as strong a mark as possible of their growing power and of the fears of Bonaparte, yet I cannot forgive them for having made it without consulting Georges or at least having an eye to his safety in the treaty.'

29. Memecourt is a mistake for Chalmel-Menlicourt, whilst Lavi Dubois is none other than L'Air du Bois.

30. A letter by General Gardanne states categorically that 'General Guidal, to whom I'd given the order to capture them dead or alive, has arrested them and will send them to Paris with a strong escort.' General Lefebvre seems to have met this column at Verneuil and had the royalist officers tried and executed in great haste.

31. Napoleon was taken aback by the numbers and decreed that all dossiers should be submitted by 3 March 1800.

32. Cadoudal, p. 230. Brune's impression of Cadoudal was that 'he was not a fervent monarchist or attached to the emigrants, but desirous of seeming the most important man in the region and the one who was in charge of the locals.' When Brune offered him the command of volunteers in republican service, Cadoudal replied 'that he could not be seen as an apostate so soon, but that in two or three months he might decide to serve the republic, and would do so with as much fervour as he had hitherto served the rebels.'

33. It stated, falsely, that he was a landowner born in Vannes and resident in Nantes.

34. Some discussion was held on 13 March as to how many officers Cadoudal wanted removing from the list of emigrants, Cadoudal proposing 19 men, including Sol de Grisolles and Saint-Réjant.

35. Martel, 1885, p. 206.

36. He covered his departure by a ruse, ordering dinner for 20 guests then sending one of his men off with his passport whilst himself climbing into a coach with a trusted lieutenant. A police spy noted: 'they say he has left for his region with Biget.'

37. Those caught by the gendarmes were incorporated into Free Companies and sent to Brest or Rochefort to form fodder for the machetes and mosquitoes of the West Indies. Napoleon had been explicit about this, telling General Gardanne on 20 February that: 'when you have collected 200 or 300 send them under escort to Brest where orders await for them to be enrolled into the troops bound for Saint Domingue.'

38. Strangely there was a rumour amongst the gossips of Paris that Napoleon was the rightful heir, being himself a descendant of the brother of Louis XIV, the famous man in the iron mask.

39. Thiry, p. 3.

40. Thiry, p. 3. Talleyrand, when asked by Montesquiou whether the letter had progressed matters, replied that 'for the present, no; for the future, yes' and that Napoleon 'was more desirous of glory than titles', making it clear that royalist hopes would have to wait.

Agents and Spies

1. Wickham, p. 38. 13 April 1797.

2. It had been bad for years although in 1798 and 1799 it had improved thanks to a generous subsidy from Czar Paul and the possible release of Marie Antoinette's unpaid dowry following the wedding of the Duke d'Angoulême to Madame Royale. If the Emperor of Austria paid up, Louis stood to gain at least 200,000 écu.

3. Louis-Hilaire de Conzié, an ultra not given to compromise and viewed as 'a liar, gossip, ignoramus, of poor judgement and always wanting to do something but without the means to achieve anything and without having thought things through' according to the king's advisers.

4. He ended up in London. There on 22 July 1812 he and his wife were murdered in their home at 27 The Terrace, Barnes, by their Italian servant, who then shot himself.

5. D'André was well connected, his contacts including Consul Lebrun, a man who had declared that he would like 'to serve the king, should a favourable opportunity present itself.'

6. Daudet, p. 172.

7. Forneron, III, p. 199.

8. From where François Mallet-Butini (or Mallet de Crécy) had him shipped over the Channel. Mallet was a Swiss officer, married to Anne Molesworth, who ran various ineffective Chouan bands along the Seine but who was, more importantly, the Royal Agency's chief point of contact in northern France.

9. *Conspiration Anglaise*, p. 8. The Institutes were a national cadre of royalists kept ready in case of a more general rising.

10. It was probably just as well that he had not heard that a doctor in Gex had written to Condé suggesting that he be allowed to introduce the plague into France to punish the republicans.

11. Hyde de Neuville, grandson of a Jacobite, had been wanted by the police since 1797. He had gone to ground in Paris, and had nearly been arrested on the Pont Saint-Michel. Only some quick-thinking by his wife, who unfurled her umbrella into the faces of the two arresting officers, and Hyde's long legs, allowed him to escape. In September 1799 Coigny saved him from further persecution by sending him to Britain to act as liaison with D'Artois.

12. He moved in to 46 Baker Street in June 1799. This allowed him to be close to the centre of power, and to his mistress, Madame de Polastron. Two months later British ministers were hoping they could move him to Jersey.

13. Indeed their plan even featured General Dumouriez, who had been in exile since 1792, landing a Danish contingent in British pay in Normandy before marching on Paris where some 300 audacious men were ready for a coup, an imaginative but impractical scheme. A second, and even more ridiculous, idea had Dumouriez go to Egypt to bribe Napoleon's abandoned army in Egypt to switch sides, and to then land it in Provence.

14. Amongst other items was an indication that Barras was open to negotiating an end to the republic.

15. Massena, the victor in Switzerland, certainly had ambition, but he told Napoleon he would not seek to replace him for fear that upon leaving the Tuileries he would be shot by the Consular Guard.

16. Hyde de Neuville would attempt to get Toustain freed but, failing that, hoped to find the names and addresses of the judges who had condemned the chevalier to death, so that there might be retribution. The royalists got the names but the office boys and clerks had been told not to pass on any addresses, and would not be bribed.

17. *Conspiration Anglaise*, p. 114.

18. Hyde communicated every Monday and Thursday, sending couriers up to Boulogne or Rouen. These were then brought over to Britain

by agents, the most unusual of which was a distant relation of Wickham's by marriage, namely Arabella Mallet, daughter of David and Lucy Mallet and widow of Major Williams of the Royal Office of Ordnance. She had been born in Geneva and had been in English service for some time, being given the codename Petit Matelot.

19. A phrase repeated to Dutheil: 'We'll treat Felix [Bonaparte] the same way we would have treated Barras and his friends.'

20. Margadel was the 'commander of a little army of insurrection in Paris which the Comte D'Artois had tried to organise,' according to Louis XVIII's agents. He was in a safe house in Saint Germaine en Laye. He received 4,832 Francs from Hyde but managed to spend 505 Francs on Champagne and 1,966 on three horses. Only 300 went on arming the band, each man getting a dagger and a pair of pistols, which suggests that it was rather a small army.

21. Daudet, 1904, p. 407. Grenville probably agreed; he had already told Windham that 'I wish the agents there [Paris] were more capable than I fear they are.'

22. Fouché's agents had infiltrated what remained of the royalist network around Augsburg and had already got wind that Willot was planning to organise a rebellion in Provence. One of Willot's agents was arrested in Paris that April and police agents confiscated some bills of exchange signed Southers being used to pay royalist agents. Further correspondence, signed with Willot's nom de guerre Mesnard, also fell into police hands.

23. Condé's inclusion in the plan was strange as he had written to Wickham asking for asylum in England, wanting nothing more than 'a country house, with a garden, and a reasonable climate, altogether something comfortable rather than magnificent'.

24. Within a year the British had pensioned off the officers and were hoping to send the 690 remaining rank-and-file to Egypt, all despite having promised the corps that they would only be employed on services useful to the restoration of Louis XVIII. The Enghien Regiment promptly passed over to Napoleon's side.

25. Although he subsequently told General Brune: 'I had a high opinion of Bonaparte. I would serve him honestly, but he won't be in power for long. I have details as to why. I'll tell Bonaparte about it if I get to see him. Siéyès wants to be rid of him, I'm certain, and he wants to put an Orléans on the throne.'

26. They crossed on 13 April and reached London on the 17th or 18th of the same month, Windham noting on 18 April 'Received note from Georges informing me of his arrival ... He has gone to Grillon's in

Brook Street [Albermarle Street] and passed under the name of Magon.'
According to Add MS 37903, Windham had known Cadoudal since
1793 and was on good terms with him. In December 1799 he had
described the Frenchman: 'Georges is a plain, farmer-like man, and
very much of that class. He is such a figure as you might see at an audit,
but very intelligent and much to be relied upon in all ways. The second
in command, too, Mercier, is a very excellent, modest young man.'

27. A raid on Houat in February led to Brune capturing information that
there was a plan to land the Russians in France. A report from Rouen
noted that 'as soon as the Anglo-Russian Army disembarks we shall
again see the province covered with Chouans.'

28. In May Willot had 1,200, most of them Swiss and remnants of the
Chasseurs de Nice seconded from Sardinian service, but also with
a few French volunteers from Austrian prisoner-of-war camps. The
army had originally been based in Turin where the officers 'were
quartered in rented rooms in order to avoid the excessive charges
levied by hotels'. Willot's plan had been to seize Elba but instead he
had to flee to Livorno in June to avoid Napoleon's soldiers. Willot
would eventually flee to Baltimore after London judged him guilty
of misappropriating State funds, fining him £25,000.

29. Napoleon was livid, telling Lebrun on 7 June that 'I think it useful to
dismiss the municipal authorities of Calais for their lack of vigilance
and for having allowed Dupeyrou to escape.'

30. Maillefert had the advantage of being a police officer. On 16 May, eleven
days after his arrest, he complained that the authorities were in breach
of Article 46 of the constitution, whereby 'if, within a period of ten
days, following a person's arrest, he is not placed at liberty or brought
to justice, then a crime of arbitrary detention has been committed.'

31. Daudet, 1885, p. 162.

32. L'Association royaliste de l'Institut philanthropique, p. 44.

33. Lanzac de Laborie, p. 146. Apart from destroying the network,
Fouché took great delight in implicating Talleyrand's secretary, Roux
de Laborie, who had been receiving letters marked 'Pour Madame
Smith' addressed to his office from Hyde and contacts in London.

34. Daudet, 1885, p. 270.

35. Cadoudal asked Frere on 19 May to remind D'Artois to send
the marquis to France. The marquis was lavished with funds by
Whitehall and eventually despatched.

36. Rohu, also Caudrillier, 1901, p. 282. Thauvenay, a royal informer in
Paris, was telling the king that June that Napoleon's disappearance
would trigger a war between the generals, allowing the king to return
as peacemaker.

37. Caudrillier, 1901, p. 281.
38. Wickham had obtained details of Napoleon's campaign plan on 18 May from a French spy and sent Count Lehrbach to carry them to Thugut, who would then transfer them to Melas in Italy. They failed to reach the Austrian commander in time owing to delays at the Austrian outposts.
39. There he met Pichegru and Pitt on 31 July and 17 August and both men left Britain on 17 September, Pichegru heading to Germany and Cadoudal returning to Brittany with a further £12,000 or £14,000 in British support.
40. BL Ms Add 37, 9222.
41. His view was that 'the greater part of those captains who received an amnesty are quiet, but their subordinates, who have a different perspective and who still wish to acquire fame and fortune, behave in quite the opposite way. Everyone protests against the government and its agents.'
42. Far away in Naples Queen Maria Carolina, who had her own spies in Paris, was telling the Marchese di Fuscaldo that 'in around a month, a bolt of lightning will set Europe on fire.'

A Fervour for Repression

1. This was at the former residency of the president of the Parlement, just around the corner from Fouché's office. It was burnt down in 1871 during the Paris Commune.
2. The Parisian police force was itself, of course, much older than the Directory and the revolution that spawned it. Louis XIV had created the role of Lieutenant of Police, and his duties included registering taxis and prohibiting double parking (Edict of 1739).
3. Commissaires would see their pay raised to 6,000 Francs, a considerable increase from the 2,500 they originally received in 1790.
4. The police were paid more regularly under Napoleon but the official responsible for administering their salaries worked for the prefect of the Seine, a rival of the prefect of police, with consequent ramifications. Dubois lamented that 'those employed in and by the prefecture of police, the wardens and prison staff and the firemen have not been paid for six months, the total owing being 601,620 Francs on 20 July 1800 ... nearly everyone is discouraged and lacking in means; their creditors persecute them from all sides, and their wives and children are dying of hunger. This unfortunate situation is nothing short of a conspiracy against public security and that of the individual.' From August onwards, the situation improved.
5. The chief casualties were Milly, Letellier and Champein of the Bureau central, sacked by the First Consul three days after his ascension to

power. There was also a limited purge of commissaires and officiers de paix in March 1800.

6. Indeed, it was only on 25 October 1800 that its powers were finally extended beyond the arrondisements of Paris to include the entire department of the Seine and most of that of the Seine-et-Oise.

7. Dubois would be created councillor of state, then count of the empire, and, increasingly, he would divide his time between policing and acting as squire of the château de Vitry-sur-Seine. He served as prefect until 1810 when he was retired to directing commissions of inquiry.

8. Torture had been banned, but the police worked around such obstacles. Louis Picot, Cadoudal's servant, arrested in 1803, described Bertrand's favoured technique: 'Citizen Bertrand, commander of the First Division of the prefecture of police, sent an officer to fetch a musket hammer ... my fingers were placed in the mechanism and were crushed with as much force as they could manage.'

9. His wife, Mademoiselle Lhardy, was cousin to the wife of General Marmont and her uncle was Perregaux, a banker and intimate of Talleyrand.

10. Le Cabinet Noir was primarily interested in correspondence and was sent letters by the *commissaire général des Postes aux lettres et aux chevaux* or intercepted them, copied them, and if necessary decoded them. Antoine de laforest, a friend of Talleyrand, had been responsible for passing the intercepted correspondence of foreign agents on to Napoleon.

11. The preferred area for soliciting was the Palais-Egalité. According to Vandal, 'girls lived in the basement and showed themselves at the windows, calling out to passers-by. Others lined the Boulevard Italien whilst ... on the Boulevard du Temple creatures aged between eight and sixteen offered themselves for corruption.'

12. The Law of the Trousers was introduced in November 1800. It stipulated that women who wished to wear male clothing, for health reasons or for ease of riding, had to have a licence issued by the prefecture. It was abolished in 2013.

13. They received bread and broth. Additional food in the Depot beneath the prefecture cost three Francs per day, firewood two Francs and rent for the bed one-and-a-half Francs.

14. There were two commissaires in the Buttes des Moulins as it was notorious on account of disturbances around the Palais Royal. Many were veteran police officers. Armand Leroux, for example, joined the Bureau central in 1798 and was retired from service in 1816. Thirty years of service guaranteed a reasonable pension.

15. The law stipulated that any French national coming from England had to be subjected to checks and enquiries at Boulogne. Mengaud's checking could be gentle. The Duchess de Guiche, arriving in June 1801, remembered how the officer asked for her valet's name and that of her maid, before adding 'permit me to accompany you to your hotel, for you must be quite fatigued.' Airport security officials please take note.

16. He had emigrated to London in 1792 along with his wife, Maria-Felicia-Thersia Macdonagh, although she died there in 1795. He returned to Paris in 1797 and lived with Clotilde Bodard, his mistress, who bore him two children.

17. The information he provided was mixed, but his police supervisors learnt that Talleyrand and Nogent were holding orgies with 'five or six women deprived of morals' and composing 'the most horrendous calumnies against the First Consul and Madame Bonaparte'.

18. Even less respectable was the spy Chevrillon who had taken 1,200 Francs from an emigrant, promising to supply him with a forged residence permit, only to denounce him to the police and then pocket a further 1,200 Francs voted to him by the grateful authorities.

19. Robbery carried out by more than two people could be tried by courts martial and the accused, if found guilty could be executed without recourse to appeal. This law was kept in place until January 1800.

20. Hue, p. 20. Letter dated 5 April 1800.

21. It is probable that some of the regiment's officers were double agents, used to trick the disaffected into saying too much and then reporting them to the authorities. A man called Pierre Fournier was denounced by Lieutenant Joseph Roux of the 45th Line for having made insulting remarks about the consul.

22. It lambasted Bonaparte for abandoning his army in Egypt, but also featured a question from the Turk regarding France's new Caesar – 'has a Brutus not come forwards?' – to which the answer was 'they shall come forwards in their thousands.'

23. Rapports officiels, p. 6.

24. Rapports officiels, p. 6.

The Revolution's Revenge

1. Barère was close to Demerville having raised him after he was orphaned, and Demerville had been living with him in Paris for four months in 1799.

2. A subscription to have his bust of the First Consul, who had had offered him state employment, transferred from Italy to Paris, began in June 1800.

3. Arch. préf. Pol. AA 271, d 11, item 225.
4. Rossignol had moved to Paris and was living in 6 Rue Dominique-Enfer, telling the minister that he was no longer involved in politics but preferred to spend the day fishing.
5. Hue, p. 42.
6. Masson, p. 25.
7. Massena was a potential rival of Napoleon. In November 1799 Grenville had been telling Wickham to probe whether any amount whatsoever might induce him to secure his services 'either to the cause of royalty or upon any other principle to which he might be willing to accede.'
8. Hue, p. 45.
9. Hue, p. 53.
10. Hue, p. 50.
11. Later D'Instrem recalled the conversation slightly differently with Demerville telling his relative 'not to go to the theatre as there might be trouble, although I can't say what exactly as I didn't want to listen and didn't pay attention.'
12. In an added twist, Demerville's mistress was sister to Frochot, Prefect of the Seine and a man loathed in the prefecture of police.
13. As did Langlois who testified that 'we were in the foyer when, after an hour, we saw someone enter; it was then that Harel said, "that's Ceracchi".'
14. Diana explained at his trial, 'I read French, and understand what I read, but I don't understand all the words when it is spoken to me.'
15. Jerome was not long for Paris. His elder brother wanted him to make up for his lost years by giving him a profession. On 23 November, escorted by Savary, Jerome was sent by stagecoach to Brest where he joined the navy as a midshipman. He was back on dry land by March 1801.
16. The *carte de civisme* was issued by the municipality. It bore the bearer's name, age, address, height and a brief description. Some had professional status too and it was rumoured that for many Chouans who had surrendered, the word brigand was entered as a description of the bearer's profession.
17. Hue, p. 168.
18. Hue, p. 115.
19. Barère, in his colourful memoirs, claims that Demerville came to him saying 'take me to the Minister of Police and I shall tell him all I know about this strange affair and, without a doubt, he will discover

a trail laid from the Tuileries by your personal enemies.' Bourrienne was Barère's personal enemy.

20. Hue, p. 122. Barère was the minister's friend, but his Jacobin credentials made him a suspect in the eyes of Dubois.

21. Procès ... Demerville, pp. 44-7.

22. Rao, p. 485.

23. Barère was not, however, one of their number, which leads one to suspect that he played an active part in police machinations, all the more so as Fouché seems to have been a close friend. Barante, in his memoirs, says 'He [Fouché] learned from Barère that Demerville, a former employee of the Committee of Public Safety, was preparing an attempt on the life of the First Consul.' But it could, of course, have been Barère's ploy all along, merely entrapping Demerville and Ceracchi, whom he also knew, to prove his loyalty.

24. Hue, p. 171.

25. A second expulsion took place on 20 January 1801.

26. Topino-Lebrun had not yet been caught.

27. Hue, p. 176.

28. Masson, p. 13. Chevalier later confessed to adding a secret ingredient which would create poisonous fumes and suffocate the First Consul.

29. The house of the Blancs-Manteaux, in the Marais district, was a former monastic building then sold off and owned by Nicolas Duval and Laurent Burloy. Duval had taken part in Babeuf's conspiracy along with Chevalier and Veycer.

30. D'Abrantes, Memoires, p. 322.

31. Rapports officiels, p. 37.

32. Rapports officiels, p. 21.

33. Rapports officiels, p. 25.

For the King

1. Cadoudal was not above such methods, sending Jean-François-Edmée La Peige de Bar (known as Debar or The Prussian) to prowl the coasts, raiding the property of known republicans, attacking gendarmes and stagecoaches. Mercier, too, was kept busy in Brittany, raising recruits or money, hunting down gendarmes and blues, menacing mayors and magistrates.

2. General Tercier, a Chouan officer, went so far as to tell him 'your conduct and behaviour have been such that you should not openly travel through the regions you once commanded, for, if you do, then a musket shot will ring out from behind one of the hedges.'

3. Martel, 1885, p. 341.
4. Report from Wickham to Grenville, 23 April 1800.
5. According to Add MS 37869, Windham was interested in how the custodianship of that fort could be held outside the jurisdiction of British law. An early example of secret rendition.
6. A police report dubbed him 'commissioner general acting with the authority of the princes'. A police informer noted that 'he was to organise a few *coups de main* which aren't quite clear as yet but which seem important.'
7. Martel, 1885, p. 277.
8. Papiers saisis, p. 363. Dutheil to Trottouin, 26 December 1800.
9. Caudrillier, 1901, p. 282.
10. Cadoudal would later state: 'I sent a few of my officers to Paris to be rid of Bonaparte as I thought it necessary, but I never gave orders as to which method to employ. They chose to detonate a device, which is criminal as innocent people were killed. But my idea had been to attack the First Consul in the open and equipped with weapons of the same kind as used by his escort.'
11. It would be wrong to think of all the Chouans as gallant gentlemen; they had killed and attempted to kill many republican officers by fair means or foul. After the Chouans had first been defeated by Hoche they thought to assassinate him. In April 1796, near Loudéac, he was shot at by a Chouan leader who had been deserted by his men. Then, in October 1796, Moriau 'The Death Blow' was sent to shoot him as he left the theatre in Rennes. Moriau missed, hitting the wall.
12. Lorédan, p. 27. Ratel was a connection much used by Hyde and the English Committee.
13. This is confirmed by a police report which stated 'they formed the plan to attack a stagecoach around Charenton, at the marker for 50 miles. The weapons for this have left Paris and it was François who got them out. Saint-Andéol de Ré and Girod are in the gang.'
14. Passports were required for internal travel. Returning royalists found it difficult, but not impossible, to obtain such documents, as Dubois noted: 'They arrive at Versailles without papers, or with forged ones. They are lodged in houses which have been recommended to them and remain there for some time before, gradually, showing themselves in the district, going on little walks. Their neighbours grow used to them and, having chatted to the grocer or tailor in their street, they use them as witnesses in order to obtain a passport.'
15. He was the same height as Napoleon, *cinq pieds, deux pouces*, or 169 centimetres.

16. Lorédan, p. 34.
17. Martel, 1870, p. 23.
18. Villeneuve, p. 88.
19. Villeneuve, p. 88.
20. The commission reviewing the cases of returning émigrés and requests for reconciliation worked under the Ministry of Justice, led by Abrial, and Fouché was determined to undermine his fellow minister, whom he viewed as unwelcome competition for jurisdiction. Thanks to Fouché withholding paperwork or swamping them with reports, the poorly managed committee of 30 had achieved indifferent results, rendered still less worthy by rumours of bribery and corruption. When Napoleon returned from Italy in July, it was clear that there was a serious problem regarding how cases were being handled, and that much money was being handed over to allow some to get to the front of the long queue. On 18 July he partly abolished the committee, irritably instructing that it be reconfigured to consist only of men who were 'just, of integrity and determined'.
21. Monsieur Lavieuville, who had helped Limoëlan find lodgings in the capital, and whose wife was a cousin of the royalist, later informed the police that 'Limoëlan seemed like someone who enjoyed the special protection of the minister of police.'
22. Villeneuve, p. 92. Letter 20 July 1800.
23. Napoleon certainly had the means to ensure that an individual received such beneficial attention, as did Josephine. Those who enjoyed the personal attention of the couple found themselves in receipt of the following note: 'Madame Bonaparte has the honour to extend her compliments to Monsieur/Madame and to inform them that they have been removed from the list.'
24. Written 3 December 1800.
25. That uncle was a former Jesuit and had, in recent months, been trying to establish the Society of the Sacred Heart of Jesus and the Heart of Mary, a secretive order based loosely on the Jesuits.
26. Lorédan, p. 33.
27. Bartholomäus Girardoni's air rifle had first been used by the Austrians at the siege of Belgrade in 1788. Whilst silent, it was also delicate, impractical and required considerable skill to use effectively.
28. Villeneuve, p. 97.
29. Notice how different this description of the suspect is when compared to that by Dubois.
30. Martel, 1870, p. 23.
31. He lists his Chouan contacts as being Luxembourg, Sougé, Chateauneuf and Lanougarède.

32. In a premonition, he had told Desmarest 'for fear of being suspected, and thus done away with, I beg you to only send letters addressed to me to Citizen Gagney, the Matignon cul-de-sac, rue des Orties, galerie du Louvre number 321.'
33. Martel, 1885, p. 246.
34. Desmarest, who knew the facts better than most, was of the opinion: 'I do not know whether the publicity surrounding the case brought against Chevalier and his machine suggested the idea of planting an explosive device but before then they had wavered in their choice of methods, at one time thinking of an attack on the way to Saint-Cloud, or whilst hunting in the woods, or at the theatre or opera house, where they had measured out distances to be sure their pistols would be within range.'
35. Jean-Baptiste had been robbed on the road to Brest, probably by Chouans, and was renting out rooms, quietly, to make up for the loss of the stolen 5,000 livres. The couple charged 36 livres a month in rent.
36. The doctor's account read 'The patient told me he had not gone to the privy for several days. I suggested various potions. I did not stay long. I did not sit down. The day after next I came back to find him better. I recommended nourishing food and wine.'
37. It bore silver bells and the medallion with the inscription 'I belong to Madame Descognets de Quintin in Brittany.'
38. Martel, 1870, p. 37.
39. Procès instruit ... Saint-Réjant, p. 47.
40. Students of social history should note that the time-honoured complication over splitting the bill was prevalent in the Paris of 1800. Alexandre Moriset paid 32 sous but Carbon, feeling generous, paid the rest.
41. Martel, 1870, p.24. That area was a haunt of royalists, many of whom attended a Masonic Lodge in the Boulevard Poissonnière.
42. Chevalier Baillif-Mesnager lived at 776 Rue Neuve-Augustin. He had been a captain the Port-au-Prince Regiment but had been wounded at Savannah during the American Revolution. He had retired to Paris in 1787 and lived off his 600-Franc pension and rental income.
43. Procès instruit ... Saint-Réjant, p. 284.
44. Some straw and powder had been used to dry the barrel out so it could be filled with gunpowder. Carbon would later deny this and say that they used the cup as a container for urine, as they were going to wash some pimples off the horse.
45. Procès instruit ... Saint-Réjant, p. 247.

Notes

Christmas Eve

1. The badly paved streets of Paris were troubling the prefect in 1800, forcing him to remark that 'it will soon be impossible to move along certain streets without the risk of injury or damage to horses, coaches and even pedestrians.'
2. The Place du Carrousel was squeezed between the Tuileries Palace, with its courtyard gates, later replaced by an arc de triomphe, opening out onto the square, and, on the eastern side, the Hotel de Longueville, converted into assembly rooms by a Directory fond of dance.
3. Or Lise Peussot, according to some accounts.
4. The theatre would take a staggering 24,000 Francs.
5. Rapp, p. 20.
6. Martel, 1885, pp. 385-6.
7. This is contradicted by mention of the grenadier a little later.
8. Her testimony is supported by Desmarest's brief account: 'the explosion took place five seconds after the coach, having found its way past the obstruction, had reached the junction of Rue de Malte and Rue Rohan [Marceau], and was out of sight.'
9. The escort was not alone in thinking it was an artillery salvo; the Chevalier du Mautort was dining just after eight when he heard the explosion, the party exclaiming 'that was quite a cannon shot!'
10. From Napoleon's *Mémorial de Sainte-Hélène*. Here he lied like a bulletin, blaming Limoëlan for lighting the fuse and stating that one of his escort had been wounded and his horse killed, and that 50 civilians were also killed.
11. According to the ordinance of 29 April 1800, unrecognised bodies had to be exhibited naked to the public for three days, 'with precautions being taken to take account of decency and morality.'

An Explosive Aftermath

1. The minister was using Bourmont for information. Luxembourg, Bourmont's friend and betrayer, added a week later 'it was certainly the Chouans and there is still time for you to help find out which ones.'
2. Napoleon was soon to remark to Berlier that 'There were good Jacobins, there was a time when all right-thinking people had to be such; I was, just as you were and thousands of other good people were. Those have held on to their liberal principles, but aren't behind the troubles. The bad ones, the incorrigible ones, are those who continue to dream of destruction, whereas now we must build.'

3. Others recalled that Napoleon added 'I would hang myself out of despair.'

4. Arch. préf. Pol. AA 282.

5. Fouché was to compose a list of those who were deemed culpable, and the First Consul and Dubois would add their own suggestions. A definitive list was then compiled by Piis, Limodin and Boisseau of the prefecture and on 4 January 1801 this document was approved by the consuls and their ministers.

6. Fauriel, p. 117. Claude Fauriel was Fouché's secretary in 1801.

7. On 18 January the police report noted that some retired officers, strolling in the Tuileries garden, had been overheard saying that they knew Harel had been offered a financial reward 'and that they were going to divulge this fact.'

8. Here the president of the court helpfully reminded the jurors that conspirators did all they could to conceal their weapons, so that not finding a dagger could not lead one to conclude that one never existed.

9. Aulard, p. 121.

10. Although the judge had ordered their immediate release, within 24 hours, the minister of justice, Abrial, told Fouché that 'as it would be dangerous to release these individuals, I have written to the court to ask that they be detained. As this cannot be in the Conciergerie, I suppose you will have to have them taken to the Temple for reasons of security.' This arbitrary kind of detention was called a *jugement administratif*. On 15 March 1801 Napoleon would have 'Diana escorted to Italy and Lavigne and the woman Fumey released.'

11. Réal's comment was that 'I would be on the list as a Babouvist too if I was not a councillor of state.'

12. Desmarest would have it that by early January there were 223 individuals detained on account of having been denounced.

13. Martel, 1885, p. 396.

14. The survivors fell into British hands when that colony was captured in 1810. One of those Valeri Hugot was blind, having lost his sight due to the intense sunshine.

15. The king was given two small artillery pieces and 40 muskets. The prisoners were disembarked with 20 sacks of biscuits, a barrel of salted beef, an axe and a frying pan, the latter donated by the officers of the ship.

16. These two, having suffered unimaginable privation, eventually found passage on an American ship bound for the barren Atlantic rock of Saint Helena and from there, after adventures that would shame Robinson Crusoe, returned to France in November 1803.

17. On 13 January Dubois ordered the governors of the Temple prison to hand over Destrem and other Jacobins in custody to Lieutenant Gaudriot and an escort of gendarmes who would transport them westwards.

18. Destrem died on 20 July 1804. He had been issued a pardon in July 1804 but it arrived after his escape.

19. Some five days after the atrocity *Le Publiciste* published a letter from Antoine-Alexis Cadet de Vaux, normally a commentator on agricultural reform but now become the voice of vengeance against the criminals behind the deed, calling for a return of hanging in gibbets or breaking the guilty on a wheel. His sentiments met with a sympathetic reception that winter.

20. The Justice of the Peace described the body as 'naked, the two arms blown off, and the brains blown out, so disfigured that no description is possible.' Cobb, p. 56.

21. Her remains were recorded as 'a female corpse deceased at number 511, at de Metz's, the hatter's, with three skirts one of Rouen cloth, a leather die and small toothbrush in her pockets, a ring and a golden earring.' Cobb, p. 56.

22. Alexandre was later awarded 800 Francs compensation so he could bring up his surviving child of two years.

23. The original breakdown is in Dubois's report of 30 October 1801 to the Minister of the Interior, Arch. préf. Pol. AA 273, see the annex for details.

24. It was perhaps typical of Napoleon to take advantage of the opportunity offered by this damage to reconfigure Paris. The Maison Bron was pulled down, as were the stables of Consul Charles-François Lebrun (his house was in Rue Saint Honoré) and the storehouses of the Opera. Many of the badly damaged houses were not repaired enabling Napoleon to clear the site and so carry out his plan to link the Louvre to the Tuileries.

25. Rumour began almost at once. Some said five men dressed in white overalls had been seen following Napoleon's coach. A butcher in a bar in the Halle 'saw five or six men in caps hurrying along at around 8 o'clock saying that the affair would be over before they got there.' A woman from Rue de Lille told a doorman two months ago words to the effect that 'they aim to blow Napoleon up on the road to Malmaison, planting a barrel of powder in a cart of hay.' Right after the explosion an individual said that he had heard a body of men marching quickly along Rue Traversiere say, in bad French, that 'he was born lucky, it isn't him, unfortunately.'

On the Trail of Treason

1. Réal, p. 46.
2. The Rue de Chartres-Saint-Honoré was renamed Rue de Malte in 1798 in honour of the capture of Malta.
3. Aulard, p. 82.
4. Aulard, p. 91.
5. Aulard, p.107.
6. *Lettre du Ministre de la police générale*, p. 4. The government transferred a sum of 24,000 Francs to a merchant called Pillier in Rennes for payment of any bounty leading to Cadoudal's arrest or death. At Le Mans additional warrants went out for known Chouans who may have been involved, including 'Debé, dit Belfort, complice de Limolan [sic]', Chandelier, Beauregard (known as Jean-bon-bougre), and Rochejaquelein whose real name was Forest.
7. General Jean Romain Conilh de Beyssac had been told that the priority was to take Cadoudal, and the most recent information was that Cadoudal was on the island of Loquelle near Auray at the time of the explosion. On 2 February they managed to catch his brother, Julien, who was shot whilst trying to escape.
8. Martel, 1885, p. 381
9. Henry of the force was to remark that 'there's something mysterious about the Hotel de Mayenne that one can't quite put one's finger on.'
10. Martel, 1870, p. 196. The scar was below his left eye, a detail provided before the first raids took place.
11. Bruslart would return to France in 1814 and the restored Bourbons made him governor of Corsica, responsible for keeping an eye on the exiled Napoleon on his miniature kingdom of Elba.
12. Fouché lamented that 'the shadows from which they operated could have been swept away by certain individuals who had been pardoned and who were in daily contact with the police and with those plotting. Yet those individuals made things more obscure.'
13. The minister also mentioned 'some of the loyal pardoned royalists have actively assisted in finding out where Georges' men are hiding.' And reported that 'Another of Georges' officers, no longer in Paris, said following the atrocity that they would blame it on the Jacobins but that they would find out later that they played no part in it.'
14. Deladouespe, p. 337. Dated 16 January 1801. The importance of this letter was underscored by General Hédouville: 'I ask you to show this letter to the First Consul as the importance of putting an end

to the great correspondence, which I believe is still being directed against his person, cannot be exaggerated.'

15. Martel, 1885, p. 315. The text of the warrant reads 'We demand and order that Citizen X [name and address] be brought before us, in conformity with the law and in order to respond to the charges that will be brought against him. Paris [date], Year x of the Republic One and Indivisible.'

16. Carbon's arrest prompted an argument in the police ranks as to who should be accorded the 12,000-Franc reward. The minister reminded Dubois that he had provided information to his agents regarding Carbon's whereabouts, but, in the end, the reward was shared out between Dubois's officers.

17. Martel, 1870, p. 20. Carbon sent a note from his cell the next day asking that the police return his cravat.

18. Lorédan, p. 107.

19. Cadoudal's nom-de-guerre. Cadoudal later denied writing the note, and denied the notion that it could have reached Paris in the four days between its date and the explosion of the bomb. But its 'we look to you and all our confidence and our hope rests in you' is unequivocal.

20. Aulard, p. 133.

21. Procès instruit … Saint-Réjant, pp. 141-142.

22. The doctor would note that the leeches had never been applied, but that the landlady had obtained some blood from a butcher and splashed a few drops on the royalist's linen, pretending that he had been treated.

23. Martel, 1870, pp. 80-81. The landlady had told her husband that the Chouan had taken a fall. Unconcerned about their lodger, he merely asked whether he had fallen down their stairs.

24. There was speculation that Saint Victor had agreed to Bourmont's request that he track the perpetrators down, Bourmont even issuing him with a semi-official warrant. This is at odds with the police raid on Saint Victor's rooms in the following days, however.

25. Evidence that Sougé, a Chouan officer known as La Musette who had spent time in Jersey, was the one to betray Saint-Réjant is confirmed by the fact that when Dubois wanted to arrest Sougé too, Fouché rebuked him: 'I authorised Citizen Sougé to reside in Paris, in the Hotel de la Mayenne, Rue du Four-Honoré, where I know he keeps quiet and which is why I have had him exonerated. Withdraw, therefore, the order you have given for his arrest or inform me as to your reasons if you still wish to go ahead.'

26. The police took offence at the implied criticism of the honesty of their agents and noted that 'the public servants charged with the arrest and the securing of all the papers in the room were honest men who had served in this position of trust for the last seven years and against whom no criticism had ever been raised.' Regarding the issue of forgery, the police were very careful to bring in handwriting experts to assess Cadoudal's letter, Augustin Oudart and François Legros analysing the style and content to find a match with examples from Cadoudal's known correspondence.

27. Procès instruit ... Saint-Réjant, p. xiv. The persons known to you probably meant Cadoudal and Mercier. His sister-in-law responded and began raising funds for the Chouan's defence.

28. Thérèse Mélanie Ropert, or Thérèse Orieulx, was, despite being pregnant with her sixth child, detained in the Madelonnettes prison. She was allowed out of prison but restricted to living in Paris until the end of April 1801 when she was finally granted permission to return to Brittany.

29. Aulard, p. 120.

30. Lorédan, p. 161.

Trial and Punishment

1. The judge's daughter, Emilie, was married, albeit unhappily, to Felix Lacoste. The couple lived in the United States where Emilie had an affair with Joseph Bonaparte and gave birth to a son, Félix-Joseph Lacoste, by him.

2. The august Doctor Joseph-Ignace Guillotin also made an appearance on behalf of Cicé as he knew her brother but his sanguine intervention was outclassed by Dr Dejussieu's florid allusion to her 'delicate state, and precarious nature of her health' and his probable exaggeration that 'he had never heard anything from her which did not merit my admiration.'

3. He was touchingly vague: 'I won't mention the torments that each man was subjected to, because they themselves will not discuss them.'

4. The relatives of those banished were indignant that, upon the true culprits being found guilty, their loved ones were not pardoned. The wives of the deported took to petitioning the authorities and launching a court case, but to no avail.

5. Procès instruit ... Saint-Réjant, II, p. 269.

6. An expedition to Saint-Domingue had been fitted out in 1801 and numerous reinforcements were sent in 1802 and 1803. The campaign

was a disaster with most of the troops and the majority of its medical officers dying of Yellow Fever.

7. Martel, 1870, p. 201.
8. The letter was signed and also bore the signature of Citizen Prétot, the jailer, who also added the text 'I certify that this bears the signature of Carbon and that it was written in my presence on 13 April 1801.'
9. Sanson, p. 44.
10. He also thought a second attempt would be made on Napoleon soon after, adding 'If Bonaparte escaped this time he won't escape another.'
11. Talleyrand had asked Hawkesbury to extradite Dutheil and Cadoudal in an elegant missive which began 'the crime designed to kill the First Consul has inflicted on the innocent population of Paris horrors which are without precedent in modern history. I am sure the First Consul is incapable of thinking the present or the former ministers of His Majesty capable of either funding or directing a crime which even the most uncivilized hordes would disavow.' Should the British refuse the French request then Otto, the representative in London, was to ask that the two individuals be sent to America.
12. Bouillé, p. 439. Hyde would deny it, writing 'The atrocity, committed on their own devising by some obscure Chouans, was used as a pretext by the minister of police to attack the royalist cause directly, and to lay blame as high as possible, right up to the most noble and best of princes, up to Monsieur!' And perhaps protested too much by adding 'Limoelan, Saint-Rejant, Carbon and two or three others were the only ones involved in the wicked and cowardly crime of 3 *nivôse*. It was with profound sadness for the royalists to learn that the crime had been committed by those drawn from amongst its ranks and who fanaticism had pushed to criminality.'

Postscript

1. He received compensation of 32,890.20 Francs, with a further 12,072.54 for his family.

INDEX